Contents

Foreword by The RSPB   4

Preface   6

INTRODUCTION   6

   How to use this book   7

   The tidal cycle   8

   How to read a tide table   11

   Where to look...   14

   The Seashore Code   20

   Keeping a nature journal   24

   What to do...   27

   The value of the coast and seas   30

   Conservation and climate change   34

SEAWEEDS   38

   Brown seaweeds   42

   Red seaweeds   53

   Green seaweeds   63

FLOWERING PLANTS   67

SPONGES   70

CNIDARIANS   76

   Sea anemones   78

   Soft and hard corals   85

   Sea firs and siphonophores   89

   Jellyfish   93

MARINE WORMS   96

MOLLUSCS   105

Chitons   109

Gastropods   112

Bivalves   132

CRUSTACEANS   142

   Barnacles   146

   Isopods and amphipods   150

   Shrimps and prawns   154

   Crabs   160

   Lobsters   170

SEA SPIDERS   173

BRYOZOANS   176

ECHINODERMS   180

   Starfish   183

   Brittlestars   189

   Sea and heart urchins   192

   Sea cucumbers   197

SEA SQUIRTS   200

SEASHORE FISH   205

THE STRANDLINE   219

Glossary   229

Further reading   233

Useful websites   234

Author acknowledgements   235

Index   236

Photographic credits   239

Foreword
by The RSPB

As Professor C.M. Yonge pointed out about our coastline over 60 years ago in his pioneering natural history entitled *The Sea Shore*, 'this narrow strip holds an interest altogether out of proportion to its extent'.

Narrow it may be, but the coast of the UK mainland unravels to more than 12,000km overall, and if we include the perimeters of all our offshore islands we end up with a total shoreline that matches the distance from London to Auckland. Moreover, this oceanic ribbon is unique in Europe for its outstanding diversity of landscapes and habitats – rock, sand and mud sculpted and bevelled by the flux of the sea and the ice ages. The tidal rise and fall, and the gradients of light penetration, overlay this geology to create a treasure trove of niches for plants and animals, in sum a halo of life that contributes in no small measure to the fact that the marine environment supports over half of the UK's biodiversity. From childhood we are drawn to this astounding richness not only as a playground, but also as a highly accessible outdoor laboratory where we can delve in the sand, explore rock pools, and begin to grasp how different animals and plants have adapted to this highly dynamic frontier between land and sea.

Maya Plass has created an inspirational handbook to the inhabitants of this briny laboratory, revealing and cataloguing their secrets with a remarkable portfolio of colour photographs, many never before depicted outside of the scientific literature. It is not accidental that her lens focuses on the cold-blooded vertebrates and invertebrates to the exclusion of the warm-blooded shorebirds. These fall outside the scope of the book, as they are all covered in detail in the companion *RSPB Handbook of British Birds*, also published by Bloomsbury.

Turnstones are common winter visitors to almost any British shore, but with a preference for rocky or shingle beaches, where they use their strong bills to eat molluscs and crustaceans like this crab. At times they may even be found on coastal grassland, harbour walls or piers.

Z924466

RSPB
HANDBOOK OF THE
SEASHORE

MAYA PLASS

B L O O M S B U R Y
LONDON · NEW DELHI · NEW YORK · SYDNEY

This book is for you, Niamh – you are my finest
and most perfect inspiration

a million
voices for
nature

The RSPB speaks out for birds and wildlife, tackling the problems that threaten our environment.
Nature is amazing – help us keep it that way.

If you would like to know more about the RSPB, visit the website at www.rspb.org.uk
or write to: The RSPB, The Lodge, Sandy, Bedfordshire, SG19 2DL; 01767 680551.

First published in 2013

Bloomsbury Publishing Plc, 50 Bedford Square, London WC1B 3DP
Bloomsbury USA, 175 Fifth Avenue, New York, NY 10010

www.bloomsbury.com
www.bloomsburyusa.com

Bloomsbury Publishing, London, New Delhi, New York and Sydney

A CIP catalogue record for this book is available from the British Library
Library of Congress Cataloging-in-Publication Data has been applied for

Commissioning Editor: Julie Bailey
Project Editor: Julie Bailey
Design by Julie Dando, Fluke Art
Diagrams by Marc Dando, Fluke Art

UK ISBN (print) 978-1-4081-7836-2

Printed in China by C & C Offset Co. Ltd.

10 9 8 7 6 5 4 3 2 1

Visit www.bloomsbury.com to find out more about our authors and their books.
You will find extracts, author interviews and our blog, and you can sign up for newsletters
to be the first to hear about our latest releases and special offers.

Apart from celebrating our seashore, this inventory serves first and foremost as an identification guide. We marvel at the exquisite colours and patterns of the Rainbow Wrack, Blue-rayed Limpet and Scarlet Lady – a nudibranch resembling a shimmering feather boa. There is still much to learn about how seashore animals live, reproduce and fit into the fabric of their ecosystem, but this book is enough to whet anyone's appetite for further exploration. One specimen of the Bootlace Worm was reportedly 55m long, the longest known animal on earth. The Ragworm, we learn, has evolved to tolerate polluted substrates by storing copper safely in its skin. The Violet Snail can change sex, while the diminutive Pistol Shrimp stuns prey by snapping shut a super-claw to generate a shockwave of overwhelming concussive force.

The Sanderling is a bird of sandy beaches. Ever-restless flocks race frenetically along the shoreline, close to the water's edge, where they probe into the wet sand to feed on marine invertebrates like this shrimp. In Britain Sanderlings are invariably seen in their strikingly pale winter plumage.

Beyond the intrigue of life history, however, the handbook sheds light on the changing ecology of the seashore and the growing threat it faces from man on a scale unimaginable in Professor Yonge's day. Two themes emerge particularly strongly. The first is the ever-increasing competition to our native species from ones invading these shores as a result of ill-conceived, deliberate introduction or else passively, often as opportunistic hitchhikers on global shipping. Thus the Slipper Limpet introduced from America is displacing oysters and other native shellfish, while the burrowing Chinese Mitten Crab is a menace, undermining dykes and embankments. We are also battling against invasive sea squirts like *Didemnum* which, like an alien from science fiction, coats every surface it colonises in a slimy gunk.

The second and not unrelated challenge of our time is climate change, which is radically transforming our oceans, so much so that it is a race against time to unfathom and tackle its insidious impacts. Sea-level rise is the most visible sign of climate change but, as the handbook shows, there are also subtler and less tractable changes, including the spread northwards of warm-water species. We also witness cold-water species like the Tortoiseshell Limpet retreating north, but in the long run sea warming will probably outstrip the capacity of some species to cling on and we will lose them from our shores altogether.

Apart from its intrinsic value and fascination, wonderfully evoked in this handbook, the seashore is the wellspring for much of our marine life, whether as spawning and nursery areas for fish and shellfish, or as feeding grounds for the Arctic waders that flock to our shores every winter. The seashore is equally critical to our own social, economic and environmental well-being and we abuse it at our peril. For all these reasons, the RSPB is proud to be associated with this handbook for highlighting so graphically our unique and fragile coastal assets. We urgently need to safeguard them by establishing Marine Protected Areas and taking other, more global action. I wholeheartedly commend this book to all who care about our seashore and its stewardship for future generations.

Euan Dunn
Head of Marine Policy, The RSPB

Preface

One of my early memories of the seashore remains clear and distinct. This was the point at which my interest, understanding and ultimately passion for the marine environment began. Despite being only five years old, I clearly remember crossing golden sands, heading to a rocky patch of seashore on the Kentish coast. Holding tightly onto my mother's hand, I precariously climbed over the rocks with their slimy and colourful seaweeds. We discovered a pool in which to dip our bare feet. In the pool I found strange creatures like crabs, starfish and anemones. This was the starting point for my journey into the marine world.

We later moved to a house by the coast, and I started to explore the seashore in greater depth. I started asking more questions, some of which my mother did not have the answers to. The more I discovered about the seashore, the more I grew curious about this alien, mysterious environment. This interest, combined with a love of being outdoors, secured my decision to become a marine biologist.

My relationship with the coast and sea has been enhanced by a multitude of books, people and experiences. The more I understand about a species, like the often-overlooked Estuary Ragworm (*Hediste diversicolor*), the more I appreciate what a wonderfully evolved and evolving beast it is. Increasing knowledge has only cemented my relationship with the seashore and its inhabitants even more.

This book will, I hope, allow seashore visitors to get more from their own journeys of discovery on the seashore. It aims to provide enough information to confidently approach the shore, by knowing when, where and how to look, taking into account the safety of both the explorer and our seashore inhabitants. The species accounts aim to familiarise seashore explorers with some of the many species that can be found around the coasts of the British Isles. The species within these pages are just some of the commonly found and identifiable ones – species that are always of interest when I take groups down to the rocky shore.

With the help of this book, I hope you will grow to appreciate what truly incredible plants and animals – from the seaweeds and worms, to the bryozoans – can be found on the coasts of the British Isles. The stories of adaptation and survival they tell are formidable and courageous. My descriptions may at times seem anthropomorphic, but my intention is always to connect you, the reader, with the amazing creatures you can discover on our shores.

Enjoy all your visits to the seashore and your journey of discovery in our marine world.

Maya Plass,
Marine and Coastal Ecologist

Spring 2013

How to use this book

The *RSPB Handbook of the Seashore* is designed to help you discover and identify a wide variety of our seashore species and to ensure that you have enjoyable, safe and considerate seaside adventures. This handbook has been written with the coasts around the British Isles in mind, and the first step to using it effectively is to take a moment to read the general introduction sections, on pages 8 to 37, and the helpful and informative texts that introduce each taxonomic subsection.

The general introduction section on **tides** (pages 8–13) helps you to plan your trips according to the best tides each month and through the year. This section provides you with the skills you need to understand tides and use tide tables to ensure safe excursions.

Tidal fluctuations produce a variety of microhabitats that allow each of our seashore inhabitants to carve out its home, sometimes literally. Different species are found according to the location of the beach and your position on the seashore (zonation), with some species being found in rather unexpected places. You can discover some of the very best places to look for all these inhabitants within the **Where to look...** section (pages 14–19).

The Seashore Code section (pages 20–23) encourages you to enjoy your visits to the seashore while considering your own safety as well as the protection of the wildlife found there. In the section that follows you will find suggestions for enriching your seashore experiences by **keeping a nature journal** (pages 24–26). Make sure you familiarise yourself with the crucial information outlined in the **What to do...** section (pages 27–29) in case you find something unusual on one of your seashore visits.

The main introduction ends with a section highlighting **the value of our coast and seas** (pages 30–33), which encourages us to appreciate the role they have to play on our society and global health, and with information about **conservation and climate change** (pages 34–37), including the consequences of human activities on the marine environment.

Each phylum – from the seaweeds to the most common seashore fish, as well as species that get washed up on the strandline – is introduced in text enhanced by detailed anatomical illustrations, offering highlights of the most interesting features of seashore species and a glimpse into their often complex life cycles.

Individual accounts are included for 208 of the most commonly seen intertidal species. Each account includes a full-colour photograph alongside a detailed description to help you easily identify the species. Concise information on each species' size, the zonation in which it can be found on the shore, its distribution around our coasts and any similar species to watch out for has been set in a helpful box for quick reference.

Both common and scientific names are provided above each description. If you see a pen and paper symbol here it indicates an unusual, invasive or rare species. Marine scientists would be keen to hear more about encounters with any of these notable species, so if you come across one please refer to the relevant part of the **What to do...** section on pages 27–29.

Following the species accounts, from page 229 to 240, a number of helpful references are included, which should help you to further your knowledge of the seashore and enhance your enjoyment of this handbook. These include a glossary of scientific terms used in the text, a list of useful seashore-related books and websites, and an index to all the species names (common and scientific) mentioned in the book.

The tidal cycle

*It is advisable to look from the tide pool to the stars
and then back to the tide pool again.*

John Steinbeck, *The Log from the Sea of Cortez* 1951

Arriving at the beach in the early hours of the morning, the sun was rising over an expansive horizon of sea. As the waves lapped at the shore, you stood barefoot where the sea meets land and felt the water come rushing over your ankles. Then, by some mysterious force, the waves rolled back and you were seemingly drawn into the deep blue. Experiences like this remain a lasting memory for so many seashore visitors.

The start of a day trip to the seashore often includes taking a moment to relax and perhaps enjoy the view, while you wait for the sea to retreat and reveal wet, glistening sand, and for seaweed-strewn rocks to start breaking through the surface of the water. As the day progresses the character of the beach keeps changing. Shallow waters morph from a serene, mysterious, visually impenetrable surface to a glistening, rugged terrain bursting with colour, life and texture. You are witnessing the magic of the tide and the powers of the moon.

The tides are capable of shaping the seashore, creating unique habitats and providing shelter for species that have perfectly evolved to live in this harsh and changeable environment. To understand and explore this area between the high and low tides we must first understand the tidal cycles – only then can we hope to make the most of these wonderful windows of exploration between the tides.

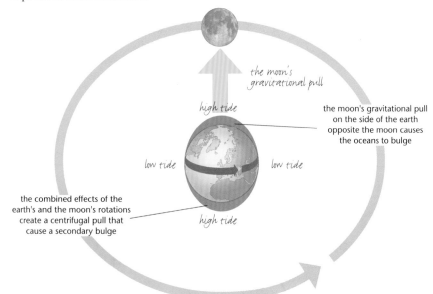

the moon's gravitational pull

high tide

the moon's gravitational pull on the side of the earth opposite the moon causes the oceans to bulge

low tide

low tide

the combined effects of the earth's and the moon's rotations create a centrifugal pull that cause a secondary bulge

high tide

The moon has a powerful influence on the tides.

It has long been known that the cyclical rise and fall of the tides was related to the moon. This could be deduced from simple observation by anyone who spent time on the coast. And in many cultures phases of the moon correlate with the times thought best to fish, harvest or plant. This might seem far-fetched until we start to look carefully at the significance of lunar cycles on nature's rhythms, which is so evident on our coastal intertidal regions.

To understand daily tidal cycles, we have to start with some basics. A solar day is almost exactly 24 hours. The moon orbits the earth in the same direction as the earth rotates on its axis, and it takes slightly more than a solar day – about 24 hours and 50 minutes – for the moon to return to the same location in the sky. Within each of these cycles there are usually two high tides and two low tides around the UK. Since this daily tidal cycle takes longer than our 24-hour (solar) day lasts, with every rotation of the earth the times of tides move approximately 50 minutes later.

The powerful gravitational forces of both the moon and sun have a huge and wondrous effect on our coasts. They cause our oceanic waters to 'bulge' both on the side of the earth opposite the moon, and on the side of the earth facing the moon. As the earth rotates these shifting bulges result in the rise and fall of the tides and the creation of a unique habitat. We are guaranteed a different scene on every day that we happen upon the shore.

On the coast lives are not only dictated by the daily tidal cycle, but also by the lunar and solar alignments that create our 'spring' and 'neap' tides through the month. When the sun, earth and moon are in a straight line, at the full and new moons, we experience tides with the strongest gravitational forces placed upon them. At these times we experience very *low* low tides and very *high* high tides because, like a coiled spring, the tides are pulled to their biggest strong magnitudes. These are our spring tides and they provide an optimum time to

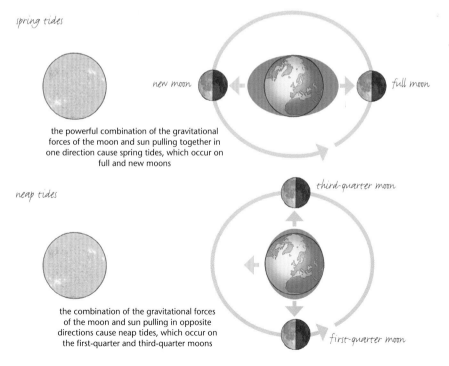

spring tides

new moon

full moon

the powerful combination of the gravitational forces of the moon and sun pulling together in one direction cause spring tides, which occur on full and new moons

neap tides

third-quarter moon

first-quarter moon

the combination of the gravitational forces of the moon and sun pulling in opposite directions cause neap tides, which occur on the first-quarter and third-quarter moons

Changes in the positions of the sun and the moon in relation to the earth cause spring and neap tides.

The lives of seashore species are dictated by the lunar-driven tides.

go rockpooling. When the moon, earth and sun are at right angles, at quarter-moon phases, we see weak or neap tides, and experience *low* high tides and *high* low tides. From one spring tide to the next is a 14-day cycle, and many of the species of the intertidal zone echo this cycle within their biorhythms.

Yet this is only the beginning of a complex story. The spring tidal heights can also vary. They are at their very *lowest* low tides close to the equinoxes on 21 March and 21 September, when the sun, moon and earth are at the very nearest to a linear arrangement. These times provide the best opportunities for exploring the lower reaches of the shore that are rarely exposed. There we can observe seldom-seen species that spend the vast majority of their lives submerged.

With only a few hours to reach the low tide and start exploring, we are given just a tantalising window for exploration each day. In practical terms, rockpooling on a low tide gives us a chance to explore new territory, but this opportunity also comes with additional risks.

During the spring tides there is a greater volume of water rushing in and out of estuaries, and on and off the seashore. Because of this these regions can become particularly treacherous should you get stranded in the period of fastest movement, which happens between high and low water in the third and fourth hour after 'slack water'. Slack water is when there are periods of still water. It occurs when the tide is at its highest just before it drops, or at the lowest tidal point. These interim periods of fast movement also make rip tides and currents particularly dangerous. Always check local information panels and boards for details of the local seashore you are visiting, as one region in the British Isles will not share similar tide times as a region at the opposite end of the country.

Tidal times differ because of variations in coastline and also due to the depth of the sea. As a result, you need a tide table that is up to date and has been written specifically for the area you are visiting. Regional tidal books list the variations of local tide times, and advise you how many minutes you need to add to or subtract from them, depending on your exact seashore location. A local tide table is an essential piece of kit that will give you all the information you need on tidal heights and times so you do not miss out on the best opportunities for exploration.

There is an even greater tidal cycle worth briefly mentioning. It is called the lunar nodal cycle and it repeats every 18.6 years. In 1997 we experienced the highest and lowest spring tides and we should do so again in 2015. Other factors like the weather may affect overall tidal heights but, generally speaking, 2015 (and every 18.6 years thereafter) should be a great year for rockpooling.

How to read a tide table

Time and tide wait for no man.

William Shakespeare, *Macbeth* 1606

A tide table is an essential part of your low-tide exploration. If you are planning a coastal holiday focused on rockpooling, it might be wise to look ahead at the local tide table in order to organise your holiday around the best available tides. Tide tables give you the information you need to plan a day's rockpooling around the tide times. It is always worth arriving well before low tide. The best plan is to follow out the tide, allowing you maximum time to explore on the lower shore.

Take care not to get so carried away discovering new species that you do not notice the tide rushing into the gullies around where you stand. The incoming tide may well fill gullies that allowed you access to the lower shore. This can result in a slightly wetter journey home than originally expected. To avoid this ask local people for advice on the local tides and currents, and allow plenty of time to return to the beach before the tide comes rushing in.

Knowing the tide times is an important part of planning a seashore trip.

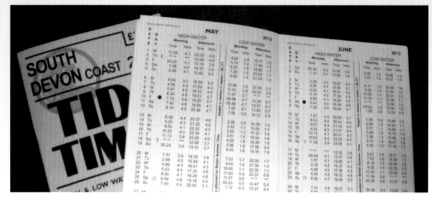

A typical page from a tide table includes times and tidal heights of both high and low tides.

SEPTEMBER	HIGH TIDE				LOW TIDE			
	am		pm		am		pm	
	Time	Height (m)	Time	Height (m)	Time	Height (m)	Time	Height (m)
5 Tues	10.55	4.44	23.32	4.20	04.40	1.30	16.15	1.40
29 Thurs	06.53	5.40	19.11	5.50	00.41	0.40	13.03	0.40

The two dates given in the section of a tide table above are an example of a neap tide on 5 September and a spring tide on 29 September. A transect of a rocky shore is the easiest way to illustrate what these tidal heights mean.

The variation in neap and spring tides makes a signficant difference to the amount of shore exposed for rockpooling.

The illustration shows how a low spring tide exposes more rocky shores and therefore new species that may not be seen during the lesser neap tides. Standing at the lowest point of a spring tide the water may barely touch your feet, while at the same spot on a neap tide of 0.4m you would be wading up to your knees in water. If the shore is very steep this difference in tidal heights results in far less seashore to explore – this is why low spring tides provide the best opportunities to find species like the Spotted Cowrie (*Trivia monacha*) clinging to rocky walls covered in Jewel Anemones (*Corynactis viridis*) and sponges.

It is worth noting that the wind and barometric pressure both also alter tidal heights from those given in your tables. Strong onshore winds (from sea to land) cause water to surge higher than usual, and vice versa for offshore winds. When we are experiencing poor weather and low pressure the sea is pushed down onto the shore, with high pressure having the opposite effect. Tide tables assume an atmospheric pressure of 1013 mmHg (millibars). If there is a particularly high pressure of 1040 mmHg the tide will be approximately 30cm lower. If a region experiences low pressure the tide will be higher. Tidal heights vary by about 1cm for every 1 millibar of pressure.

These first two sections contain only a simplified explanation of the tidal cycle, with suggestions on how to maximise its opportunities. As with most things, what can be covered in a page or two can be explained in much finer detail in an entire book. A good way to gain an appreciation of the extreme variations of the tidal cycle is to walk along an estuary on a low spring tide (though only if you know the area well and are sure of your own safety) and try to imagine the 4 or 5m of water that would be over your head about six hours later in the same spot. Though we now have a logical explanation for this phenomenon, it is still difficult to comprehend the immense power of the astronomical forces exerted on our small aquatic planet.

limit of low neap tide

limit of low spring tide

Where to look...

If man cannot discover for himself the evident beauty and design and knowledge which exist in every rock-pool and every weed-covered stone, no amount of talking or writing will drive the palpable fact into his head.

George Tugwell, *A Manual of the Commonly Found Sea-Anemones on the English Coast* 1856

Now that you have a clearer idea of the best times to go rockpooling, the next step is knowing where to look for all the weird and wonderful species on the seashore.

There is not a rock, seaweed, gully or boulder on the seashore that does not offer perfect conditions for something to live. The range of seashore habitats is suitable for species that burrow in sediment or sand, or in types of shingle, mud or pebbles. The more we familiarise ourselves with how many different habitats there are within the seashore, the more species we are likely to find.

The first and least obvious place to look is in the water itself. A handful of seawater in your cupped hands contains the basis of all life, in the seas and on land. Plankton are the ocean-drifting algae, animals and bacteria that go with the oceanic currents and tides and are the foundation of the marine food web. Phytoplankton are found in the photic zone, where the sun's energy can easily penetrate. These photosynthetic plankton make good use of the

Every handful of seawater is full of plankton – the basis for life in the oceans and a source of oxygen on earth.

Different rockpool species can be found sheltering under or attached to boulders and rocks.

sunlight for survival just like our terrestrial plants do, producing oxygen in the process. It is to these microscopic algae in our seas and oceans that we owe approximately half of our atmospheric oxygen.

Plankton also includes animal plankton or zooplankton. Some zooplankton species remain as plankton throughout their lives, but others undergo incredible transformations into some of our more recognisable intertidal species, such as the Shore Crab (*Carcinus maenas*) and Common Starfish (*Asterias rubens*). Many of the species found in the intertidal zone start their lives as larval planktonic stages. It is only as they grow that they settle and start to take on adult form. Spring is the peak time for plankton growth; there is also a second, lesser autumnal peak that is influenced by variations in sea temperature and the availability of sunlight and nutrients for growth.

Thankfully for the seashore observer, no two shores are ever the same. The gradation of the shore, the tidal range, the exposure to wind and waves, the type of rocky substrate or coarseness of sand and local weather conditions are just some of the factors that help create diversity on the seashore. All these factors work together to create thousands of kilometres of varied coastline with thousands of different species.

Where there is little exposure to wind and waves, the shoreline shows distinct and different zones. Each contains species that can tolerate living within differing regions and their specific conditions. Closer to the low-tide mark, species spend more time in their natural marine environment and less time out of the water. Higher up the shore, towards the high-tide mark, species have to withstand being left high and dry over the tidal cycle and have adapted to suit these conditions and their associated stresses.

The diagram below illustrates the variation in species found in the typical intertidal zones. You will first discover the splash zone, or supralittoral fringe, where you will find, amongst others, lichens and the Rough Periwinkle (*Littorina saxatilis*). As you move towards the sea you will find resilient seaweeds like the Channelled Wrack (*Pelvetia canaliculata*) on the upper shore. Even nearer the sea you come to the mid shore, or eulittoral zone, which is dominated by wracks such as the Spiral Wrack (*Fucus spiralis*) and Egg Wrack (*Ascophyllum nodosum*), and where you will find species attached to the rocks such as limpets and anemones. Next you reach the lower shore and here you can see red seaweeds, the long tendrils of Thongweed (*Himanthalia elongata*) and the blades of kelp emerging out of the water, with Cushion Stars (*Asterina gibbosa*) and Common Starfish (*Asterias rubens*) sheltering on the rocks below. Finally, you reach the subtidal region, where the deeper water species live. This zone is least affected by tides, but is also inaccessible by foot. If the gradient of the rocks is steep you may find you do not have to go very far to discover this region, but if the gradient is shallow you could have a mini-adventure ahead of you and a snorkel can come in handy.

For species that live between the tides temperatures can vary widely, not only because of the seasons but also because of the tides. The temperature of a pool may vary by up to 10°C in the summer months. As pools get warmer their salinity and quantity of available dissolved gases changes. The pH or acidity of the water also changes over a tidal cycle. As well as contending with these variables the species that live here also have to deal with aggressive waves on both the high and low tide, and with aquatic, avian and/or terrestrial predators.

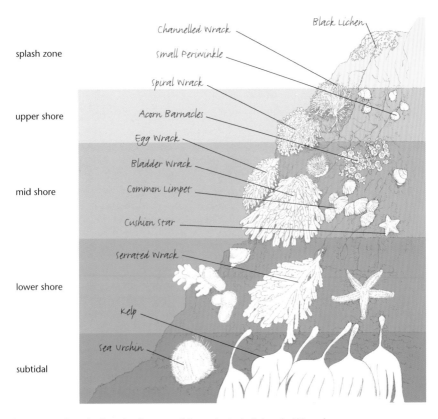

The zonation of a rocky shore showing some of the species typically found within each zone.

water

The most unexpected places, like the undersides of pontoons, are full of marine life.

You can now see why Britain's coasts have a collection of such apparently alien species that are so perfectly adapted to this uniquely beautiful but harsh aquatic environment. Moreover, the coastline offers a never-ending supply of new and different territories to explore. The rockpooling experience is therefore never dull, and the few hours offered by the tidal cycle never seem quite long enough time to investigate rockpools fully.

To see interesting species that might be difficult to capture in a bucket, allow yourself some time for quiet observation sitting on the edge of a rockpool. Species in rockpools are sensitive to vibrations, and the stamping of feet on nearby rocks will ensure most head for the closest crevice, potentially never to be seen again. By taking a moment to sit down and watch quietly you might see some of those species re-emerge, and witness interesting behaviour that might otherwise be missed.

There are species suited to shady areas, such as the Breadcrumb Sponge (*Hallichondria panicea*), which covers large areas of rocky substrate. They dry out very quickly on sunny surfaces, so you will discover them under rocky overhangs. In areas permanently in shade, species are found that are less well adapted to the heat and drying effects of direct sunlight.

On the sunny surfaces of the rocks you may find species like the Common Limpet (*Patella vulgata*) or Acorn Barnacle (*Balanus balanoides*), which cling tightly to the rock or have rocky plates that protect them from the heat, cold and predators on this exposed and potentially vulnerable patch of seashore.

Other hardy types can be found clinging onto the cooler undersides of rocks. They are able to withstand the buffeting of the boulders, moving with the tidal and wave surges. Here you may find the beautiful Star Ascidian (*Botryllus schlosseri*), looking like a well-crafted piece of glasswork, or the Broad-clawed Porcelain Crab (*Porcellana platycheles*), perfectly camouflaged on the underside of a rock, holding fast.

Under the boulders moulting crabs may be sheltering in safety until their shells harden. Many of the rockpool fish like the Shore Clingfish (*Lepadogaster purpurea*) can make their nests under the rocks, where they look after their progeny until they hatch. This makes it vitally important to return any species and rocks that you move to the places where you found them.

The sediment on our shores can include fine shingle under boulders or within the sand or silt in estuaries. On the beach it is the material that settles on the sea floor, made up of organic matter, shell, rock and bone fragments, and these areas can be surprisingly rich in life. There are bivalves that burrow into the sediment, such as the Common Cockle (*Cerastoderma edule*) and large, rare Fan Mussel (*Atrina fragilis*). On more gravelly bottoms you could find some of the marvellous marine worms like the impressive Bootlace Worm (*Lineus longissima*). If you watch the receding tide you may notice the sand fizzing and squirting, evidence of burrowing bivalves. Their siphons project just above the sand, filtering water and food.

There are also some fish that lie in wait camouflaged in the sand. The Lesser Weever Fish (*Echiichthys vipera*), for example, will unfortunately be felt before it can be seen. If you accidentally stand on one it will inject your foot with a small amount of venom from its dorsal fin, which can sometimes cause considerable pain.

Despite aggressive tidal action, rocky gullies are home to a range of hardy species.

In addition to exploring the natural surfaces and sediments, it is worth visiting some man-made structures. Harbours are prolific havens, with interesting species living hidden on the undersides of floating pontoons, jetties and neglected boats. In fast-flowing areas, many larvae-born species settle on these structures and grow into their adult forms, filtering nutrients from the moving water. You may be lucky enough to discover the soft coral Dead Man's Fingers (*Alcyonium digitata*), or some bright white, feathery looking puffs that are the Plumose Anemone (*Metridium senile*).

On a low tide you may also find that the hulls of boats have their own assemblage of species that have settled over time. Barnacles are often some of the first to settle, along with microscopic algae that provide a suitable surface for the larval stages of mussels, for example, to settle. It is important to remember that every area, corner and structure within the intertidal and marine environment is a niche in which different species with different adaptations can settle and thrive.

The British Isles are fortunate enough to lie between two distinct biogeographical regions. To the south-west the British Isles are influenced by the warm North Atlantic drift, which brings with it species that are found in the Atlantic and Mediterranean, also known as the Lusitanian species. In the north and north-east the British Isles are influenced by the cooler polar 'slope current' from the Iberian region. Therefore, the northern and eastern reaches are more often home to the Boreo-Arctic species from cooler climates.

The Snakelocks Anemone (*Actinia equina*), for example, is found in the southerly reaches of the British Isles, but not in the north and north-east. However, with changes in sea temperatures and shifts in currents, the distribution of some of the Lusitanian species may shift northwards. We could even lose some species in the north that are no longer suited to the changing water temperatures and conditions around the British Isles.

The strandline, or the line of flotsam and jetsam deposited by the tides and waves, also provides an opportunity to find species that are often not found between the tides. The rotting, decaying seaweed is home to many invertebrates that are great sources of food for both marine animals, such as fish (when submerged), and also for mammals, such as shrews, bats and even hedgehogs, all of which have been known to frequent the strandline. Within this valuable habitat lurks a variety of marine-related treasures such as mermaid's purses, cuttlefish bones and sea wash balls.

There is a huge variety of marine species to be found in disparate parts of the British Isles. The overall number of marine flora and fauna, excluding the bacteria and viruses, stands at close to 10,000 species. This should be enough to keep even the most avid and conscientious rockpooler busy for many years. However, to ensure that we maintain this diversity for the next visitor – and hopefully for many generations of seashore visitors to come – it is important that we take care of all our seashore species and ourselves by following a few simple rules, commonly referred to as the Seashore Code.

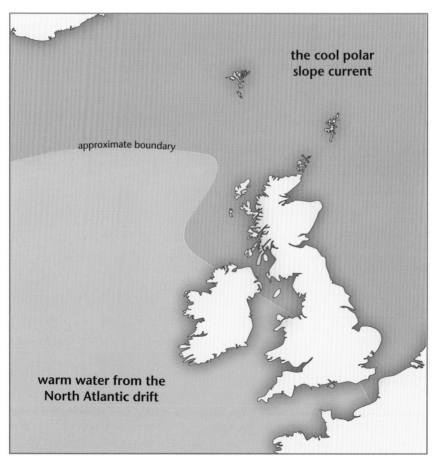

The British Isles is situated on a biogeographical boundary of warm water and cool water species, some of which have migrated northwards as sea temperatures have increased.

The Seashore Code

Hug the shore; let others try the deep.

Virgil, *The Aeneid* 19BC

In historical seashore guides readers would be positively encouraged to collect uncommon seashore animals and plants for their aquariums. However, today we have a greater awareness about the vulnerability of our natural environment, and we know we must take better care of both the wildlife and ourselves. We are often wisely encouraged to take only photographs and leave only footprints.

Having said that, there is little better than the sight of an intertidal rocky shore smothered in sunshine and people rockpooling. However, it is important for all seashore visitors to aim to ensure that the next time the tide retreats to allow glimpses of marine life, we can find the same healthy species as we discovered here on previous explorations. We must follow what is commonly called the Seashore Code. This ensures not only your own safety, but also that of the beautiful species you are likely to find lurking in rocky crevices and under swathes of seaweeds.

The beauty of rockpooling is that it only requires a bucket and a little consideration.

Wearing appropriate clothing ensures a fun day on the seashore whatever the season.

Dress for the occasion

The first step is to make sure you are prepared for the day out by getting properly dressed for the elements. The seashore has a habit of amplifying weather conditions. The sun's rays are strong when reflected off seawater, and so too are the winds when they are blown onshore from that vast seascape. It is also advisable to wear sturdy footwear that will protect you from the sharp rocks and bony plates of barnacles.

Tides, weather and timing

Check your tide table for the best time to visit the shore. Tide tables are only a guide and it is important to remember other factors that could affect your trip, including the weather, currents and the type of beach you are visiting. Other factors that affect tides include strong winds, changes in weather pressure and the local conditions. It is always best to ask locals for advice on currents and the best spots for rockpooling, and to check for any information panels on the beach.

Tread gently

As you traverse the rocky seashore, be aware of your footing and take your time. In summer, when seaweeds shroud the shoreline and the sun has not had the opportunity to dry them out, rocks can be very slippery. Be careful not to dislodge any species from their positions as you walk – limpets can rarely find their 'home scars' again if you accidentally remove them from the safety of their individual positions on the shore.

Equipment

Rockpooling organisations often recommend that nets should not be used when exploring the seashore. They tend to be very destructive because of their 'remote' nature. When we use our hands to collect specimens we are far more likely to take care of ourselves and, as a result, this will also ensure the safety of the species we are trying to pick up. The best bits of kit you could invest in are some sample pots or a transparent bucket. These are simple, but brilliant tools that can help you look closely at some of the other-worldly features of the marine species you find as you explore the seashore. A clear bucket or pot allows you to take a really good look at a species' anatomy before returning it safely to the place where you found it.

When using buckets, trays or pots, it is important not to keep a variety of species in the same pot. If you did this, there would be a good chance that a food chain would be created in the pot and that your species would end up eating one another. The water in the bucket must also be changed regularly, as the temperature of such as small volume of liquid can increase rapidly on a hot summer's day.

Protecting species

The intertidal environment is a harsh one even without our intrusion, so it is important to give these highly adapted and unique species a fighting chance of survival. As in all habitats species have evolved to cope with specific locations. In rockpools, for example, the Snakelocks Anemone (*Actinia equina*) needs sunshine for the algae that live within its tentacles, whereas chitons hide from direct sunlight. If you turn over a rock to look at a species on the underside or below it, make sure you put the rock back in the position you found it. Moulting crabs, for example, are highly vulnerable to predation if they are not returned to the safety of a protective rock.

Coastal birds and seals

In some regions of the coastal seashore you may find roosting birds during the winter months; you may also see them on their summer breeding grounds, particularly on shingle beaches. You may even spot an area where seals are congregating with their pups. Take note of where these areas are and give the animals the space they need to protect and raise their offspring.

Give nesting birds on shingle beaches a wide berth. This is a Little Tern, one of our rarest coastal seabirds.

Beach cleans are a great way of helping to keep our coast clean and safe.

Marine litter

The strandline on the seashore has changed dramatically over the last century. With the advent of plastic we are finding plastic materials of every description on the strandline and beaches. This has implications for marine health and you must ensure that you remove any litter that you take down to the beach with you. If you take a spare bag in your pocket you could perhaps also help remove any plastic on the beach left by others. Take extra care if you come across any sharp or unsanitary items that turn up on the shoreline. There are often organised beach-cleaning events which are great social occasions and a brilliant way of helping to free the seas of plastic.

At home

While it is evident that you can do your bit on the seashore to protect these wonderful species, you can also protect them from the comfort of your home. Do not buy marine souvenirs from seaside shops – starfish, shells and seahorses are likely to have been gathered alive. You can also help preserve the health of the seas and coastal regions by using phosphate-free detergents, and by not pouring any oils or solvents into the drainage systems. You will also help support the marine environment by only eating seafood that has been sustainably sourced – your fishmonger should be able to help you with this.

If you are able to follow this advice, not only will you discover one of the most satisfying and exciting of nature's playgrounds, but you will also be able to do your bit to protect it.

Keeping a
nature journal

*The average human... looks without seeing, listens without hearing, touches
without feeling, eats without tasting, moves without physical awareness,
inhales without awareness of odour or fragrance, and talks without thinking.*

Leonardo Da Vinci, quoted in *Leonardo's Notebooks* 15th century

Now we know how to tread gently we can explore ways of preserving our memories and
enhancing our experiences of the seashore. Keeping a nature journal provides a great way
of gaining a deeper perspective of the natural world around you.

There are no rules for writing a nature journal, but if you want to use it for future records
and comparison it is useful to keep a note of the date, and the tidal and weather conditions
of the visit you are recording. You could also include a rough illustration of the shoreline to
remind you of its generic qualities. Besides these loose guidelines a nature journal is a means
of recording your exploration of the seashore using your own words, illustrations and style.

After several months or even years of keeping a journal, you may find patterns emerging, or
even new theories developing from your personal jottings. There are some great exercises you
can do to help you explore the natural world around you. You could start by exploring with
your senses and developing a multi-dimensional sensory appreciation of this aquatic habitat.

Nature or field journals can help you to gain a greater perspective of the natural world around you.

You could spend one day on the seashore exploring with your sense of touch alone. On this day forget about which species you may find. Instead just explore how they all feel. Spend some time exploring the different textures of the seaweeds. They may vary from slimy but firm in the case of kelps, to soft and delicate when it comes to tufted weed that grows attached to Egg Wrack (*Ascophyllum nodosum*). You might sense a Cushion Star (*Asterina gibbosa*), with its rough upper surface but softer underside. As you explore with your sense of touch you may come up with questions you had never previously considered. What makes that seaweed slimy? What benefit does a rougher upper surface have for a starfish? The answers to these questions could just take you on a new journey of appreciation for the seaweeds and other organisms of the seashore.

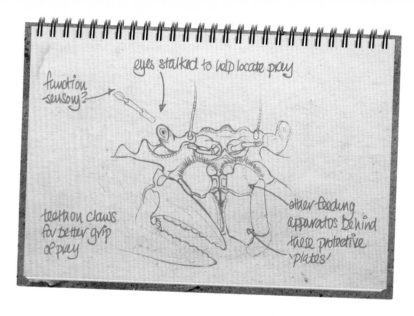

Drawing the detail of a crab's feeding structures can help you understand how they work.

This closer examination of the seashore can be the birthplace of a scientific mind of enquiry. If we take a moment to really examine what is before us we begin to question what we touch, feel and smell. As we explore the questions – and digest the answers – our understanding of the seashore grows. To help with your exploration, try finding creative ways of remembering your discoveries through your nature journals. This could include drawing what you find or even using other art materials to record your experiences.

Illustrating what you see is a fun way of gaining a better understanding of the anatomy of seashore species. In practice it is always useful to spend a long time observing before putting pencil to paper. Over time watch how a species moves, how it feeds and how it protects itself from impending danger. Details in this handbook on particular species can help you with this. Keep asking yourself questions about your observations. These questions will make you look further still at the detail of the species you are studying. You might then recognise, for example, the detailed feeding parts that are necessary for a crab to feed. Examination you carry out for illustration purposes could help you identify the qualifying features that set one species apart from another. Your illustrations could also be a useful reference source for other readers.

Many modern technologies and media can play a part in keeping a nature journal. Simple things like noting whether you took photographs or videos of unusual behaviour can enhance a journal entry. There are also lots of online resources that can help you map a seashore trip. You can obtain accurate grid references to add to your journal entry, and you can even pinpoint your latest discoveries on useful websites like Google Earth.

Social media are ideal for sharing our experiences and are an opportunity to inspire others to do the same. Nature blogs are an excellent way of keeping a record of your explorations and allowing others to recognise species you find. Readers of your blog could even helpfully correct identification or add to your understanding in other ways.

Reading nature journals from bygone eras is not only a delightful opportunity to gain a sense of somebody's experience; many such journals are also of scientific importance. Books by nineteenth-century naturalists who recorded which species they saw on a certain shore are still used today to give an indication of how species abundance and distribution might have changed. You never know how or why your findings could become of scientific importance now or in the future. If there is something you feel may have particular significance it is always incredibly useful to inform the relevant organisations. With every seashore visit we can be the eyes and ears on behalf of scientists and our findings could prove invaluable in progressing everyone's understanding of the seashore.

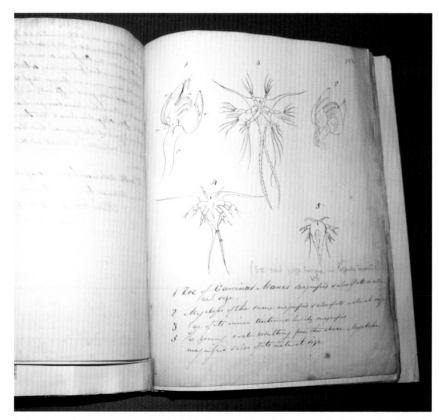

In the nineteenth century, naturalist Richard Quiller Couch used his field journal to help explore and understand the larval stages of the Shore Crab.

What to do...

As a visitor to the seashore you are in a position to provide valuable information to scientists, organisations and charities that work towards the protection and conservation of our coast. With your assistance they can gather useful data to promote changes in policy that will help further protect our coastline and its inhabitants.

...if you discover an unusual or interesting species

Some species are of particular significance to scientists because they are classed as climate indicators, or as non-native or invasive species. Such species are indicated in this handbook via a pen and paper symbol alongside their names. They are of specific interest to marine ecologists who research the impact of climate change and human influence on the natural environment. By recording your sightings you can help them gain a better understanding of the health of our seas (www.marlin.ac.uk/rml).

The arrival of invasive species like this Chinese Mitten Crab (*Eriocheir sinensis*) is becoming more frequent on our shores.

...if you spot a pollution incident

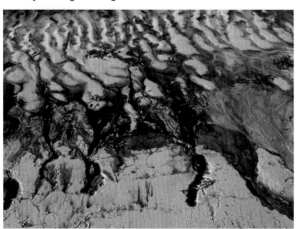

If you are on the beach and discover a pollution incident, contact the Environment Agency's free pollution hotline for England, Wales, Scotland or Northern Ireland – 0800 807060.

Prompt reporting of pollution incidents helps speedy response and action.

...if you find mermaid's purses

Every year The Shark Trust organises various events to gather data on the egg cases of sharks and rays that helps us to study the health of their populations. You can find out about these events, download identification guides and report your sightings on the trust's site dedicated to mermaid's purses: www.eggcase.org

Mermaid's purses can be found fresh and pale or darkened in the sun. They are egg cases of sharks and rays.

...if you see a jellyfish (dead or alive)

If it is in UK waters report it to the Marine Conservation Society at www.mcsuk.org
On their website you will find information on how to report your jellyfish sighting as well as a helpful identification guide.

Jellyfish, like these Moon Jellyfish (*Aurelia aurita*), come in to shallower waters in great swarms or smacks.

...if you spot a Basking Shark

For information on what to do if you see a Basking Shark, go to www.baskingsharks.org. Here you will find great resources, including codes of conduct for when you are in the water, and advice on reporting a sighting. For all other shark-related information visit www. sharktrust.org

Basking Sharks can be spotted in the summer months – mouths agape, feeding on plankton.

...if you spot a whale or dolphin

You can report your sighting on the Sea Foundation website (www.seawatchfoundation.org.uk), or contact them directly by phone or on email (01545 561227 or strandings@ seawatchfoundation.org.uk).

Harbour Porpoises are frequent visitors to estuaries and coastal waters.

...if you find a live stranding

www.ukstrandings.org provides you with advice and details about what to do in the event of a stranding. British Divers Marine Life Rescue are a team of volunteers who mobilise volunteers to help return animals to the sea should that be its best option.
UK Stranding Hotline: 0800 652 0333 (for live or dead marine strandings in Scotland, England, Wales and Northern Ireland.)
Irish Seal Sanctuary: 01835 4370
Irish Whale & Dolphin Group: www.iwdg.ie
South Coast Ireland: 087 699 5314
West Coast Ireland: 086 854 5450.

The British Divers Marine Life Rescue team are well trained to deal with live strandings.

...if you find a dead stranding

It is vitally important that dead strandings be reported as quickly as possible, so that the cause of death can be established while a corpse is still fresh. Do take care around dead strandings as they can carry disease. If the stranding has a tag attached to it this means it has already been reported to the relevant organisation and no further action is required.
UK Stranding site/hotline: www.ukstrandings.org/ 0800 652 0333
Wales Stranding Network: www.strandings.com
Scotland Stranding Network www.strandings.org
Ireland's Whale and Dolphin Conservation: www.iwdg.ie

The quicker you report a dead stranding the more can be done to investigate its death.

The value of the coast and seas

There is a pleasure in the pathless woods,
There is a rapture on the lonely shore,
There is society, where none intrudes,
By the deep sea, and music in its roar:
I love not man the less, but Nature more…

Lord George G. Byron, *Childe Harold's Pilgrimage* 1812

So why should we care about the coast and seas? What value does the aquatic world have to terrestrial society? There is an obvious intrinsic value in maintaining a stunning and varied coastline – so we may discover a plethora of weird and wonderful species. However, there is a more tangible economic benefit from the coast and seas too, as an invaluable resource on a local and global scale.

The sea is an integral part of our island community.

If you are reading this book there is a good chance that you have already had an opportunity to experience the real value of our beautiful coastline. From the moment we get our first glimpse of the sea we fall under its spell. On the coast the air we breathe seems somehow purer and our senses are more fully engaged. With every trip to the seashore we are treated to a different experience due to the variability of the seasons, weather and tides. Whatever the draw, our coastline has attracted people for countless generations.

Coastal tourism is fantastic for our island nation's economy, but it relies on attractive and unspoilt coastal countryside and on providing a safe and clean environment to swim, surf and sail.

Other coastal communities rely on fisheries and their related activities for income. The sustainability of the fisheries depends on a host of complex issues. The commercial fisheries all rely on one common factor: healthy, clean, well-managed and productive seas. Many commercial species depend on our coastal habitats for spawning and for nurturing and protecting juveniles.

The contents of this book include details on how marine species hold the key to medicinal cures, engineering conundrums and all manner of discoveries that may yet benefit us. These discoveries rely on healthy, productive and biodiverse coasts and seas. If we do not maintain such conditions, we may be in danger of losing species before we realise their potential.

There is a pattern clearly emerging – if we do not protect and manage the seas we will lose an incredibly valuable aspect of our global environment. This is without beginning to consider the value of the seas for the transportation of goods, and as a source of marine aggregates and other materials used to produce everyday products for houses, homes and vehicles.

The coast is also involved in larger cyclical systems, which create a hospitable, pleasant and healthy environment for the global system. We rarely acknowledge – or we choose not to observe – the role the marine environment plays in global weather systems. We are seldom taught about or have little or no comprehension of the ocean's ability to produce and sink (absorb) gases. Recycling of gas, minerals and nutrients has gone on naturally for millennia. Recycling is a lesson taught by nature. Life's 'nutrients' are limited and are recycled by biological, physical and chemical processes – or biogeochemical processes. Here are some examples of the cycles of life to give an indication of the value of the seas and coast on a global scale.

One thing we share with all living organisms is our reliance on water. It keeps us alive and maintains our own biogeochemical processes as it does for the earth. The availability of water is down to the hydrological cycle, in which most of our water is evaporated in warmer equatorial waters. After the water falls on the land it meanders back to sea, through rivers and streams. It takes with it minerals, organic substances and man-made pollution. Ultimately, if we pollute the seas involved in these great global cycles, we serve only to create a less healthy environment for ourselves.

Our beautiful seas and oceans are a source and sink of atmospheric gases and minerals, sustaining life on earth.

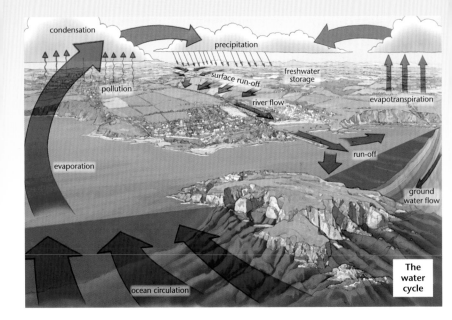

The water cycle

Carbon is an elementary aspect of life on earth. It is in life's building blocks – our carbohydrates, proteins, lipids and nucleic acids. Carbon dioxide is a critical factor for the growth of the marine producers at the base of the food chain. Just as terrestrial plants photosynthesise, so too do phytoplankton. They use the carbon dioxide dissolved in sea water to make carbohydrates and produce oxygen.

As the carbon dioxide dissolves in sea water it produces bicarbonate ions which, when combined with calcium, make marine skeletons in the vertebrates and shells in the

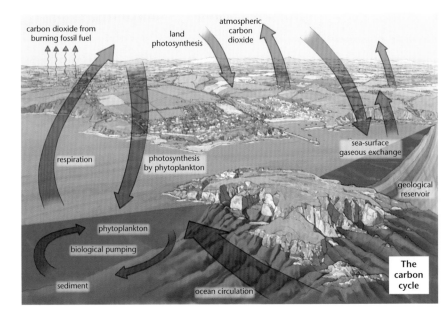

The carbon cycle

invertebrates. When excessive carbon dioxide is pumped into the atmosphere, through industrial activity and the burning of fossil fuels, the sea mops this up and absorbs this gas. The ocean then creates more bicarbonate ions but also more of the hydrogen ions that are produced when carbon dioxide dissolves in sea water. This process – called ocean acidification – is acidifying our oceanic waters. It has potentially serious ramifications for marine species and marine habitats.

Nitrogen is also needed for life and for making proteins in the plants and marine algae that form the basis of the food web. When these producers die they release nitrogen, which is used again by other producers. Vast quantities of dead organisms drop to the ocean floor, where the nutrients collect in a way that is not dissimilar to leaf litter on a forest floor. As a result of winds and ocean currents the nutrients are brought to the surface of the sea and provide a source of food, resulting in a phytoplankton bloom. In our rich temperate waters this is a seasonal process that peaks in the spring, with a lesser but still obvious peak in the autumn. Because of this excess of nutrients the plankton grow well and the species that rely on them for food move into our waters. It is shortly after these blooms start that we start seeing the mackerel and the enigmatic leviathans – the Basking Sharks (*Cetorhinus maximus*).

Excess nitrogen from agricultural fertilisers can run off the land into freshwater systems and then into the seas. High levels of nutrients from human activities like this promote excessive algal growth, decay and consumption of oxygen, which can lead to 'dead zones'. Here there is not enough oxygen for phytoplankton growth, which has a knock-on effect on the food web; it causes a negative impact on entire ecosystems, including potential commercial fisheries.

This section only touches on some of the processes in the global ecosystem, but hopefully it demonstrates not just the value but also the integral importance of our seas and coast to life on land. We must safeguard our aquatic systems for their intrinsic environmental and societal value. Intertidal species rely on these systems for their health, as does the human population. In the end, though, we must protect the marine environment because all life is connected.

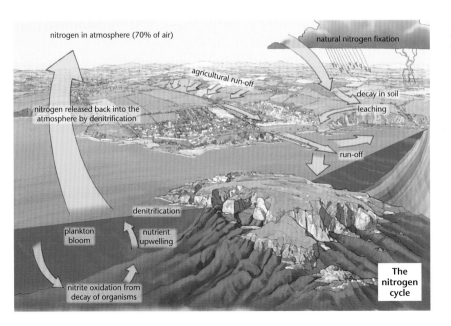

Conservation and climate change

In the end, we will conserve only what we love, we will love only what we understand, and we will understand only what we are taught.

Baba Dioum, speaking in 1968 to the General Assembly of the International Union for the Conservation of Nature

We have discovered that coastal and marine habitats are connected to the health of other systems on land, and that their conservation is therefore of vital importance. The seashore represents a highly biodiverse region. Rocky shores are an important habitat for biodiversity, feeding and spawning, and as a resting place for our much-loved seals. The health of coastal regions has an impact on the seas, which in turn affects our lives on land through the cyclical nature of our global system. Unfortunately, we have the ability to upset nature's balance.

The seashore is an incredibly dynamic zone, and many species living here can cope with quite extreme and variable conditions and are particularly resilient to change. Many are very capable of sensing and responding to natural changes in their environment. The ability of

The coast is susceptible to agricultural run-off and to a variety of other human activity.

Invasive species like the Slipper Limpet (*Crepidula fornicata*) can spread rapidly, outcompeting our native species.

the larvae of a large number of species to disperse with tides and currents allows them to re-populate areas that have been affected by natural or man-made incidents. Their survival relies on healthy neighbouring representative patches of different habitats. Unfortunately, because intertidal species are situated in the area where land physically meets the sea they are particularly susceptible to pollution from both land and water.

The cocktail of pollutants and human impacts varies from plastics, agricultural run-off and industrial effluents, to increased carbon dioxide emissions and the associated effects from climate change. These all work together to create changes in the coastal environment that, in turn, can affect our ability to enjoy the seashore and all it offers, ultimately affecting our economy.

During a time when more development around estuaries is likely, there is an increased chance of siltation from building works. As we increasingly import and export goods there has been a corresponding increase in non-native, often invasive, species. This has been exacerbated by warming sea temperatures, which increased the likelihood of warmer water species settling and colonising.

Our coasts and seashores are changing because of the introduction of these non-native species, which have moved or been introduced from their original native geographical range. They have the potential to damage our ecology and our economy, at which point they are classed as invasive. This is often a natural phenomenon. However, we also provide mechanisms that increase the rate and chances of it happening. Some species can inadvertently hitch a ride in ballast water or on boat hulls that are transported across our oceans in the shipping industry. Species have also been introduced through the aquaculture industry – young oysters, for example, can have larvae of other species attached to or within their exteriors.

There continue to be incidents of oil pollution around the global coasts, which can have a huge impact on local economies as well as killing wildlife. Coastal waters are also hit by large volumes of nitrates and phosphates from agricultural run-off. The nitrates and phosphates are fertilisers used in the agricultural industry to help boost depleted soils. After heavy rains, the chemicals and soil can run from the fields and reach the rivers and eventually the seas.

The quality of the global marine environment as a whole is affected by other human influences. The fishing industry can affect the quality of habitats through the types of fishing gear used. Boats dragging heavy trawls along the sea bed can destroy valuable habitats. Fishing can also change the balance of species in our waters by removing an excess of individual species. This could involve the eradication of top predators, like shark and tuna, or the large-scale removal of species lower down the food web, like Krill, to be used as a food base for the aquaculture industry. Such losses will have an impact on how marine ecosystems function.

In order to understand ocean acidification, place some Coral Weed in a small beaker of household vinegar. The seaweed's chalky calcium carbonate skeleton bubbles away as the acid breaks it down.

Then there are changes in sea temperature and acidity caused by human activities. Recent research has shown that increases in temperature and decreases in the acidity of our seas have a large and varied impact on the species that live within them. In lobster species, increased temperature and decreased acidity has been shown to produce smaller lobsters with normal size claws and rostrum (the section covering the head), but a smaller thorax (main body). How this might affect the health of the populations is still the subject of research and the impact on commercial fisheries is unknown.

A simple experiment demonstrates the potential effect of acidification. If a small piece of Coral Weed (*Corralina officinalis*) is taken from the strandline and placed in a dish with some household vinegar, the acid can be seen to dissolve the calcareous exoskeleton of the Coral Weed. While this is an extreme example, it gives an indication of the effects of acidifying seas.

The range or distribution of species around the coast is also changing due to the changes in sea temperatures. There is a general northwards migration of species around the British Isles. There are specific species that have been classed as 'climate change indicators'. These will help show the rate at which our coastal waters are changing due to climate change. Along with other species important to science, they are highlighted in this book with a pen and paper symbol.

To maintain a variety of species that will support a healthy and diverse ecosystem, it is important to conserve a variety of habitats that home a larger variety of species. A network of Marine Protected Areas has been established. These protected habitats work together to create an ecologically coherent network of protected sites, ultimately conserving a variety of species and habitats. This will then benefit the marine system as a whole and its ability to cope with climate change and pollution episodes, and will help affected regions to recover.

The protected areas include habitats that act as breeding and nursery grounds for different species for their ecological and commercial value. They also include areas that are protected from harmful human activities such as oil drilling, fishing and mineral exploration or dredging. These established networks can improve biodiversity, allow for habitat recovery, produce larger species (that produce more offspring), increase the larval distribution of species, improve fisheries stocks, enhance tourism, and help the economy to grow.

Marine scientists, researchers and government policy makers help manage, measure and reduce the effects of harmful human activities and gain a better understanding of the condition of natural habitats. We can contribute to marine conservation through supporting local and national management efforts, becoming involved in beach cleans, buying sustainable seafood and generally becoming more careful consumers. There are many steps we can take to support and promote conservation in marine areas, but the very first and perhaps most important step is to enjoy become familiar with and enjoy the wonderful plants and animals that are found around the spectacular British coastline.

Enjoy your journey of discovery on the British seashore.

SEAWEEDS

Oh! Call us not weeds, but flowers of the sea,
For lovely, and gay, and bright tinted are we!
Our blush is as deep as the role of thy bowers –
Then Call us not weeds, we are ocean's gay flowers.

Mary M. Howard, *Ocean Flowers and Their Teachings* 1846

As you approach the sheltered rocky seashore on a low tide, the glistening seaweeds lie flat on the rocks, attached by their holdfasts and laid down where the waves and swell left them as the tide receded. Within this flattened seaweed, many other species conceal themselves from predators and the heat of the sun. On a hot summer's day the seaweeds become so dry and crisp that it is hard to believe they will recover. As you approach the tidal pools the spectacular and vibrant green of the Sea Lettuce (*Ulva lactuca*) stands out. Other seaweeds might include the branching fronds of Irish Moss (*Chondrus crispus*), the tips of which reflect the sun and seem to glow metallic blue.

Kelp forests are rich habitats sheltering many species.

During the summer months the seaweeds have grown so successfully that some pools are obscured by vast curtains of the invasive Wireweed (*Sargassum muticum*). This proliferation of seaweeds provides protection from predators for the creatures that live in the pools but sadly also prevents the rockpooler from clearly seeing them. On summer days when the low tides reveal pools filled to the brim with seaweeds and wracks the rocky shore becomes almost two-dimensional.

However, if the same rocky shore were snorkelled over on a high tide it would present a very different picture. On the high tide the seaweeds stand erect and tall. They use sunlight to grow, so have evolved to reach up towards the sun. The rocky shore is transformed into a marine forest, allowing snorkelers to glide over the canopy and gain a bird's eye view of what goes on in the 'undergrowth'. From this perspective, views of the rocky shore are more three-dimensional, packed with colourful seaweeds both short and tall, and the fish and invertebrates that live within this vibrant community.

Seaweeds are marine algae that are split into three main groups – the red, brown and green seaweeds. Confusingly, the red and green seaweeds are thought to be closely related to terrestrial plants while the brown ones are not. They do, however, share common structures and features. Seaweeds do not have roots but most have holdfasts to firmly grip on to a suitable surface; some do not attach to anything at all. They do photosynthesise like terrestrial plants, and use pigments that are ideally suited to the different quality of sunlight in the sea and its ability to penetrate to different depths. The colours of the seaweed fronds are no less beautiful than a flowering meadow. Seaweeds offer a colourful palate on the seashore and are an invaluable part of the seashore ecosystem, as well as offering much to our lives on dry land.

To help identify and examine the seaweeds, it is useful to familiarise yourself with some seaweed descriptions and general morphological terms.

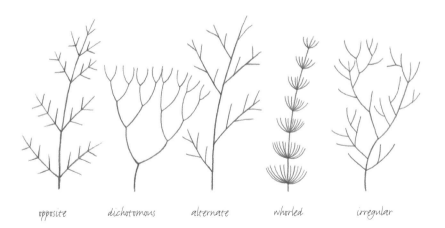

opposite   *dichotomous*   *alternate*   *whorled*   *irregular*

The terms used to describe the branching patterns of seaweeds.

The holdfast of a seaweed acts as an attachment mechanism, whether this is to a shell, another seaweed, a hard man-made structure or the more usual rocky surface. It does not use the holdfast for absorbing nutrients, as do the roots of terrestrial plants, but merely as an incredibly strong anchor. This is clearly evident when kelps are washed up on to the seashore. The tangled mass reveals that the holdfast has been ripped off the rocks, and it often still has some of the bedrock firmly attached to it.

The distribution of seaweeds that we find on the seashore is affected by their ability to cope with desiccation, the season, the availability of light and the exposure to waves and storms. The thinner seaweeds are prone to damage by storms and wave action. They are more likely to be found in sheltered pools and on less exposed beaches. There is a range of sizes and forms of seaweed, from small species that encrust rocks to longer tendrils that extend to the sea surface on the high tide for a couple of metres. The taller species may have evolved to include air bladders, which help them to float to their most erect position, maximising the light available to them.

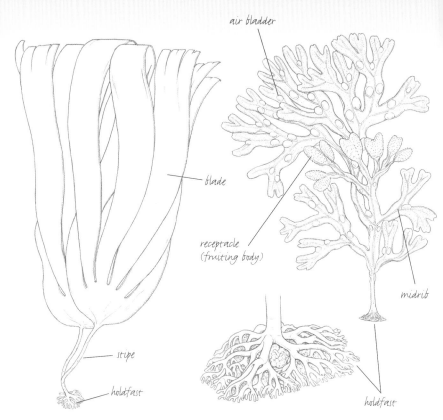

The forms and structures of seaweeds.

Seaweeds have been and are still of great value to our society. There are records of seaweed being used for cattle fodder going back to the times of Horatus at the turn of the first century. More recently and even today, laver cakes are made from harvested Purple Laver (*Porphyra umbilicalis*). Irish Moss (*Chondrus crispus*) has been used to make jellies and blancmanges because its carrageen is a great substitute for gelatine. However, it is worth noting that seaweeds are very good at absorbing heavy metals from industry, so can contain high levels of chemicals. It is also interesting to note that seaweeds have slightly different bonds in their carbohydrate molecules than do those of terrestrial plants, which render them indigestible to humans. Limpets and other gastropods benefit from an enzyme that is capable of breaking down these carbohydrates. However, marine algae are packed with minerals and nutrients and they do taste rather good.

Seaweeds have also been used by farmers as fertiliser. In the past they were used to help nourish the soil for growing potatoes. There are even seaweed 'farms' of varying structure and scale in this country and abroad, although seaweed farms in the UK tend to be on a small scale. Seaweeds are used for foods such as Wakame in sushi. The alginates, agar and carrageen derived from seaweeds are used as thickening agents for the pharmaceutical, cosmetic and food industries.

Perhaps the real value of marine algae is attributable to its place in the seashore ecosystem. Seaweeds provide food and shelter in the intertidal zone for many creatures such as the Blue-rayed Limpet (*Patella pellucida*). Looking closely at the blades of the laminarians it is often possible to find the neon-blue lines of this small but beautiful limpet. Even when detached by storms, the seaweeds are an important habitat. They float in masses as flotsam and create rafts that serve as refuges for juvenile fish. Once on shore, they become the rotting strandline. This then becomes host to a range of surprising marine, avian and terrestrial visitors.

This book covers the macroscopic species that you can see without the use of a microscope. If you take time to learn some of the most common species you will find great pleasure in their many shapes, colours and diversity.

A variety of red, brown and green seaweeds can be found washed up onto the shore after storms.

Brown seaweeds

And hidden within thy depths, the seaweed creep,
And grow beneath the surf that widely raves,
Unmindful of the storms that o'er them leap,
And the rude winds that lash the dreadful waves.

Mary Anne Browne, *Ocean* 1827

Brown seaweeds belong to the class Ochrophyta and your first sight of them might be the huge piles of weather-beaten seaweeds on an autumnal trip to the seashore. Here, on the high tide, great rafts of wracks and kelps (amongst others) have been deposited on the beach by storms and waves. Progressing down the shore, the seaweeds are held tight to the intertidal rocks by their holdfasts. At the very lowest point of the tide, the ability of brown seaweeds to withstand the hot drying sun decreases, as is the case of the kelps. As a result, it is possible to identify the seaweeds through their positions on the shore as well as through their morphology.

You will find the curved fronds of the Channelled Wrack (*Pelvetia canaliculata*) at the upper reaches of the tide, with other wracks dominating the lower shore region. The broad, large blades of kelps are on the very lowest reaches, where the large, flat surface area of the blade would cause rapid dehydration from extended periods of exposure on the higher shore. The kelps create great 'forests' of protection, food and opportunity for marine species. Historically, kelp was an incredibly valuable commodity, an important source of soda, potash and iodine. These were used in industry, to make soap and glass, and the iodine was also widely used in medicine.

Swathes of brown seaweeds, like this Egg Wrack (*Ascophyllum nodosum*), cover the rocky shore.

On the low tide on cooler, wetter days the brown seaweeds stay wet, slimy and potentially dangerous for the intrepid rockpool explorer. Regardless of the weather conditions, there are cooler, moister habitats under the piles of seaweed which create an ideal safe haven for species more prone to desiccation (drying out) or predation. The brown seaweeds are the most plentiful of all the seaweeds and you should quickly be able to familiarise yourself with some of the easily distinguishable features of these relatively large brown macro-algae.

To succinctly explain the life cycle of all of the brown seaweeds is not an easy task. However, it is possible to see some of the different phases of the life cycle of the brown seaweeds with the naked eye. An apple tree has a very large amount of vegetative tissue – the roots, trunk, branches and leaves. It then has the reproductive tissue – the fruit or the apples. The seaweeds also have 'fruit' in the form of receptacles or fruiting bodies. These are more obvious in some of the seaweeds than in others. In Thongweed (*Himanthalia elongata*), for example, 98% of the seaweed is the fruiting body and only 2% the vegetative tissue. In others the 'fruit' may show as swollen, gel-filled tips, as seen in many of the wracks.

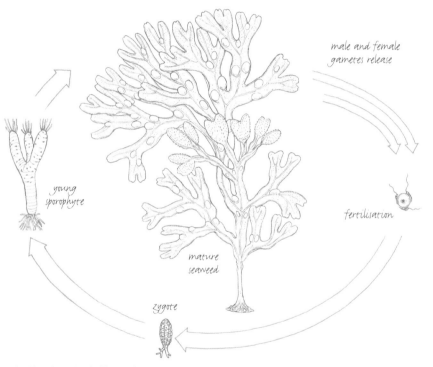

male and female gametes release

young sporophyte

fertilisation

mature seaweed

zygote

The life cycle of the Bladder Wrack (*Fucus vesiculosus*).

One of the simpler life cycles is that of the Bladder Wrack (*Fucus vesiculosus*). In the early winter months the Bladder Wrack grows its fruiting bodies or receptacles. This seaweed is dioecious, meaning that a single plant produces both male and female gametes. Both are produced in 'conceptacles', which are found in the fruiting receptacles of the seaweed. They are released in the summer months in considerable quantities, with up to a million eggs being produced by one plant. This release often happens in calm waters. After release the zygote forms from the fertilised egg and the young seaweed may begin to settle and grow on the rocks. The early stages of the seaweed must survive both predation and the action of the tide and waves for it to reach maturity.

Channelled Wrack   *Pelvetia canaliculata*

This species can be found on the very highest of tides all around the British Isles. The Channelled Wrack is easily identified by its position on the shore and its in-rolled fronds. It is perfectly adapted to long periods out of water, the rolling of the fronds reducing the rate of desiccation. When left out of the water for long periods it turns a very dark black and becomes brittle. When this seaweed is fruiting it has swollen receptacles at the ends of its dichotomously branching fronds, growing up to 15cm long. In Scotland it has been used for cattle fodder and as a result is also known as 'Cow Tang'.

LENGTH Up to 15cm
ZONE Splash zone to upper shore
DISTRIBUTION All of British Isles
SIMILAR SPECIES None

Spiral Wrack   *Fucus spiralis*

The Spiral Wrack is found all around the British and Irish coasts just below the region dominated by the Channelled Wrack on the upper shore. The fronds are flattened, with a prominent midrib and dichotomous branching. Spiral Wrack also has a tendency to have a twisted shape, an adaptation that reduces evaporation. It can grow up to 20cm long and has no gas bladders. When the fruiting bodies are present they have visibly swollen tips (receptacles) to their fronds. These gel-filled receptacles were once thought to be a cure for corns. Within the spiral wrack both sexes are found in the same individual.

LENGTH Up to 20cm
ZONE Upper shore
DISTRIBUTION All of British Isles
SIMILAR SPECIES *Fucus serratus*

Serrated Wrack   *Fucus serratus*

The Serrated Wrack or Toothed Wrack is found all around the British Isles on the lower shore region of sheltered to semi-sheltered shores. As its name suggests, this seaweed has a toothed edge to its flattened fronds, which also have midribs and grow to 60cm long. In the winter the fronds are a little swollen with fruiting bodies that make the fronds bumpy in appearance and texture. In the case of the Serrated Wrack the male and female are found in separate individuals. This wrack covers rocks, creating a sheltered spot for many invertebrates. Often you will find the small white worm casing of the Spiral Worm attached to the fronds.

LENGTH Up to 60cm
ZONE Lower shore
DISTRIBUTION All of British Isles
SIMILAR SPECIES *Fucus spiralis, F. vesiculosus*

Bladder Wrack   *Fucus vesiculosus*

The Bladder Wrack is common around the British Isles and is, in fact, the most common of all the wracks. It is found between the belts of Spiral and Toothed Wracks. It has characteristic bladders which are found in pairs along the length of the dichotomously splitting fronds (up to 1m long). The bladders are bead-like flotation devices that allow the seaweed to float as close to the surface as possible, making good use of sunlight for photosynthesis. The tips of the seaweed form forked or singular swollen fruiting bodies. On highly exposed shores you may also find variations that have no bladders, which are easy to confuse with the Spiral Wrack.

LENGTH Up to 1m
ZONE Mid shore
DISTRIBUTION All of British Isles
SIMILAR SPECIES *Fucus serratus, F. spiralis*

Egg or Knotted Wrack   *Ascophyllum nodosum*

This seaweed, previously known as 'Sailor's Whistle', is found on sheltered shores around the British Isles in the middle zone. Historically, the large bladders found along the long, thin, yellow-green stem-like fronds would be made into flute-like whistles. The bladder size varies, with the more sheltered shorelines producing larger bladders than exposed shores. Fronds can grow as long as 1.5m and the fruiting bodies are found along the length of the frond on short branches. It is possible to age this wrack as one bladder is produced per year along the main stem-like frond.

LENGTH Up to 1.5m
ZONE Mid shore
DISTRIBUTION All of British Isles
SIMILAR SPECIES *Fucus vesiculosus*

Sea Oak   *Halidrys siliquosa*

This seaweed is common on all coasts around the British Isles on very low spring tides and below the tidal range. It is a highly alternate-branching, large, bushy seaweed of up to 1m in length that creates a zigzag-like structure. The Sea Oak is attached to the rocks by a disc-shaped holdfast. It has swollen bladders on the tips of its fronds. The bladders are lance shaped and divided by internal walls that can be seen from the outside. The oblong fruiting bodies grow at the apex of the fronds.

LENGTH Up to 1m
ZONE Lower shore to subtidal
DISTRIBUTION All of British Isles
SIMILAR SPECIES None

Thongweed *Himanthalia elongata*

The Thongweed is found around all the British Isles except in the east and south-east of England. It is common on lower shores above the kelps and below the Serrated Wrack. It is an intriguing species in that 98% of its tissue is reproductive. The initial vegetative tissue appears as a small button on the rocks in early spring. As the sea temperature increases from February to May the olive-green fruiting receptacles grow, reaching up to 1m-long tendrils with dichotomous branching. The Thongweed releases its reproductive gametes from June and continues until it starts to die off or gets broken off by autumnal storms and waves.

LENGTH Up to 1m
ZONE Lower shore
DISTRIBUTION All of British Isles
SIMILAR SPECIES *Chorda filum*

Rainbow Wrack *Cystoseira tamariscifolia*

This stunning but increasingly rare seaweed grows on the lower regions of the shore. The Rainbow Wrack is only found in the south-west of England, perhaps because it is often out-competed by the Wireweed. When seen in the water, it is the most beautiful of seaweeds, with its bright iridescent blues and greens. When out of the water it loses this property and appears as a muted, olive-green seaweed. It is highly branched with short spines, and has small air bladders at the ends of the branches. It grows to approximately 40cm tall.

LENGTH Up to 40cm
ZONE Lower shore
DISTRIBUTION SW British Isles
SIMILAR SPECIES None

Sugar Kelp *Saccharina latissima*

The Sugar Kelp is found on the very lowest part of the shore all around the British Isles. It can be seen on the lowest of spring tides and at depths of up to 30m, or detached on the foreshore after heavy storms. It has long blades up to 4m long. The blade can be very broad, with bumpy surfaces and undulating margins. It attaches to the rocks with a branched holdfast and a smooth, short stipe. The Sugar Kelp is also called 'Poor Man's Weather Vane', from the tradition of hanging it from fishermen's cottages to forecast rain.

LENGTH Up to 4m
ZONE Lower shore
DISTRIBUTION All of British Isles
SIMILAR SPECIES None

Dabberlocks *Alaria esculenta*

The Dabberlocks can be found on the lowest of shores down to depths of 35m, predominantly on the west and north of the British Isles. *Alaria esculenta* rather poetically and accurately translates as 'edible wings'. It has a long blade similar to that of the Sugar Kelp, but the Dabberlocks has a midrib that makes it resemble a large feather. Both the young, supple stipe and midribs are edible. The seaweed attaches to the rocks with a branching holdfast. The blade is thin and in storms can be ripped off the stipe, leaving behind a skeletal seaweed consisting of only the stipe and midrib.

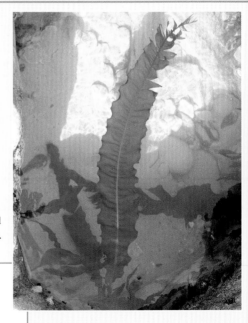

LENGTH Up to 1.5m
ZONE Lower shore
DISTRIBUTION N and W British Isles
SIMILAR SPECIES *Undaria pinnatifida*

Bootlace   *Chorda filum*

The Bootlace can be found commonly around the British Isles on the lower shore down to depths of 5m. This long seaweed can grow up to 8m long and about 0.5cm wide. If snorkelling through these long, unbranched seaweeds you will see why it is sometimes known as 'Mermaid's Tresses', or the more macabre 'Dead Men's Ropes'. It feels rather slimy to the touch and has very fine hairs covering its length. In the summer months it grows well, but it breaks down in the autumn months and disappears through the winter.

LENGTH Up to 8m
ZONE Lower shore
DISTRIBUTION All of British Isles
SIMILAR SPECIES *Himanthalia elongata*

Oarweed   *Laminaria digitata*

This low-tide and subtidal seaweed is found along most of the coasts of the British Isles except for the east and south-east of England. The Oarweed has a large, leathery, paddle-like dark brown blade that is split into 'fingers' and held up by a long oval stipe. On the lowest of tides it collapses on to the rocks, unlike the other laminarians, which remain more erect. It attaches to the rock by a tangled-looking, branching holdfast. If washed up on the shore, check the holdfast for other species that may have sought protection within the safety of the tangled 'nest'.

LENGTH Up to 1.5m
ZONE Lower shore to subtidal
DISTRIBUTION N, S and W of British Isles
SIMILAR SPECIES *Laminaria hyperborea, L. ochroleuca*

Cuvie   *Laminaria hyberborea*

Cuvie is often called Forest Kelp and Northern Kelp because kelp forests are common in northern regions of the British Isles; this seaweed can be found all around Britain, but is less common in the south-east of England. Cuvie is very similar to the Oarweed but differs in that it has a more erect, round stipe that if bent will snap. It can be up to 3.5m long and the stipe is often covered in other, red seaweeds. It has a branched and tangled holdfast that attaches to the rocks. The stipes are very slimy and are a good source of alginic acids.

LENGTH Up to 3.5m
ZONE Lower shore to subtidal
DISTRIBUTION N, S and W of British Isles
SIMILAR SPECIES *Laminaria digitata, L. ochroleuca*

Furbellows   *Saccorhiza polyschides*

The Furbellows is found on the lowest of spring tides, below the Cuvie on the shore, on unstable and exposed rocky shores all around the British Isles apart from the east and south-east. It can grow up to 4m long. This seaweed is sometimes found on the strandline broken into separate pieces. After storms a large, brown, warty lump (that resembles the brain of a sea monster) can be found. This 'lump' is found just above the branching holdfast of the Furbellows. Shortly beyond this there is an undulating, thick wavy stipe at the base, which develops into a strap-like stipe. This seaweed has a large blade that splits into leathery, flat fingers.

LENGTH Up to 4m
ZONE Lower shore to subtidal
DISTRIBUTION All of British Isles
SIMILAR SPECIES None

Wakame   *Undaria pinnatifida*

The Wakame was first found on the Solent Estuary in 1994 and since then has been noted in ports and on pontoons on the southern coasts of England. This seaweed is native to Asiatic waters, where it is harvested for food. It is similar to the Dabberlocks, but the stipe of the Wakame has a much more furrowed edge. The species has a thin membranous frond growing up to 2m long. On its home shores it creates forests from low tide to 15m deep, depending on the clarity of the water. It can outcompete native kelps and is therefore considered an invasive species.

LENGTH Up to 2m
ZONE Subtidal (pontoons)
DISTRIBUTION S England
SIMILAR SPECIES None

Wireweed   *Sargassum muticum*

The Wireweed came to the British Isles from Asiatic waters. In 1973 it was found on the Isle of Wight. Since then it has spread across much of the coast of southern England, up to the Welsh coast, across to Ireland and up to the east coast of Scotland. In the summer months it fills rockpools and is also found in the shallow subtidal region. It is a bushy brown seaweed that can grow up to 2m long and create large forests of erect seaweed. It differs from the bushy *Cystoseira* species because it has stalked air bladders that hold it very erect in the water. It is an invasive species and can compete with important habitats such as seagrass.

LENGTH Up to 2m
ZONE Lower shore and subtidal
DISTRIBUTION S and W of British Isles
SIMILAR SPECIES *Cystoseira* species

Oyster Thief *Colpomenia peregrina*

The Oyster Thief is found mostly on the western coasts of the British Isles. This seaweed is often washed on to the strandline and mistaken for an egg case. The common name derives from its habit of this olive-green seaweed of growing on young oyster shells. The seaweed is a hollow ball that can float up lifting oyster shells from its substrate, hence 'Oyster Thief'. It can grow up to 9cm in diameter and is 'epiphytic' as it grows on other species. The Oyster Thief originated in the Pacific Ocean and may have been introduced with the Pacific Oyster.

DIAMETER Up to 9cm
ZONE Upper to lower shore
DISTRIBUTION W of British Isles
SIMILAR SPECIES *Leathesia difformis*

Peacock's Tail *Padina pavonica*

The Peacock's Tail is found, at its most northern distribution, on the southern coasts of England and Ireland. This species bears little resemblance to any other seaweed. It creates flat, cream-coloured lobes up to 10cm in diameter. It has a slimy surface and 'hairs' running in lines across the lobes. It can be found on the rocky substrate and in pools from the mid shore to the lower shore. The seaweed is incredibly pale and looks rather like an albino peacock's tail or as represented by its other common name, like a 'Turkey Feather'.

DIAMETER Up to 10cm
ZONE Mid to lower shore
DISTRIBUTION S England, Wales and Ireland
SIMILAR SPECIES None

Red seaweeds

Say, do the sea-nymphs find thee,
Thy roseate leaves unfold,
And round their tresses bind thee,
As oaken wreaths of old?

J. Mackness, *To the Oak Leaved* Delesseria 19th century

The red seaweeds add a vibrant splash of colour to the seashore. Strictly speaking they are not always red – their colours include the pale pinks of the Coral Weed (*Corralina officinalis*), the shocking pink of the Sea Beech (*Delesseria sanguinea*), the deep rusty-red of the Dulse (*Palmaria palmata*) and even the deep purple of the Irish Moss (*Chondrus crispus*). The pigments they contain are capable of utilising relatively low light intensities and as a result they are often found on the lowest of shores. However, they are delivered to beaches after heavy storms, so it is always worth checking amongst the piles of kelps and wracks for the flash of colour of the red seaweeds.

The red seaweeds belong to the class Rhodophyta, are incredibly diverse and the vast majority are marine. They do not, however, grow as large as the brown kelp forests. The largest of the red seaweeds is the Dulse, which usually reaches a comparatively small 50cm, but may grow as tall as 1m. Red seaweeds use (amongst others) phycobiloprotein pigments, which give them their characteristic colours and absorb green light in the colour spectrum. The red marine macro-algae are found on rocks, boulders and pebbles, and attached to the larger kelps. They can be encrusted mats of lichen-like appearance, red foliose leaves like that of an oak tree and even bony skeletal, segmented algae resembling coral.

The striking red seaweeds include the Rainbow Weed (*Drachiella spectabilis*), which has a blue and violet iridescence underwater.

As a result of their thin, cellular surface, which reflects light from the short wavelength of the spectrum, some of the red seaweeds are also iridescent. The iridescence is so pronounced that when exploring the rocky shore you may have your breath taken away when you discover the blue-purple 'glow' of the Irish Moss on a sunny summer's day. Many of the red seaweeds tend to be quite slimy because they have double cell walls that contain slimy gels; these are used to produce the thickening agents agar and carrageen.

The eminent phycologist Dr Gerald Boalch remembers collecting seaweed as a child during the Second World War: 'I started looking at seaweeds when I was about 9. During the war as school children we collected seaweed at Beer "for the war effort". When I was doing my PhD I discovered that our collections were used to make a substitute for agar-agar. During the war penicillin was grown on agar-agar and the only source of agar-agar was Japan so it was necessary to find a substitute. This was carrageen, which was found in *Chondrus crispus*.'

The life cycles of the red seaweeds are complex and at times astonishing. For example, you may see the small, leaf-like blade of Dulse attached to the stipe of Oarweed (*Laminaria digitata*) and other kelps. At the base of the 'leaves' attached to the stipe of the kelp you could see a red, encrusting seaweed. This is also the Dulse. The small, red leafy blades are the male gamete-producing phase of the seaweed, whereas the encrusting mat is the gamete-producing female. The 'leafy' male phase produces heavy gametes that drop onto the encrusting female for fertilisation. Suffice to say this is a greatly simplified version of the life history of the Dulse.

Dulse (*Palmaria palmata*) has a complex life cycle which includes a foliose male gamete-producing phase and an encrusting female both of which can be seen on the stipes of kelp.

Pepper Dulse   *Osmundea pinnatifida*

The Pepper Dulse is common on rocky surfaces on coasts around all of the British Isles. It can be very yellow-green and is often mistaken for juvenile wracks. The more available sunlight there is, such as in the higher and mid-shore regions, the more yellow-green the seaweed becomes. On the lower shore it is more characteristic of 'red seaweed', appearing dark red-brown. It has flattened broad, irregular-branching fronds of up to 8cm in length. When dried, it can be used to season food as a substitute for black pepper.

LENGTH Up to 8cm
ZONE Mid to lower shore
DISTRIBUTION All of British Isles
SIMILAR SPECIES *Osmundea hybrida*, *O. oederi*, *O. osmunda* and *O. truncata*

Irish Moss or Carrageen   *Chondrus crispus*

The Irish Moss can be found all around the British Isles and is especially common on Irish coasts. It has a disc-shaped holdfast from which grow leafy blades of up to 25cm long. The blades are dichotomously branching and the flattened fronds are usually a deep red-purple colour. However, the branches can also be thickened and narrow and, in areas of intense light, more yellow-green. When the seaweed is submerged it can show bright blue prismatic hues. The gelling agent carrageen is produced from Irish Moss for use in the cosmetics and food industry. In the past, Carrageen has also been used as a medicine for coughs and colds.

LENGTH Up to 25cm
ZONE Mid to lower shore
DISTRIBUTION All of British Isles
SIMILAR SPECIES *Mastocarpus stellatus*

Fan Weed *Callophyllis laciniata*

This red seaweed occurs all around the British Isles except in the east and south-east of England. The Fan Weed is found attached to other seaweeds and on rocks, in kelp forests and to depths of 30m in clear waters. It is attached by a very small holdfast from which the fan-shaped seaweed develops with no visible stipe. The forked branches range in colour from bright pink to brown-red and brown, and grow up to 25cm in length. The tips of the weed are fringed and branch irregularly. The Fan Weed does not demonstrate any iridescence underwater.

LENGTH Up to 25cm
ZONE Lower shore to subtidal
DISTRIBUTION All of British Isles
SIMILAR SPECIES *Ahnfeltiopsis devoniensis, Chondrus crispus, Cryptopleura ramosa*

Rainbow Weed *Drachiella spectabilis*

This very beautiful seaweed is found in Cuvie (kelp) forests. Its distribution is restricted to the west and south-west coasts of the British Isles. Due to its location in lower shore regions it may be difficult to find, but keep an eye out for it in low shore rockpools. It produces very flat, thin, pellucid blades of red and pink seaweed that grow up to 7cm long, and are attached to a disc-shaped holdfast and a small stipe. The edges of the seaweed are split and the tips can even bend down to the rocky substrate and reattach. This seaweed has a radiant blue-purple iridescence that is characteristic of the species.

DIAMETER Up to 7cm
ZONE Lower shore to subtidal
DISTRIBUTION W and SW of British Isles
SIMILAR SPECIES *Drachiella heterocarpa*

Sea Beech   *Delesseria sanguinea*

This leaf-like seaweed occurs throughout the British Isles in lower shore regions. It is often found in kelp forests on bedrock, but can also attach to the stipes of kelps. The holdfast is thick and disc-like, with a thick, tough midrib from which arise the beech-like 'leaves'. The deep magenta, red-brown blades are up to 35cm long with defined midribs and are paired, (with opposite veins running along the length of the blade). Further finer veins run from the main veins. The thin blades can be ripped off in storms, leaving skeletal blades of only the midribs and veins.

LENGTH Up to 35cm
ZONE Lower shore to subtidal
DISTRIBUTION All of British Isles
SIMILAR SPECIES *Phycodrys rubens*

Batters or Sea Oak   *Phycodrys rubens*

The Sea Oak is distributed around the British Isles, but is less commonly found in the east of England. It often occurs on the stipes of kelps in the lower shore regions and can be seen washed up on shores. Like Sea Beech, this seaweed has leaf-like blades that run from a midrib. The blade has rougher, serrated edges, closely resembles the leaf of an oak tree, and grows up to 25cm. The species has pale pink to pink-brown coloration and becomes skeletal when the blades have been removed by storms. The names Sea Oak and Sea Beech have historically been interchangeable, so clarification is sometimes needed to ensure which seaweed is being described.

LENGTH Up to 25cm
ZONE Lower shore to subtidal
DISTRIBUTION All of British Isles
SIMILAR SPECIES *Delesseria sanguinea*

Red Rags   *Dilsea carnosa*

The Red Rags is found on the lowest point of the shore, often on rocky and vertical surfaces. It is common around the British Isles, but most common in the south. It has a small, disc-shaped holdfast and a thin, short stipe from which develops an egg-shaped thick, leathery inedible blade. During storms and as a result of wave action, the blade often becomes split into strips. The species has a deep red or dark brown-red coloration and is one of the larger seaweeds in the British Isles, reaching lengths of up to 50cm.

LENGTH Up to 50cm
ZONE Lower shore to subtidal
DISTRIBUTION All of British Isles
SIMILAR SPECIES *Meredithia microphylla, Schizymenia dubyi, Palmaria palmata*

Dulse   *Palmaria palmata*

The Dulse can be found throughout the British Isles except in the east of England. It is a thinner seaweed than the Red Rags and has more dichotomous branching. It arises from a disc-shaped holdfast and has a deep purple-brown coloration. As discussed on page 54, this seaweed has an interesting life cycle. It commonly occurs on the stipes of kelps, where the different male and female forms can be found. The more visible male form is flat-bladed and grows up to 50cm long, occasionally to 1m. The Dulse is an edible seaweed and is packed with minerals and vitamins. Historically it has been used to treat fever in the northernmost Scottish isles.

LENGTH Up to 50cm
ZONE Lower shore
DISTRIBUTION All of British Isles
SIMILAR SPECIES *Dilsea carnosa*

Purple Laver   *Porphyra umbilicalis*

Many *Porphyra* species are found throughout the British Isles. The Purple Laver occurs on rocks from higher shore to lower shore regions. It is an edible seaweed most commonly eaten in Wales. The seaweed is boiled for a long time, chopped and made into laver cakes or added to stews and soups. A very thin seaweed, it resembles the green Sea Lettuce but is a rich brown-red to purple colour with a very small holdfast, a height of 13cm and a breadth of 20cm. When the tide recedes it covers the rocks and has been described by some as having a 'snot-like' appearance.

LENGTH Up to 13cm
ZONE Higher to lower shore
DISTRIBUTION All of British Isles
SIMILAR SPECIES *Porphyra dioica,
P. leucostucta, P. linearis, P. purpurea*

Polysiphonia lanosa

This seaweed has not developed a common name, but is commonly found attached to the stipes of Egg Wracks in filamentous tufts all around the coasts of the British Isles. There are many *Polysiphonia* species, which are difficult to individually identify on the seashore. This species not only lives on the surface of the Egg Wrack, but also actually grows into the wrack, penetrating its surface. It forms short, thick tufts of red-brown seaweeds, and is recognisable by its association with the Egg Wrack.

LENGTH Up to 7cm
ZONE Mid shore
DISTRIBUTION All of British Isles
SIMILAR SPECIES *Griffithsia devoniensis,
Polysiphonia atlantica, P. devoniensis*

Sand Binder *Rhodothamniella floridula*

This seaweed is found on sandy, rocky substrates from the mid shore down to the lower shore region. It occurs all around the British Isles, often under the Toothed Wrack. It appears as a carpet of red filamentous algae which, as the name suggests, binds sand together creating a turf. It is spongy to the touch and the red filamentous alga covers the rocks to such an extent that it prevents other species from living in the same area. This seaweed can live for between 5 and 15 years.

LENGTH Up to 3cm
ZONE Mid to lower shore
DISTRIBUTION All of British Isles
SIMILAR SPECIES *Rhodochorton purpureum*

Heterosiphonia plumosa

This delicate deep crimson seaweed is most commonly found on the southern and western shores of the British Isles. It occurs on rocks and growing on kelps from the lower shore down into the subtidal. It attaches through a small disc holdfast and has Christmas-tree-like branches that taper towards the tips. Overall it can grow up to 20cm tall. The alternate and irregular branching of this crimson seaweed can look like tufts out of the water.

LENGTH Up to 20cm
ZONE Lower shore to subtidal
DISTRIBUTION S and W of British Isles
SIMILAR SPECIES *Asparagopsis armata*

Coral Weed   *Corralina officinalis*

The Coral Weed is found throughout the British Isles in pools from the mid-shore region down into the subtidal region. This seaweed has a bony, skeletal texture and on close examination is segmented in appearance. It shows irregular branching of its thin fronds that grow up to 20cm long. Its skeletal feel is the result of chalky deposits in its cell walls. When detached, you can place a small piece in a dish with some vinegar and watch the calcium deposits bubble away, hereby demonstrating the potential effects of ocean acidification (see page 36).

LENGTH Up to 20cm
ZONE Mid shore to subtidal
DISTRIBUTION All of British Isles
SIMILAR SPECIES *Jania rubens*

Maerl   *Phymatolithon calcareum*

Maerl beds are found in the south, west and north of the British Isles. The Maerl is another calcareous red seaweed species that is slow growing. It does not attach to anything but creates loose nodules, like irregular-shaped 'jacks', and balls of pink, calcareous algae. Maerl beds are an important diverse habitat, containing many different and some unique species. Until quite recently, Maerl have been dredged from the sea to be used as a soil conditioner and to treat acidic water. Fishing practices and dredging, which disturb the sea beds can make Maerl beds vulnerable habitats.

DIAMETER Up to 2cm
ZONE Strandline, subtidal
DISTRIBUTION All of British Isles
SIMILAR SPECIES *Lithothamnion corraloides, L. graciale, Lithophyllum dentatum*

Paint Weed *Lithophyllum incrustans*

The Paint Weed can be found all around the British Isles. It grows from the low shore down into the subtidal regions depending on the water clarity and, therefore, light penetration. The Paint Weed is an encrusting calcareous seaweed covering rocky surfaces in what looks like pink paint. There are several species, which are difficult to identify without a microscope. This species can be found in thick and lumpy patches. Some paint weed species, such as *Titanoderma pustulatum*, grow on other larger red and brown seaweeds.

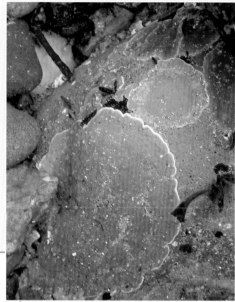

ENCRUSTING SHEET
ZONE Upper shore to subtidal
DISTRIBUTION All of British Isles
SIMILAR SPECIES *Phymatolithon purpureum*

Harpoon Weed *Asparagopsis armata*

This non-native red seaweed was first found in Irish waters in 1939 and has since spread to much of the south and west of the British Isles. There it can be found in deep pools attached to other seaweeds. If this seaweed is held horizontally between two hands, barbed 'rhizoids' can be seen hanging from the main stem. These harpoon-like hooks are distinctive to this species and are the means by which it attaches to other seaweeds. The Harpoon Weed is a bushy red seaweed with pyramidal tufts and it grows up to 30cm in length.

LENGTH Up to 30cm
ZONE Lower shore to subtidal
DISTRIBUTION S and W of British Isles
SIMILAR SPECIES *Bonnemaisonia hamifera*, *Heterosiphonia plumosa*

Green seaweeds

Oh the dry and sterile rocks,
See, Conferva* hangs her locks;
There she waves her tresses fair
Soft as infant's silken hair;

Now floating in tufts of silv'ry green,
Floating on the tide serene;
Small sea-insects in its bow'r
Sporting in the summer hour.

Ellen Roberts, *Ocean Flowers and their Teachings* 19th century

*Conferva rupestris is now known as *Cladophora rupestris*

The vibrant green seaweeds are a pleasant sight on the seashore. They belong to the class Chlorophycae and can often be found on the shore where there is a source of fresh water, because they thrive and grow particularly well as a result of the enriched waters. If a beach has a steady flow of agricultural run-off then the Gutweed (*Ulva intestinalis*) and other green seaweeds will dominate.

Green seaweeds are a varied group. As well as the thin, almost transparent green seaweeds that are only one cell thick, there is the robust-looking, but soft Velvet Horn (*Codium tomentosum*), which tends to be found hanging from the walls of deep pools. It has an incredibly soft

Green seaweeds like the Gutweed grow very well in areas of freshwater run-off and in nutrient-rich water.

texture and is an unusual but exciting find. Green-and-white patchy seaweeds are also sometimes found on the strandline, which can cause confusion, but the coloration of these is merely a result of the sun bleaching green seaweeds.

The chlorophytes, as green seaweeds are also known, are not as numerous as the brown and red seaweeds, with only around 100 green seaweed species. Many of them are very similar and difficult to identify without using a microscope to look at their cellular structure. Red, brown and green seaweeds use different pigments for different qualities of light in the water. The green seaweeds use chlorophylls, beta-carotene and xanthophylls to harness energy from the sun.

The life cycles of the green seaweeds are all complex and the Sea Lettuce (*Ulva lactuca*) is no exception. It has an isomorphic life cycle, which means that different phases of its life cycle look identical. The Sea Lettuce has a sporophyte phase and a gametophyte phase that look identical when you find them on the shore. The sporophyte is the asexual form of the seaweed, which produces the gametophyte through a spore that does not fuse. The gametophyte is the phase that produces the gametes, and the zygote (which is the result of gamete fusion) grows into the sporophyte.

Both the Sea Lettuce and Gutweed are edible, but if you are going to try eating them, it is always advisable to be familiar with the local water quality and to clean seaweeds carefully and well. When gathering seaweeds take only what you need, snipping off just small pieces or, better still, collect seaweed that has been freshly deposited on the strandline.
The Gutweed can be prolific on the seashore and with little preparation and just a few additional ingredients can make for a delicious and authentic 'crispy seaweed'.

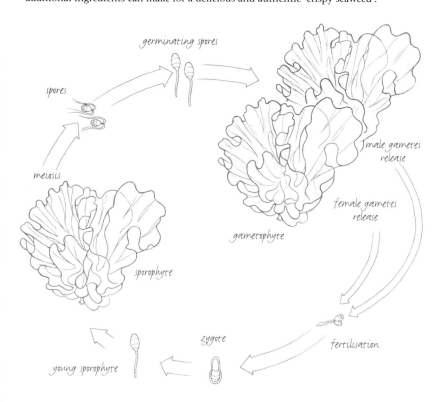

germinating spores

spores

male gametes release

female gametes release

meiosis

gametophyte

sporophyte

zygote

fertilisation

young sporophyte

The life cycle of the Sea Lettuce.

Sea Lettuce   *Ulva lactuca*

The Sea Lettuce is commonly found all around the British Isles at different tidal heights on the seashore, in estuaries and extending even into deeper waters. Scientists and naturalists often name things as they appear, hence the name Sea Lettuce. It is also commonly called 'Green Laver'. If cleaned thoroughly this seaweed can be eaten raw. It is fairly easy to identify because of its thin, bright green, broad leaves (of up to 30cm in length), which are only two cell layers thick. The Sea Lettuce has a very short stipe with a small circular holdfast.

LENGTH Up to 100cm
ZONE Upper to lower shore
DISTRIBUTION All of British Isles
SIMILAR SPECIES *Monostroma grevillei*, *Ulva rigida*

Gutweed   *Ulva intestinalis*

The Gutweed is common on all shores around the British Isles. It is frequnetly found in estuaries and in areas of low salinity, as well as on the intertidal shore. The Gutweed, despite its unappetising name, is a very tasty seaweed. It has tubular-shaped strands of up to 7.5cm long and these can become 'inflated' in the water, looking rather like semi-inflated intestines, hence its common name 'Gutweed'. It is attached by a small holdfast although it can also be free floating. Excessive growth of Gutweed is sometimes an indication of eutrophication from excess nitrates and phosphates.

LENGTH Up to 30cm
ZONE Upper to lower shore
DISTRIBUTION All of British Isles
SIMILAR SPECIES *Ulva compressa*, *U. intestinaloides*, *U. linza*

Cladophora rupestris

This tufted seaweed is common on shores of the British Isles. It is found from the mid shore to the lower shore region, and often occurs under larger brown seaweeds, in rockpools and floating in the water in large tufts. As there has been no historical use of this seaweed, nor is it readily recognisable, to date it has not developed a common name. It is a fine, filamentous seaweed that creates dense, thick tufts is deep green in colour and can grow up to 20cm tall.

LENGTH Up to 20cm
ZONE Mid to lower shore
DISTRIBUTION All of British Isles
SIMILAR SPECIES *Cladophora pellucida, Spongomorpha aeruginosa*

Velvet Horn   *Codium tomentosum*

This seaweed can be found mainly in the south and west of Britain and Ireland, although it has been recorded as far north as the Orkneys. The Velvet Horn occurs on the middle and lower shore, commonly on the walls of deeper pools. It is a rich dark green and has a shape and velvety texture that resemble reindeer antlers. The Velvet Horn has dichotomous branching and can grow up to 30cm long. Because of various factors, including competition from the invasive *Codium fragile*, the Velvet Horn is quite rare. It is difficult to distinguish the two *Codium* species, but *C. tomentosum* tends to have more rounded tips than *C. fragile*.

LENGTH Up to 30cm
ZONE Mid to lower shore
DISTRIBUTION S and W of British Isles
SIMILAR SPECIES *Codium fragile, C. bursa*

FLOWERING PLANTS

Half way down
Hangs one that gathers samphire, dreadful trade!
Methinks he seems no bigger than his head:
The fishermen that walk upon the beach
Appear like mice.

William Shakespeare, *King Lear* 1608

The flowering plants or angiosperms belong to the class Anthophyta and are a surprising phylum to find in a marine environment. One might imagine that flowering plants would need insects to pollinate the flowers, or wind to disperse airborne seeds. However, some incredibly well-adapted flowering plants not only live in the marine environment, but also actually create extremely important marine habitats. There are coastal plants that tolerate salty spray, such as some of the saltmarsh plants, which may encounter sporadic submersion during extreme low spring tides. There are also coastal plants that contribute towards the stabilisation of sand dunes, allowing successive plants to grow. However, the plants considered in this section are those that are regularly submerged and most commonly found on the coast and in estuaries of the British Isles.

Seagrass (*Zostera marina*) beds are a vital nursery area and habitat for a broad range of species like these juvenile Corkwing Wrasse (*Crenalibus melops*).

Seagrass or Eelgrass beds are a vital and important ecosystem for local marine health and also for global health. The Seagrass is a very well-adapted plant, able to grow in Arctic conditions and even to survive under ice. Yet it is under threat from human activities and with the potential loss of this humble flowering plant would come a host of losses to our marine and global ecosystem and ultimately to us.

To ensure its survival in the marine environment the Seagrass reproduces both by flowering in summer months, producing seeds, and by vegetative reproduction where the rhizomes (the underground stem of the plant) will spread. Despite their ability to reproduce well, Seagrass meadows have become endangered. The Seagrass is threatened if, for example, it is smothered in silt as a result of coastal development or dredging, or if its habitat is destroyed by anchors or other estuarial or harbour developments, such as pontoons. Excessive nutrients from agriculture can also be a threat to the species. Sadly, it is estimated that a football pitch of Seagrass meadows is lost every half-hour due to human activities.

In addition to all this, the invasive Wireweed (*Sargassum muticum*) is thought to be able to potentially outcompete the Seagrass in British waters. The Wireweed grows in long tendrils, shading out surrounding plants, so in scoured areas of disturbance in Seagrass beds the Wireweed quickly establishes itself before the Seagrass has a chance to take hold.

The Seagrass habitat is an important area for many animals, such as seahorses, stalked jellyfish and other crustaceans, worms and gastropods. The beds are a spawning ground for commercial fish, cuttlefish and invertebrates such as Sea Hares (*Aplysia punctata*), amongst many others. The benefits of the marine meadows are not restricted to marine species, but also extend to feeding wildfowl such as Brent Geese (*Branta bernicla*), Wigeon (*Anas penelope*) and swans.

Seagrass meadows also act as a sink for atmospheric carbon dioxide. Recent research has shown that as much as 83,000 metric tonnes of carbon can be stored in 1 square kilometre of Seagrass, compared to 30,000 metric tonnes for the same size of forest on land. To further add to their merit, while land forests store the carbon for up to 60 years in the soil, Seagrass beds can store carbon for thousands of years. Despite these benefits, we have lost in the region of 29% of global Seagrass habitats in the last century.

The Spiny Seahorse (*Hippocampus guttulatus*) can be found in Seagrass beds wrapping its tail around the Seagrass blades.

To do your bit to protect this vital habitat, care must be taken to avoid anchoring boats or walking in it. If you carefully walk around the peripheral regions of the Seagrass you might see a host of species such as heart urchins, burrowing bivalves and stalked jellyfish. If you have the opportunity to snorkel you may even see the eggs of cuttlefish attached to the blades, or perhaps even a seahorse clinging on with its prehensile tail.

Seagrass   *Zostera marina*

The Seagrass occurs around the British Isles in areas of low turbidity, where the water remains clear enough for good sun penetration. The species can be found as far north as Orkney and Shetland. It has long, grass-like, dark green blades with rounded tips. The blades can grow to 1m in height and 1cm in width. The roots of the Seagrass penetrate and anchor into the sediment, preventing and minimising coastal erosion. The seeds of the Seagrass can be seen growing along the length of the blades after the summer months.

HEIGHT Up to 1m
ZONE Lower shore
DISTRIBUTION All of British Isles
SIMILAR SPECIES *Zostera noltii*

Marsh Samphire   *Salicornia europaea*

The Marsh Samphire can be found in mud-flats and soft sand around the British Isles. This succulent, branched, erect plant has a flowering stage that is hard to see with the naked eye. In the winter it dies back, to emerge again in the early spring. If collected it is advisable to snip bits off to avoid removing the stabilising roots. Also known as Common Glasswort, it was used in the past to make silica-rich ash for glass production. Samphire was historically used to garnish fish dishes and called 'Poor Man's Asparagus', and it is now popular and commonly used in gourmet restaurants. Samphire seeds are also an important food for wildfowl.

HEIGHT Up to 30cm
ZONE Upper shore
DISTRIBUTION All of British Isles
SIMILAR SPECIES None

SPONGES

let the word sponge bring to mind...
the wonderfully colourful race of living creatures...
much as clumps of violets and marigolds, brighten our terrestrial gardens.

William Beebe, *Half Mile Down* 1934

In otherwise dark and shaded spots in rocky crevices and overhangs, you might spot the bright orange, soft and bouncy texture of a marine sponge. Although sponges may resemble algae or lichen they are in fact animals. Their phylum name Porifera roughly translates as 'pore bearers', which neatly describes their physical appearance. They are very simple animals, with no digestive, circulatory or nervous systems.

Their method of sustaining life is simple but effective. They obtain their nutrients and oxygen from a constant flow of water, and as water leaves a sponge any waste materials are excreted along with the water. The water leaves the sponge through a large opening called the osculum (or oscule) at some speed, recorded at 8.4cm per second. The pores through which sponges draw water are called ostia and these are often visible to the naked eye.

Sponges draw the water into their pores by flagellating choanocytes, cells with beating hair-like strands that help pull the water into the ostia, trapping food matter in the process.

Sponges are found attached to the surfaces of rocks and seaweeds, and often occur amongst convoluted masses of kelp holdfasts. On a low tide, it is well worth looking under pontoons and hard structures – because many sponges have large surface areas, they dry out easily, so are often found in areas away from the drying actions of the sun and wind.

Sponges are not only colourful, but also possess chemicals with anti-cancer properties.

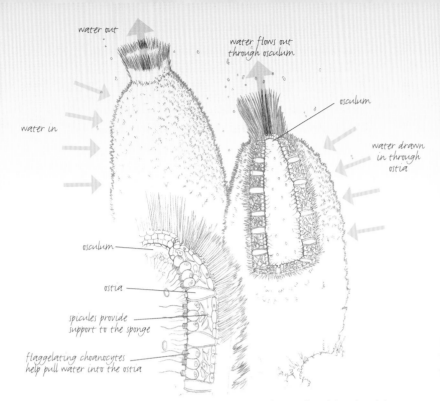

water out

water flows out
through osculum

osculum

water in

water drawn
in through
ostia

osculum

ostia

spicules provide
support to the sponge

flaggelating choanocytes
help pull water into the ostia

A sponge obtains nutrients and oxygen from a constant flow of water drawn in through its ostia and then expelled, along with waste material, through its osculum.

The soft bodies of most sponges are supported by 'spicules', which may be made from calcium or silica, or may contain a protein called sponging that gives them structure. The spicules vary enormously in shape and some sponges can only be correctly identified by examining their spicules under a microscope. Some species use the spicules to bore holes into shells, such as the boring sponges. You can tell if a hole in a shell has been created by a boring sponge by placing the bored shell in a mineral acid. The acid will dissolve the calcareous shell, but traces of silica spicules from the sponge will be left in the liquid. The spicules can then be placed under a microscope for further investigation.

The poriferans are split into three groups: sponges with silica spicules are called glass sponges or Hexactinellida; sponges with calcium spicules are most likely to be found on the shore and are called Calcarea; while sponges with silica spicules and/or sponging are called Demospongiae.

Sponges reproduce both sexually and asexually. A colony that is made up of single cells also has incredible powers of regeneration. It is possible to push a sponge through a sieve and the pieces will reform, with no obvious ill effect, after a couple of days. In the wild, this regeneration from small pieces is a form of asexual reproduction, but sponges also create and release a cell cluster called a gemmule in a process known as asexual budding. The gemmules also create new sponges through asexual reproduction.

Having a variety of reproductive methods ensures the longevity of a species in the marine environment, where larval distribution can result in a lack neighbours to share genes with. When there are suitable neighbours, sponges reproduce sexually in a variety of ways.

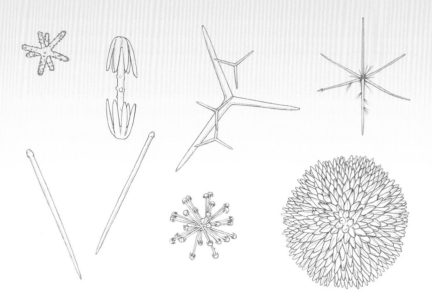

Spicules provide support for most sponges and occur in a variety of shapes.

One sponge colony will release sperm, which is then drawn into neighbouring sponges through their ostia. The sperm then fertilise the eggs inside the sponge and often the larvae develop inside the sponge. However, in some cases the developing fertilised larvae, or 'planulae', are released, becoming planktonic before settling to grow into their adult forms.

Sponges and their skeletal forms have formed an important industry in the West Indies and the Mediterranean. Bath sponges are traditionally made by hanging up living sponges to allow the flesh to rot off. In the sun, the skeleton is bleached and dries out, producing what we would recognise as the natural bath sponge.

Sponges are also of particular interest to medicinal researchers. Some sponges contain a special molecule that is believed to act as a chemical defence, preventing them from being eaten by predators. To a soft-bodied organism that spend its lifetime stuck in one place, this has obvious evolutionary advantages. Remarkably researchers have discovered that the same molecule has the potential to stop the growth of cancers in humans. Today we already have drugs used for cancer treatment whose active ingredients are derived from the molecules of tropical sponges. Researchers have also recently confirmed that the medicinal properties of sponges are not limited to tropical species. In 2005 for the first time sponges that occur around the British coast were also found to have anti-cancer properties.

Between 2008 and 2011 a survey of British sponges identified 128 poriferan species, of which 29 were completely new to science. Dr Alex White – who researches the medicinal properties of marine organisms at Cardiff University – said, "Previously our knowledge of British sponges was mostly based on work from the nineteenth century. British sponges and their medicinal properties are largely unexplored, and have untapped potential for the discovery of new drugs."

Many species of sponge can be found on the British seashore and many are difficult to identify. Finding them also requires being able to look under rocky overhangs and deep into rocky crevices. The accounts that follow present a sample of some of the key species of sponge you may find between the highest and lowest points of the tide.

Breadcrumb Sponge *Halichondria panicea*

The Breadcrumb Sponge can be found commonly in the south and west of England and occasionally in Scotland and Ireland. This sponge grows on a variety of surfaces, from rocks and boulders to the stipes of kelps and Sea Oaks. Its appearance can also vary widely from an orange pitted crust to a thick form up to 25cm deep. It grows fairly rapidly in the summer months, approximately 1mm per day. When seen on the sheltered rocky shore it is often orange, but it can also be green when algae are living within the sponge. In deeper waters it can also be a paler, cream-coloured sponge.

ENCRUSTING Up to 20cm diameter
ZONE Mid to lower shore
DISTRIBUTION S and W England
SIMILAR SPECIES *Hemimycale columella, Hymeniacidon perleve*

Purse Sponge *Grantia compressa*

The Purse Sponge can be found in rocky, shaded areas within the lower shore and subtidal regions around all coasts of the British Isles. It has a cream-coloured, flattened, cocoon-like shape, with the base attached to a rock or seaweed, and an obvious osculum at the uppermost tip of the sponge. The Purse Sponge is often found in groups of several individuals. It is short-lived, dying in the early spring after producing larvae that settle and grow over the summer months.

LENGTH Up to 2cm
ZONE Lower shore to subtidal
DISTRIBUTION All of British Isles
SIMILAR SPECIES *Scypha ciliata*

Golfball Sponge   *Tethya aurantium*

The Golfball Sponge can be found around the coasts of Ireland and Wales and the west coasts of Scotland and England. It occurs in the lower shore region, hanging from rocks and boulders in shaded areas and on rocks amongst kelp forests. As the name suggests, it looks like a round golf ball with a warty, almost spiky appearance. It can grow to a diameter of up to 10cm and is found either as solitary individuals or in colonies. It varies in colour from yellow to orange. A Golfball Sponge normally has one obvious osculum at the top of its spherical shape.

DIAMETER Up to 10cm
ZONE Lower shore to subtidal
DISTRIBUTION All coasts except E England
SIMILAR SPECIES None

Pencil Sponge   *Ciocalypta penicillus*

The Pencil Sponge occurs most commonly around the south-west coasts of Britain and most Irish coasts. It is found on the lowest of tides, attached to a rocky substrate with a sand or gravel bottom. The pencil-tip-like structures grow on upwards-facing rocks pointing up to the sky. They are approximately 5cm long and 0.5cm in diameter, and are a translucent yellow to brown colour. As well as having stalagmite-like projections the Pencil Sponge also forms a carpet-like covering over the rocks, although the 'carpeting' structure may be hidden under silt or gravel.

HEIGHT Up to 5cm
ZONE Lower shore
DISTRIBUTION All of Irish coast, SW Britain
SIMILAR SPECIES *Polymastia penicillus*

Oscarella lobularis

This sponge occurs commonly all around the British Isles. It can be found on the rocky shore throughout the intertidal zone and down to the lower shore. This sponge can be seen on rocks, boulders and also on large seaweeds such as kelps. Its colour varies, from red to green, blue or violet, but it is usually yellow or brown. It forms a 3cm-thick carpet up to 30cm wide. There are large 'lobules' over the surface of the thick sponge that are 1cm in diameter and have a large central osculum.

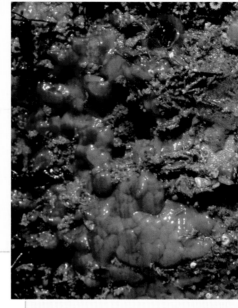

ENCRUSTING Up to 30cm diameter
ZONE Lower shore to subtidal
DISTRIBUTION All of British Isles
SIMILAR SPECIES *Dysidea fragilis*

Boring Sponge   *Cliona celata*

The Boring Sponge can be found all around the British Isles. In spite of its ambiguous common name, this is an interesting sponge that grows into two distinct forms. Its flatter form can bore into calcareous rocks and shells using its silica spicules. When the flatter form of this sponge has no more space to bore it grows into its second form, an upright wall-like structure up to 1m wide and 50cm high. This massive form has large oscula on its surface which can be red from the presence of algae. Oysters and Slipper Limpets are more often victims of the Boring Sponge than they are of any other molluscs.

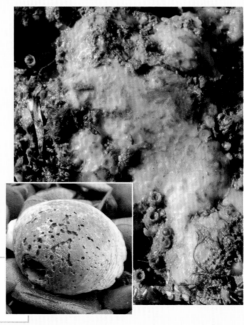

ENCRUSTING Up to 1m diameter
ZONE Lower shore to subtidal
DISTRIBUTION All of British Isles
SIMILAR SPECIES *Cliona lobata*

CNIDARIANS

And tremulous opal-hued anemones,
Will wave their purple fingers where we tread.

Oscar Wilde, *Charmides* 1881

The phylum Cnidaria is a primitive and diverse group of animals. Cnidaria were once known as coelenterates, which translates as 'full bellied'. This loosely describes the hollow body cavity found in members of the Cnidaria. The term cnidarian refers to the characteristic cnidocytes or stinging cells the organisms commonly use to capture their prey. The cnidarians are recognised by their symmetry, which is usually biradial.

There are two broad types of cnidarian. The first type is the anthozoans, which attach themselves to rocks, algae and substrate and are 'sessile' or mostly immobile, and which are known as polyps. A polyp has a mouth at its terminal end. Polyps include the anemones, sea fans, sea pens and corals, which are all in the class Anthozoa. The second type of cnidarian is the hydrozoans, which have a combination of both polyp and medusa phases. They include the Portuguese Man o'War (*Physalia physalis*) and sea firs. The medusa is a free-swimming form that has a down-turned bell with the mouth and tentacles situated on the underside of a bell-shaped cavity. The medusa form includes both the Scyphozoa and Cubozoa classes, encompassing the jellyfish and tropical box jellyfish respectively.

The basic structure of a cnidarian is that of a sac-like gut with a mouth that also acts an anus. The mouth is surrounded by tentacles that can sting and capture prey. The body wall comprises two layers of cells between which the mesoglea – a translucent, jelly-like substance – is found. The mesoglea is different in each class of cnidarian. In the hydroids it creates a non-cellular membrane. In the anemones it is a thick fibrous layer, and the medusoids have a jelly-like filling.

Cnidarians include free-swimming jellyfish and 'sessile' or attached anemones such as the Snakelocks Anemone.

As mentioned, all cnidarians share the defining feature of being armed with stinging cells, essential to their survival and their ability to capture prey. How else might a jelly-shaped blob capture large prey that has a mouth and cutting body parts? Cnidarians' stinging cells not only help them capture prey, but also act as a form of defence against predators and can even, in some forms, inject toxins that can paralyse their prey.

The stinging cells or nematocysts are held behind a trapdoor or operculum. When the cells are triggered, by touch or by chemical stimulus, the trapdoor opens. From within the cell a coiled, harpoon-like tube is fired, which penetrates the victim's skin at 10,000 times the force of gravity. The stinging cells do not normally fire their harpoon-like tubules into their own species as this would be a considerable waste of energy. Jellyfish can fire their stinging cells whether they are alive or dead, so handling jellyfish should be avoided at all times.

The Compass Jellyfish (*Chrysaora hysoscella*) and Snakelocks Anemone (*Anemonia viridis*) are both cnidarians, so both are armed with stinging tentacles. Anemones, however, are sessile anthozoans, while jellyfish are free-swimming hydrozoans.

Cnidarians reproduce sexually and asexually. It is uncommon for the medusa types of cnidarian to bud, but the polyp forms bud and will also reproduce sexually. Larval stages of marine organisms may get carried by currents and tides where they might settle, so having the potential to reproduce asexually enables single individuals to succeed in colonising new areas where no opportunities exist for exchanging gametes. Individuals that rely on sexual reproduction do not have the opportunity to ensure species survival in the same conditions.

The two sections that follow help you to identify the anthozoan sea anemones and corals found in intertidal zones of the British Isles. The next two sections describe some of the hydrozoan sea firs, siphonophores and scyphozoan jellyfish that occasionally get washed up onto shores.

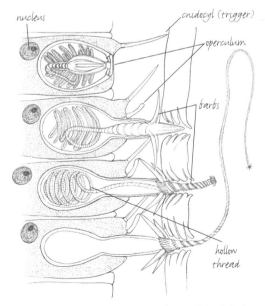

nucleus

cnidocyl (trigger)

operculum

barbs

hollow thread

This sequence shows (from top to bottom) how cnidarians' stinging cells fire.

Sea anemones

At last it becomes quite helpless, the anemone folds its arms over it, pushes it down into its mouth, and that is the end of poor Mr Shrimp.

F. Martin Duncan, *The Sea Shore: A Book for Boys and Girls* 1912

Sea anemones are single polyps that can be found decorating rockpools, but are also commonly seen on structures like shipwrecks that are submerged at great depth. When submerged in rockpools anemones appear as open symmetrical flowers, which is why they were named after the colourful garden anemone.

The majority of sea anemones are firmly attached to the substrate by pedal discs, so that even the strongest of waves and swells are unable to move them. The column is the long, neck-like part of an anemone, which contains the gastrovascular cavity or gut, the gonads and the retractor muscles. At the top of the column is the collar, another sphincter muscle. The action of the retractor muscles within the column and the sphincter column around the collar act together to pull the tentacles inside the cavity of many anemones. There are a few anemones that do not attach to any substrate and instead have gas within their gastrovascular cavities to keep them afloat.

On the upper surface of an anemone the mouth is attached to the internal pharynx, which passes food to the gut. Close to the mouth are atrial openings, which draw water into the anemone. Circling the mouth are the stinging tentacles. These maximise the chances for immobile anemones to catch potential victims by reaching out their tentacles and capturing prey with their stinging cells.

This voracious Beadlet Anemone (*Actinia equina*) is consuming a jellyfish considerably larger than itself.

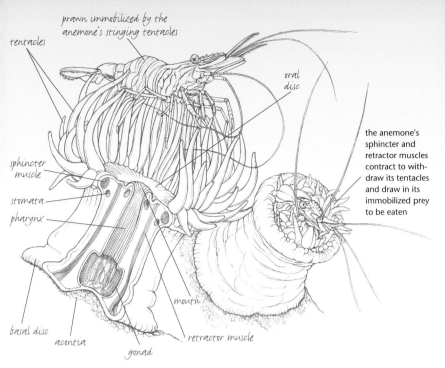

The anatomy of an anemone, shown here capturing a prawn using its stinging tentacles.

Labels on figure:
- tentacles
- prawn immobilized by the anemone's stinging tentacles
- oral disc
- the anemone's sphincter and retractor muscles contract to withdraw its tentacles and draw in its immobilized prey to be eaten
- sphincter muscle
- stomata
- pharynx
- mouth
- basal disc
- acontia
- gonad
- retractor muscle

If you were to brush your finger over the tentacles of an anemone they would appear sticky. This stickiness is actually the anemone firing stinging cells at you. Anemones can also use neurotoxins to stun their prey. Their stunned prey (small fish and shrimps, for example) is then passed to the mouth, which is in the centre of the column. After it has digested its prey an anemone uses its mouth to pass unwanted waste materials back out into the water.

Anemone reproduction can be sexual, asexual or both. An anemone can produce gametes which exit from the 'mouth', but it can also reproduce without the need for gametes and 'buds'. It does so by splitting and recreating a perfect form of itself. This form of asexual reproduction can also take place from a small portion of the attaching 'foot' or 'pedal disc'. When anemones are found in clusters, this is likely to be the result of an anemone that has reproduced by fission; whereas sexually reproducing anemones have a greater tendency to be solitary.

On the low tide, when the water drops and the sun becomes more of a threat, some anemones benefit from the ability to withdraw their tentacles, thereby reducing their surface area. Once this has happened, an anemone looks like a shiny fruit gum attached to the rocks. Children can sometimes be seen prodding anemones to produce a jet of water – while this proves their ability to contain water it also increases their chances of desiccation and ultimately death, so it should be discouraged.

Anemones are aggressive to one another and if anemones come too close to each other they will sting their neighbours to make them move to a position where there is less competition for food. The Beadlet Anemone has additional defence in the form of its bright blue acrorhagi or tubercles, specialised tentacles situated around the edge of the collar of the anemone, near the sphincter muscle and outside the feeding tentacle crown. Should another anemone come close, the acrorhagi swell and the anemone wages war against the invader.

An individual Beadlet Anemone can aggressively maintain its ideal situation, protecting its territory and the good currents and feeding opportunities.

Anemones are mostly sessile and the majority live attached to rocks, however some attach themselves to crabs. This arrangement suits the crab, as it can use the anemone's stinging ability to its own advantage, while the attached anemone can benefit from the crab's messy feeding habits. There are also a few anemone species that float, but most settle in a fixed place unless a predator or conditions necessitate a move, at which point an anemone can detach itself and move to a new, improved position.

Anemones have few predators as a result of their stinging cells. Grey Slugs (*Aeolida papillosa*), however, are one of the few ingenious nudibranchs (sea slugs) that may prey upon anemones. When they do they recycle the anemones' stinging cells within their own tentacles, or cerata, henceforth using them to deter predators themselves.

Anemones capable of withdrawing their tentacles can be found on the upper shore, whereas on the lower shore you will find species that cannot cope with long periods out of water. Pontoons are also great places to look for them, as the fast-flowing currents in tidal estuaries and harbours offer great feeding potential. Here you may find the pristine white form of the cloud-like Plumose Anemone (*Metridium senile*).

Dahlia Anemones (*Urticina felina*) are a source of colour and beautiful symmetry on the seashore.

Strawberry Anemone   *Actinia fragacea*

The Strawberry Anemone is found on the lower points of the shore around the south and west coasts of Britain. This anemone is able to easily retract its tentacles, which is what gives it its name – the column of the anemone has yellow-green spots (which look like strawberry pips) on a vivid crimson background. The tentacles, once extended, are also bright crimson. Strawberry Anemones have pale blue to pink acrorhagi that are not always clearly visible. The foot of the anemone can be as large as 10cm in diameter.

SPAN OF TENTACLES 10cm
ZONE Lower shore
DISTRIBUTION SW of British Isles
SIMILAR SPECIES *Actinia equina*

Beadlet Anemone   *Actinia equina*

The Beadlet Anemone is the most common of the anemones on the rocky shores found all around the British Isles. It withdraws its tentacles when out of water. It is found from the upper shore, where it can cope well with the higher temperatures and chances of drying out, down to the lower shore. The foot of the anemone is up to 5cm in diameter and has a smooth, solid colour. Beadlet Anemones can appear red, brown, green or orange, and have many tentacles of the same colour. These anemones are thought to be quite aggressive and will fire their nematocysts from their blue acrorhagi at other anemones that come too close.

SPAN OF TENTACLES 7cm
ZONE Upper to lower shore
DISTRIBUTION All of British Isles
SIMILAR SPECIES *Actinia fragacea, A. prasina, Sagartia elegans*

Snakelocks Anemone   *Anemonia viridis*

The Snakelocks Anemone can be found on the west coasts of Britain, from the mid to the lower shore, submerged in pools that prevent it from drying out. It has long, swaying green tentacles with purple tips and a pale brown column with a disc that is broader than it is long. The base can be up to 7cm across and the tentacles can be as long as 18cm. The Snakelocks Anemone can vary in colour, with some having brown tentacles as opposed to green with purple tips. It is thought that these two forms may be separate species. The tentacles are capable of withdrawing but this is rarely observed.

SPAN OF TENTACLES 18cm
ZONE Mid to lower shore
DISTRIBUTION S and W British Isles
SIMILAR SPECIES *Actinia prasina*

Gem Anemone   *Aulactinia verrucosa*

The Gem Anemone is found on the south and west shores of England, Wales and Scotland, and on all Irish coasts. It is well camouflaged as a result of its transparent tentacles, which number up to 48 (and are always divisible by 6) and have a mottled appearance with white, grey or green stripes or bands. The base is approximately 2.5cm wide and the column has cream-coloured warts, hence its '*verrucosa*' name. When the anemone is disturbed it retracts its tentacles, leaving a dome-shaped, warty urchin with clearly defined lines of warts running from the apex.

SPAN OF TENTACLES 6cm
ZONE Mid to lower shore
DISTRIBUTION S and W England
SIMILAR SPECIES *Anthopleura ballii*, *A. rubripunctata*, *A. thallia*

Jewel Anemone   *Corynactis viridis*

Jewel Anemones are found on the south and west coasts of England, in Wales and Scotland, and on all Irish coasts, its most northerly limit being Shetland. They are found from the lower shore down into subtidal regions and commonly found on vertical rocks or areas with little light. This is an intensely colourful anemone of green, pink, orange, red or white, with contrasting tentacles and a disc approximately 1cm in diameter. It has up to 100 tentacles, each with a small, round knob at the tip. Jewel Anemones undergo longitudinal fission and are often found in great swathes, lighting up rocky surfaces like tiny jewels.

SPAN OF TENTACLES 1cm
ZONE Lower shore to subtidal
DISTRIBUTION S and W of British Isles
SIMILAR SPECIES *Caryophyllia smithii*

Dahlia Anemone   *Urticina felina*

The Dahlia Anemone can be found all around exposed British shores from the lower shore to subtidal regions. It is named after its resemblance to the colourful garden dahlias. It can be a variety of colours, but the most common form has a red column with red stripes at the bases of the tentacles. The base is up to 15cm in diameter and the tentacles are short (2cm), numerous (up to 160) and stocky. It is an impressive anemone, which has even been observed eating mussels. When the tentacles are retracted the column is often covered in fragments of shell, stone and sediment.

SPAN OF TENTACLES 20cm
ZONE Lower shore to subtidal
DISTRIBUTION All of British Isles
SIMILAR SPECIES *Cereus pedunculatus, Urticina eques*

Plumose Anemone *Metridium senile*

The Plumose Anemone can be found all around Britain and Ireland on the lower shore, and attached to piers, rock walls and submerged wrecks. The base of the anemone is wider than the long and slender column, which has a cloud-like 'tuft' of white tentacles. There are two forms, the *pallidus* form has a shorter column and long and slender tentacles, while the *dianthus* form is far taller, with more filamentous tentacles that give the anemone a fluffy appearance. This anemone can grow to 30cm high, with a wide base, sometimes 12cm across. It is often white, pale yellow or cream.

SPAN OF TENTACLES 15cm
ZONE Lower shore to subtidal
DISTRIBUTION All of British Isles
SIMILAR SPECIES *Actinothoe sphyrodeta*, *Sagartia elegans*

Fried Egg Anemone *Actinothoe sphyrodeta*

The Fried Egg Anemone is common around all of the British Isles except for the east coast. It can be found in shaded areas on the lower shore, and commonly on pontoons or man-made structures. The column of this anemone is often very pale, almost white, with pale stripes that led to it sometimes being called the Sandalled Anemone. It has a crown of numerous fine white tentacles and a centre that is often deep orange or yellow, resulting in the common name of Fried Egg Anemone. There are, however, some individuals that are completely white.

SPAN OF TENTACLES 5cm
ZONE Lower shore to subtidal
DISTRIBUTION All of British Isles, except E coast
SIMILAR SPECIES *Metridium senile*

Soft and hard corals

Then far below, in the peaceful sea,
The purple mullet and gold-fish rove,
Where the waters murmur tranquilly,
Through the bending twigs of the coral grove.

James Percival, *Ocean Flowers and their Teachings* 1863

Corals are in the same class as the sea anemones: the Anthozoa. Corals are often assumed to be tropical species, but 12 species of intertidal corals have been recorded in the British Isles and their surrounding seas, and in the deep, dark depths of the seas around Scotland and Ireland cold-water coral reefs have also been discovered. Historically our knowledge of cold-water coral reefs would have come from fishermen who had accidentally caught coral in their nets. Today we have incredible technology that allows researchers to gain a better and fuller understanding of the extent and diversity of cold-water corals in the north-west Atlantic.

Off the coastal waters of Scotland, in Rockall Bank, there are extensive *Lophelia* coral reefs. *Lophelia* is a stony reef-forming coral that grows from depths of 50m down to abyssal depths of 3,000m. The cold- and deep-water corals are thought to be hundreds of years old, and we are still discovering exactly which species live within this unique habitat. However, just like their tropical relatives, British corals are also under threat from human activity. Tropical shallow corals face pressure from increased sea temperatures, ocean acidification and

The British seashore has its very own coral reefs, including those comprising the soft coral Dead Man's Fingers (*Alcyonium digitatum*).

siltation (amongst other pressures), and our own coral-reef habitats face damage from deep-sea trawling, and oil and gas exploration. Recognition of the threat to our cold-water corals has led to the creation of a 100-square-kilometre protected area called Darwin Mounds, off the north-west tip of mainland Scotland, set up to preserve a vast field of *Lophelia* coral reef.

Soft corals such as Dead Man's Fingers do not have calcium carbonate skeletons as do stony corals. They do have 'sclerites' that keep the soft coral supported. The Dead Man's Fingers is a colonial coral, so within one structure you may find hundreds of polyps (the anemone-like protrusions), which in favourable conditions emerge to collect food. The polyps share resources as a colony, for excreting waste for example. The Dead Man's Fingers tend to close down in cooler winter water temperatures, retracting their polyps from feeding and going into a dormant state. During this dormant period they may not be instantly recognisable because of the algal covering on their surface.

Closer to shore, in the area between the high and low tides, it is possible to discover corals without even getting wet – it just requires a little perseverance. We have a variety of cup corals that retreat into limestone cup-shaped skeletons. When the tentacles are not retracted in self-defence it is easy to mistake these solitary stony corals for their relatives, the anemones, but when retracted into their stony cups it is easy to see their characterisitc coral-like form. This calcareous external skeleton seen in the cup is how we characterise corals.

Looking for cup corals can remind us to take a close look at what we discover on and under rocks and boulders. Things are not always quite as they seem, and what we might think is an anemone could in fact be a cup coral.

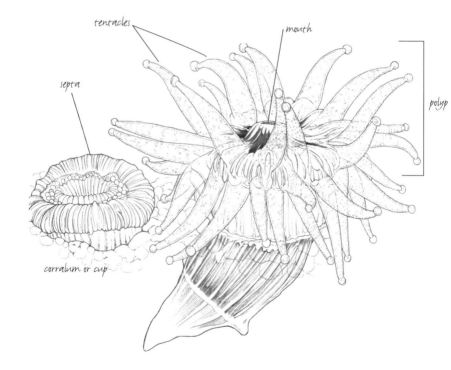

The anatomy of a cup coral showing the polyp retracted into the corralum (left) and extended (right).

Devonshire Cup Coral   *Caryophyllia smithii*

This cup coral was discovered in Devon, but it can be found on most coasts of the British Isles except for much of the east coast. It is a solitary cup-shaped coral that occurs in deep pools and shaded regions of the lower shore, most commonly in the subtidal region. The cup of the coral is 2.5cm across and when the tentacles are retracted a protruding, smooth partition is visible. The tentacles are translucent and numerous (up to 80) with small spherical knobs. The disc can be a variety of colours including white, pink, orange, green or red.

DIAMETER OF CUP 2.5cm
ZONE Lower shore to subtidal
DISTRIBUTION All of British Isles, except E
SIMILAR SPECIES *Caryophyllia inornata, Corynactis viridis*

Sunset Cup Coral   *Leptopsammia pruvoti*

The striking Sunset Cup Coral has been found in locations around the south-west of England, on overhangs of rocks in caves and gullies attached to bedrock. This cup coral is usually solitary, but can occasionally be found in small groups. The tentacles are yellow to orange and number up to 96 in total. The coralline 'cup' can be quite tall, growing up to 6cm and with a diameter of around 1.5cm.

DIAMETER OF CUP 1.5cm
ZONE Lower shore to subtidal
DISTRIBUTION SW England
SIMILAR SPECIES *Balanophyllia regia*

Scarlet and Gold Star Coral *Balanophyllia regia*

This bright yellow-orange solitary cup coral can be found around the south-west of England and Wales. It occurs on the lower shore and subtidally in overhangs, caves and gullies. The tentacles grow in rings of six and the coral may have up to 48 tentacles in total. This cup coral is brightly coloured with an orange-scarlet disc and translucent orange tentacles. The corraline 'cup' structure is softer in texture than that of other cup corals.

DIAMETER OF CUP 2.5cm
ZONE Lower shore to subtidal
DISTRIBUTION SW England and Wales
SIMILAR SPECIES *Leptopsammia pruvoti*

Dead Man's Fingers *Alcyonium digitatum*

The Dead Man's Fingers can be found on all coasts around the British Isles. Thought to resemble decomposing fingers, hence its name, in fact in the water the brilliant white and emergent polyps make it an attractive soft coral. It can also be orange or even brown in colour in inactive winter periods. Each polyp has eight tentacles, which emerge to feed. Dead Man's Fingers are often found under piers, on jetties and on rocky vertical surfaces where there is a fast flow of nutrient-rich water. The polyps can grow to 10cm across and 20cm in length.

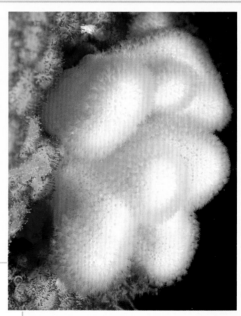

LENGTH OF FINGERS 25cm
ZONE Lower shore to subtidal
DISTRIBUTION All of British Isles
SIMILAR SPECIES *Alcyonium glomeratum*

Sea firs and siphonophores

As for your pretty little seed-cups or vases, they are a sweet confirmation of the pleasure Nature seems to take in superadding an elegance of form to most of her works, wherever you find them.

William Hogarth, *A Selection of the Correspondence of Linnaeus and other Naturalists* 1821

Sea firs and siphonophores both belong to the class **Hydrozoa**. Hydrozoans can have either a polyp or a medusa phase, but they usually have both. Hydrozoan polyps that live together in a colony are different from the sponges that live as colonies. In a sponge each cell performs mostly the same function, whereas hydrozoan polyps have different functions.

There are polyps within many hydrozoans that are used for feeding, which are called gastrozooids. Polyps that undertake the role of reproduction are called gonozooids, while the defensive and offensive polyps are known as nematophores. Some hydroids are able to float at sea and these are perhaps the best known. They include the Portuguese Man o'War (*Physalia physalis*) and By-the-Wind Sailor (*Velella velella*). These are not jellyfish as one might assume (a jellyfish consists of a single medusa); instead they are colonies of polyps, and they are classed as siphonophores and floating colonial hydroids.

A siphonophore is a single organism made up of several colonies that have different functions. The Portuguese Man o'War is made up of four colonies that act as one organism, and each of the polyps could not live separately or independently. Only one of the four colonies is responsible for locomotion: the gas-filled bladder that floats on the surface of the sea, which is propelled by winds, tides and currents across the ocean. A second colony is responsible for reproduction, a third for digestion and a fourth for defence (the stinging part of the siphonophore, that is the tentacles).

While the Portuguese Man o'War is a rare visitor to our coasts, under certain weather conditions it can be found washed up on shores. When submerged the tentacles have the ability to coil up like a spring, visually relax, lengthen, then recoil, a process that can be

The infamous Portuguese Man o'War, despite resembling a jellyfish, is actually a siphonophore.

pneumatophore
dactyloids
gastrozooids
nematocysts

In the Portuguese Man o'War the pneumatophore acts as a sail. Its tentacles hang from the sail alongside the digestive polyps. The stinging cells are found in the bead-like structures of the tentacles.

incredibly hypnotic to witness. However, it is worth noting that the tentacles can trail for several metres and they should never be approached as the sting of this siphonophore can be extremely painful.

Sea firs are also hydroids, and many can be found in the intertidal zone, attached to shells, rocks and seaweeds. Sea firs are very difficult to identify without the use of a microscope. If you discover filamentous strands attached to shells, it is always worth looking closely to see whether these seaweed-looking strands may in fact be hydrozoans. There are some with miniature tree-like branching structures that share a tree-like trunk called a stolon. The stolon anchors the sea fir, and around the outside of the stolon is a stronger sheath called a perisarc.

There are athecate and thecate types of hydroid, which show interesting and different anatomies.

Tubularia indivisa is an athecate hydroid and cannot withdraw its flower-like 'hydranths'. However, thecates such as *Dynamena pumila* are able to retract their feeding apparatus into a special microscopic cup-like structure called the hydrotheca. The hydranths of *Tubularia indivisa* are also the point from which the medusa phase is released as part of its reproductive cycle, which includes both a swimming medusa and sessile polyp phase. Within athecates like *Tubularia indivisa* the perisarc supports and protects only the interconnecting strands of the hydrozoan, not the flower-like hydranth, which always remains everted.

Whatever their structure, whether it be the athecate and thecate hydroids or the floating colonial zooids, the sea firs and siphonophores are all worthy of close inspection of their intricate and beautiful anatomical details.

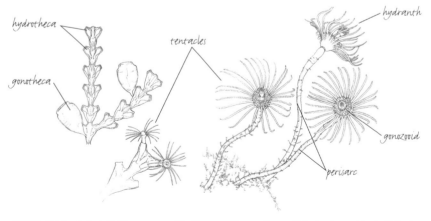

hydrotheca
gonotheca
tentacles
hydranth
gonozooid
perisarc

Anatomy of a thecate hydroid (*Dynamena pumila*) with cocoon-like gonotheca, with hydranths capable of withdrawing into hydrothecae, and an athecate hydroid (*Tubularia indivisa*), with the gonozooids found amongst the tentacles.

Dynamena pumila

Dynamena pumila is often found attached to the Toothed Wrack and other kelps. This thecate hydroid is common on all coasts around the British Isles. It is particularly abundant on relavtively exposed shores with strong waves and tidal currents.

The stems of the hydroid arise from the stolon and are short. They are occasionally branched with cups on alternate sides that hold the feeding polyps or hydranths. The stems also have pear-shaped gonotheca, the capsules containing the reproductive gonozooid polyps.

HEIGHT 3cm
ZONE Lower shore to subtidal
DISTRIBUTION All of British Isles
SIMILAR SPECIES *Obelia longissima*

Tubularia indivisa

Tubularia indivisa is found all around the British coast, attached to rocks, stones and shells on low spring tides, and more commonly in deeper waters. This species is an example of an athecate hydroid. It can grow up to 15cm tall with a long perisarc that attaches to a tangled stolon. The feeding polyp or hydranth is pink with white tentacles. It has a stalk-like body with an anemone-like head that is used to collect food. The reproductive polyps or gonozooids are found between the tentacles of the polyps, and are often visible.

HEIGHT 15cm
ZONE Lower shore to subtidal
DISTRIBUTION All of British Isles
SIMILAR SPECIES None

Sea Fir   *Obelia longissima*

The Sea Fir is found all around the British Isles, on the lower shore and in sheltered pools, attached to rocks, seaweed and shells. This colony of hydroids has short, straight branches growing from a darker main stem. The feeding polyp, resembling a microscopic anemone, is held within a cup-like hydrotheca along the branches. The polyps, like those of many cnidarians, have stinging cells within the tentacles which help trap their planktonic food.

LENGTH 20cm
ZONE Lower shore
DISTRIBUTION All of British Isles
SIMILAR SPECIES *Dynamena pumila*

Portuguese Man o'War   *Physalia physalis*

The Portuguese Man o'War mainly washes up on the south-west coast of the British Isles. This is an aggressively stinging siphonophore, common to warmer waters, which can occasionally be brought to our shores on the right prevailing winds. It has a gas-filled 'pneumatophore' sail that resembles a blue balloon, with a ridge along the upper edge that helps it to catch the wind. A vivid blue to purple in colour, below its sail this cnidarian has a collection of stinging nematocysts on its tentacles which are both coiled and straight, retractable and of the most intense blue and turquoise colour.

WIDTH OF FLOAT 30cm
ZONE Strandline
DISTRIBUTION SW British Isles
SIMILAR SPECIES None

Jellyfish

Yet, small though it may be, it is gorgeous enough to be the diadem of sea-fairies, and sufficiently graceful to be the night-cap of the tiniest and prettiest of mermaidens.

Edward Forbes, *British Naked-eyed Medusae* 1848

Jellyfish are perhaps the best known of the cnidarians. Those in our waters are of the class Scyphozoa, often found in great swarms or as a 'smack', as they are collectively known. The scyphozoans swim by contracting and pulsating their bell-shaped bodies, with these actions propelling them through the water. They are simple species in that they do not have a nervous system, just a nerve net that detects movement. They have no digestive system either; instead they have a mouth below the bell that opens into a gastrovascular cavity, or open gut, where prey that they catch with their stinging tentacles is carried for digestion and absorption.

The Moon Jellyfish (*Aurelia aurita*) is fairly typical of the scyphoid jellyfish. The bell or hood of the Moon Jellyfish narrows from a much thicker central bell to a thinner, tapered margin. The oral arms of the jellyfish can be clearly seen at the centre of the underside of the bell. The longer oral arms of the jellyfish are not to be confused with the tentacles, which are very short in the Moon Jellyfish and are found around the edge of its bell. This jellyfish is actually a filter feeder rather than a predator. Predatory jellyfish need longer stinging tentacles. The adult Moon Jellyfish feeds by trapping plankton underneath the bell in mucus it creates. The microscopic 'flagellae' or whip-like structures found under the bell and on the oral arms, combined with the swimming action, act to bring the plankton to the mouth on the underside of the bell.

This larval stage of the Moon Jellyfish is called an ephyra.

Jellyfish often swarm in thousands, with increased levels of swarming recorded in some areas recently. This is thought to be related to climate change and other human actions that are creating changes in our seas. High numbers of jellyfish swarms are linked to a reduction in predators as a result of the fishing industry, and with more nutrient-rich (from farming run-off) but oxygen-poor waters, in which the jellyfish thrive. Jellyfish are difficult to sample and study for research because of their soft jelly structure and their stings. Because of this research into and our understanding of jellyfish is not as advanced as is the case with other more readily sampled marine invertebrates and vertebrates.

The scyphpoid jellyfish have a fascinating life cycle and go through both an attached and sessile polyp stage, from which they can asexually reproduce or bud, and also a swimming medusa sexually reproducing stage. In the case of the Moon Jellyfish the gonads are clearly visible as four circular markings on the bell of the jellyfish. The gametes are released from the male with the female jellyfish, in effect, ingesting the sperm through her mouth. The fertilised gametes are released as developing embryos into brood chambers, and the embryos gradually travel the length of the arms to the tips. The planula larvae are then released from the tips of the arms in autumn. A swimming planula larva soon settles and a scyphistoma develops.

The scyphistoma settles as a polyp and will develop into a stack of developing ephyra larvae. Through the process of fission the planula larvae produce small, jellyfish-like, pulsating, radially symmetrical and perfectly formed ephyra, which are released into the water in the summer months. They pop off the scyphistoma stack and develop into the adult medusa form of the Moon Jellyfish.

In addition to the two jellyfish described on the following page, other jellyfish to look out for in British waters include the Lion's Mane Jellyfish (*Cyanea capillata*), Blue Jellyfish (*Cyanea lamarckii*), Mauve Stinger (*Pelagia noctiluca*) and Barrel Jellyfish (*Rhizostoma octopus*).

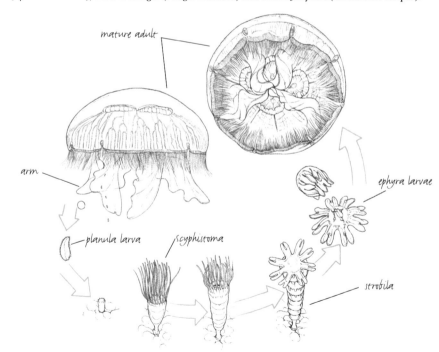

mature adult

arm

planula larva

scyphistoma

ephyra larvae

strobila

The life cycle of the Moon Jellyfish.

Compass Jellyfish   *Chrysaora hysoscella*

Compass Jellyfish are found all around the British Isles, but most commonly in the south and west and during the warmer summer months. This jellyfish has a distinguishable pattern on the bell that resembles the radial pattern of a compass. In the centre of the cream-coloured bell is a brown circle, and from this V-shaped lines radiate to the outer edge of the bell. Compass Jellyfish reach approximately 30cm in diameter and have 32 lobes around the edge of the bell. Their tentacles are in sets of three with a sensory organ between each set. These stinging tentacles are capable of causing itchiness or a rash.

WIDTH Up to 30cm
ZONE Strandline and subtidal
DISTRIBUTION All of British Isles
SIMILAR SPECIES *Aurelia aurita*

Moon Jellyfish   *Aurelia aurita*

Moon Jellyfish are common on all coasts around the British Isles. Also called Common Jellyfish, they have a transparent bell that can grow up to 40cm across. They have four distinctive incomplete rings at the centre of the bell – these are in fact the gonads. The species has short tentacles which it uses to catch its prey, and four arms that help to bring the stunned food to its mouth. The bell of the Moon Jellyfish has short stinging tentacles on its periphery and eight indentations that are its sensory organs.

WIDTH Up to 40cm
ZONE Strandline and subtidal
DISTRIBUTION All of British Isles
SIMILAR SPECIES *Chrysaora hysoscella*

MARINE WORMS

Both men and angels, worms and gods.
Exist in universal love.

William Johnson Fox, *Life is Love* 1895

When considering marine worms it is important to leave behind preconceived ideas about what they might look like, especially in relation to more familiar and arguably less interesting terrestrial worms. The marine worms are both beautiful and diverse, with an incredible array of weird and wonderful body shapes. While some might be considered less attractive than others, they all have incredible stories of adaptation and survival to tell.

The generic term and heading of marine worms used here actually describes the four phyla of the annelids, priapulids, nemerteans and platyhelminthes. The annelids include the polychaetes, among them the beautiful Sea Mouse (*Aphrodita eculeata*) and the Lugworm (*Arenicola marina*), which is perhaps more useful for fishing than it is attractive. Annelids are characterised by their segments which, if not hidden within a calcium casing or gravel tube, are visible from the outside. The priapulids, or penis worms as they are commonly called, are an unlikely discovery for the seashore naturalist. They tend to live in deep waters except

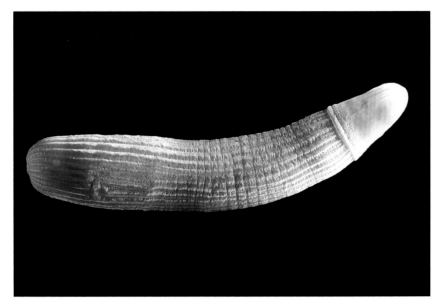

Priapulus caudatus belongs to the worm phylum of the priapulids which tend to be found in deep waters.

for the occasional intertidal discovery of *Priapulus caudatus*, which feed on polychaetes like the Sea Mouse. Priapulids have a trunk and a retractable proboscis that is covered in spines. The nemerteans include the formidable and potentially longest animal on our planet, the Bootlace Worm (*Lineus longissimus*). Nemerteans tend to be long with bilateral symmetry and an eversible proboscis. They are also called ribbon worms. Finally the platyhelminthes, or flatworms, are flattened with a bilateral symmetry, and have a mouth but no anus. The delicately beautiful Candy Striped Worm (*Prostheceraeus vittatus*) is typical of this phylum, as are the parasitic flukes and tapeworms.

Within the intertidal worms there are reef-forming worms, like the Honeycomb Worm (*Sabellaria spinulosa*), and worms that can be found unattached in the gravel and sand sediments or attached to rocky substrates. Some worms create defensive masonry tubes constructed from shell and stone fragments with great architectural accuracy. Similarly other worms create a calcium carbonate tube that can be seen attached to seaweeds, shells and rocks. The vulnerable worms are soft-bodied, so they protect themselves from predation through many methods of self-defence. The high risk of predation justifies the extraordinary efforts and energy that worms invest in burrowing, building or parasitism.

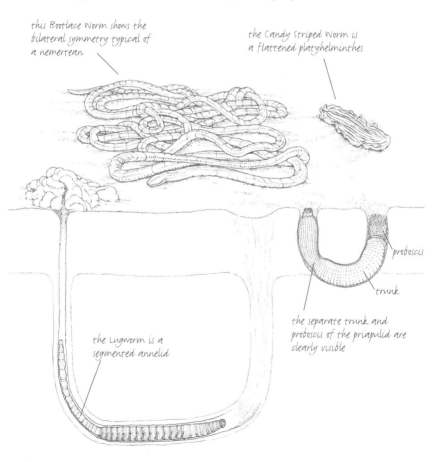

this Bootlace Worm shows the bilateral symmetry typical of a nemertean

the Candy Striped Worm is a flattened platyhelminthes

proboscis

trunk

the separate trunk and proboscis of the priapulid are clearly visible

the Lugworm is a segmented annelid

Marine worms are extremely diverse animals, as can be seen in the above examples of the four marine worm phyla, the annelid Lugworm, priapulid *Priapulus caudatus*, nemertean Bootlace Worm and platyhelminthes Candy Striped Worm.

The Biodiversity Action Plan is a national plan to help manage, conserve and enhance important natural habitats and species. Habitats considered to be of conservation concern, including intertidal and subtidal habitats, have been given the term 'priority habitats'. Honeycomb Worm (*Sabellaria spinulosa*) reefs are classed as a priority habitat and are considered important because of the way in which these polychaete worms create a stable environment by securing loose gravel and substrate. This stable and, at times, vast habitat provides a great location for other species to grow and thrive in. A rich biodiverse habitat, a honeycomb reef has many species living within it, encouraging birds that feed within the intertidal reefs. Like many habitats within our coastal environment, these reefs are under threat from fishery-related dredging and aggregate dredging, which can cause direct destruction and also smother the reefs with sediment.

The Estuary Ragworm (*Hediste diversicolor*) is a worm species of particular interest, which shows some incredible traits. This humble worm 'decides' whether to reproduce at the autumn equinox, then breeds in the spring and subsequently dies. This process is thought to be driven by the need to balance the chances of predation against the benefits of having high numbers of healthy reproductive gametes as the species matures. The Estuary Ragworm also has the ability to 'tell the time' through an internal molecular clock that helps it to synchronise breeding. One population of harbour-dwelling Estuary Ragworms has developed the ability to withstand copper pollution. In a British harbour in an area with a history of copper mining, the levels of copper have built up over time, but the Estuary Ragworms inhabiting the harbour have evolved the ability to store copper in inert capsules under the skin, preventing the metal from causing harm to their vital organs.

Marine worms represent important diverse habitats as well as interesting stories of evolutionary adaptation. These species can be beautiful and surprising in appearance, and are worthy of a low-tide exploration dedicated purely to the pursuit of marine worms.

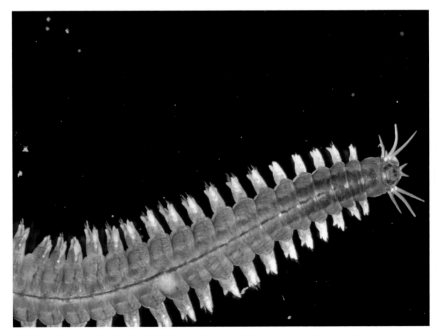

The Estuary Ragworm (*Hediste diversicolor*) showing its segmented body and paired parapodia.

Sea Mouse   *Aphrodita aculeata*

The Sea Mouse occurs around the
British Isles. This annelid tends to
be found below low tide, but can get
washed up into lower tidal pools and
on to the strandline. This attractive
'mouse' derives its Latin name from
the Greek goddess of love and beauty,
Aphrodite. Bristles cover its oval,
segmented body. Some of the bristles
glow with an electric, iridescent palette
of colour. The head is well covered
and hidden, but there are two 'palps'
that look like horns protruding from
the head end. The species can grow to
20cm long and 6cm wide, and has a
soft, yellow and bumpy underside.

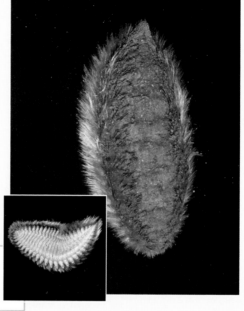

LENGTH Up to 20cm
ZONE Strandline, lower shore to subtidal
DISTRIBUTION All of British Isles
SIMILAR SPECIES None

Estuary Ragworm   *Hediste diversicolor*

The Estuary Ragworm can be found all
around the British Isles on the mid to
lower shore, in deep, U-shaped burrows
or under rocks in loose sediment. This
worm has many segments (up to 120)
and grows up to 12cm in length. Each
segment has paired parapodia which
are used for locomotion. The head
end has two antennae, four pairs of
tentacles and two palps. The species
can feed on phytoplankton by spinning
a net at the opening of its burrow to
entrap the tiny plankton. It also feeds
on invertebrates and grazes on algae.
Its colour varies from orange to green,
becoming greener as it matures.

LENGTH Up to 12cm
ZONE Mid to lower shore
DISTRIBUTION All of British Isles
SIMILAR SPECIES *Nereis pelagica, N. virens,
Platynereis dumerilii*

Green Leaf Worm   *Eulalia clavigera*

The Green Leaf Worm is common on British coasts in a variety of habitats, from mussel and barnacle beds to coarse sediment. It may also be found crawling on rocky substrates in the intertidal zone. Previously mistaken for *Eulalia viridis*, the Green Leaf Worm is a characteristic bright green colour, has up to 200 segments and measures up to 15cm long. It has parapodia for locomotion, which are more flattened and paddle-shaped than those of the Estuary Ragworm. It uses an extendable proboscis to feed. The Green Leaf Worm produces bright green, gelatinous blobs of egg masses in early spring.

LENGTH Up to 15cm
ZONE Lower shore
DISTRIBUTION All of British Isles
SIMILAR SPECIES *Eulalia viridis*, *Eumidia punctifera*

Lugworm   *Arenicola marina*

The Lugworm can be up to 20cm long and occurs around the British Isles from the high to the low shore. It is commonly found in estuaries in muddy, sandy sediment in a 20cm-deep, U-shaped burrow. On the surface of the sand above the head end there will be a small depression, and approximately 10cm away there will be a small wriggly 'cast' that the Lugworm has defecated after extracting the detritus and micro-organisms. The worm itself varies in colour, but is most commonly dark brown/black. It has a small head with 19 parapodia on the body, 13 of which have frilly-looking gills, and a smooth and segmented tail.

LENGTH Up to 20cm
ZONE Upper to lower shore
DISTRIBUTION All of British Isles
SIMILAR SPECIES *Arenicola defodiens*

Spiral Worm   *Spirorbis spirorbis*

The Spiral Worm can be found within the wrack-dominated intertidal zones of the shore all around the British Isles. The spiral, white, calcium carbonate protective tubes of this segmented worm are found attached to seaweeds, particularly the Serrated Wrack and Bladder Wrack. It is also occasionally found on stones and shells and the carapaces of crustaceans. The sinistral, spiral coil is 3–4mm wide. The segmented worm lives inside the calcium tube in relative safety. The worm itself is only a few millimetres long, and orange to red in colour.

LENGTH Up to 0.5cm

ZONE Mid to lower shore

DISTRIBUTION All of British Isles

SIMILAR SPECIES *Janua pagenstecheri, Pomatoceros triqueter, Spirorbis corrallinae, S. rupestris, S. tridentatus*

Keel Worm   *Pomatoceros triqueter*

The calcareous cast of the Keel Worm can be found on shells, rocks and the carapaces of crabs and lobsters on the seashore around all of the British Isles. It is irregular in shape, with a ridge running the length of the cast that can grow as long as 2.5cm. It has a 'trapdoor' or operculum at the opening of the cast from which the variably coloured, striped tentacles of the worm extend to feed. This annelid worm is thought to be very well protected against predation due to its hard casing and operculum. It feeds on detritus and organic matter, which it catches with its tentacles.

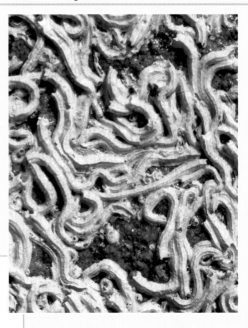

LENGTH Up to 2.5cm

ZONE Lower shore to subtidal

DISTRIBUTION All of British Isles

SIMILAR SPECIES *Janua pagenstecheri, Spirorbis spirorbis*

Sand Mason   *Lanice chonchilega*

This segmented worm is found on soft, sandy intertidal and subtidal sediments all around the British Isles. The annelid worm's self-constructed tube is made up of small fragments of sand, rock and shell held together by mucus. The worm is surprisingly lengthy, at up to 30cm, but only the head end protrudes through the tube. When the tide is high it extends its white tentacles to feed on passing organic matter that gets trapped in the tentacles. This is the part most likely to be seen, the fine tentacles covered in shell fragments, along with a section of the shell-covered tube protruding from the surface of the sand.

LENGTH Up to 30cm
ZONE Lower shore to subtidal
DISTRIBUTION All of British Isles
SIMILAR SPECIES None

Peacock Worm   *Sabella pavonina*

The Peacock Worm can be found throughout the coastal British Isles on very low tides and in the subtidal regions. As the name implies this is another colourful and attractive worm. The Peacock Worm can be up to 30cm long, but on the seashore its visible part will be the 10cm-long muddy tube from which the worm extends its red-orange, banded, feathery tentacles like a beautiful flower. The tentacles catch passing food. It retracts them when there are potential predators around.

LENGTH Up to 30cm high
ZONE Lower shore to subtidal
DISTRIBUTION All of British Isles
SIMILAR SPECIES *Bispira volutacornis, Myxicola infundibulum*

Twin Fan Worm *Bispira volutacornis*

The Twin Fan Worm is found in the south-west reaches of the British Isles, in the low-shore tidal pools, on shaded rocky overhangs and subtidally. This annelid is similar in appearance to the Peacock Worm, with an attractive fan-shaped feeding apparatus of many tentacles, but it has a bi-spiral arrangement of two whorls of tentacles. The feeding tentacles tend to be pale cream or brown. It retracts its fan into its tube when under threat. The tube, which is made from mud and mucus, is attached to the sediment or nestled into a crevice.

LENGTH Up to 10cm
ZONE Lower shore to subtidal
DISTRIBUTION All of British Isles
SIMILAR SPECIES *Myxicola infundibulum, Sabella pavonica*

Honeycomb Worm *Sabellaria spinulosa*

The Honeycomb Worm is most common on the south and west coasts of England. It is a tube-building segmented annelid worm, using fragments of coarse sand to build the tube. Honeycomb Worms aggregate on rock surfaces to form large, extensive reefs that dominate the rocky seashore and down into deeper water. These aggregations are Biodiversity Action Plan habitats valuable for feeding birds. They also act as sheltered areas for other intertidal species. The larvae are thought to settle where living or dead remains of their own species exist or have existed. The worm itself is 2–3cm long, and pale with gills running along its back.

LENGTH Up to 3cm
ZONE Mid shore to subtidal
DISTRIBUTION S and W coasts of England
SIMILAR SPECIES *Sabellaria alveolata*

Bootlace Worm *Lineus longissimus*

The Bootlace Worm can be found all around the British Isles except for the east coasts of Scotland and England. It occurs under rocks, amongst kelp and in the sediment in coiled knots. If you try to handle it, it will release a self-defensive, slightly putrid-smelling mucus. It is an unsegmented, dark brown, nemertean worm 5mm wide, with pale longitudinal lines along its length. It usually grows to 5–15m long, but in 1864 a worm was recorded measuring 55m in length, making this lowly worm the longest animal on earth, far exceeding the Blue Whale. The head end is paler in colour than the body.

LENGTH Up to 15m
ZONE Lower shore to subtidal
DISTRIBUTION All of British Isles
SIMILAR SPECIES *Lineus bilineatus*

Candy Striped Worm *Prostheceraeus vittatus*

The Candy Striped Worm can be found all around the British coast, under rocks and in pools on the lowest of tides and in the subtidal region amongst kelp forests. This worm could be mistaken for an attractive sea slug. It is in fact a beautiful and very thin, dorso-ventrally flattened flatworm, measuring up to 5cm in length. It is not segmented but has a flattened, undulating surface. At the head end the 'skirt' is split to form tentacles. The species is cream to yellow in colour, with dark longitudinal lines running along the body. The Candy Striped Worm feeds on sea squirts.

LENGTH Up to 5cm
ZONE Lower shore to subtidal
DISTRIBUTION All of British Isles
SIMILAR SPECIES None

MOLLUSCS

Each shell each crawling insect holds a rank
Important in the plan of Him, who framed
This scale of being; holds a rank which lost
Would break the chain, and leave a gap
Which Nature's self would rue.

Benjamin Stillingfleet, *Miscellaneous Tracts Relating to Natural History,*
Husbandry and Physick 1759

For thousands of years we have associated the shells of the molluscan phylum with high value. They have been used to make jewellery, as a form of currency and to indicate status. We have long perceived their form as an incredible miracle of nature. It is a source of wonder that some soft-bodied molluscs are capable of building hard, beautiful shells with intricate patterns and logarithmic spirals. The beauty of the remains of molluscs' shells and their ease of transportation are likely reasons why humans have collected them for millennia. The Victorians would take pride in their shell collections, investing great efforts to collect rare or tropical species. One can only hope they appreciated their form as much as, if not more than, the wealth they represented.

The Painted Top Shell (*Calliostoma zizyphinum*) is a striking marine mollusc found around the British Isles.

Molluscs are soft-bodied invertebrates. There are many that have external shells which we often enjoy searching for on beaches, each shell appealing to us with its own intricate beauty. There are other molluscs that have internal shells, like the Sea Hare, cuttlefish and squid. Molluscs vary in size, from the large cephalopods like the giant squid, to the smaller gastropods that are found between grains of sand. They range from the lesser known chitons, nudibranchs (sea slugs) and tusk shells, which are only found in the marine environment, to the bivalves and gastropods that are commonly found in both fresh and marine water.

The most familiar molluscs might be the edible shellfish, some of which are considered to be luxury foods, although this was not always the case. Oysters were once seen as a food for the poor; they used to be found in abundance, and native flat oysters would be consumed from the shore. However, their popularity proved to be their demise and their natural beds have since become depleted.

Today the Pacific Oyster (*Crassotrea gigas*) is grown on in bags by oyster farmers. This now invasive species was originally thought to be unable to reproduce in our cooler waters, but it was found forming substantial beds in some estuaries. The oysters that are grown in bags are seen as a sustainable low-impact fishery. They filter nutrients from surrounding waters rather than requiring food caught from the open seas, which might further deplete marine stocks. However, a number of invasive species are thought to have been transported to our coastal waters through oyster cultivation.

The molluscs are so variable that trying to offer defining characteristics is difficult. It is perhaps due to its variability that this phylum is such a success, as it has evolved many different body

Mussels have long been valued as a tasty source of protein.

shapes to suit different habitats, potential predators and feeding opportunities. A limpet has been used here to illustrate some of the key characteristics of a mollusc.

A limpet, like many molluscs, is a soft-bodied invertebrate, and its body is split into three main parts. The foot is a muscly structure used to move across surfaces, with the help of a lubricating mucus. The mantle is the area found above the 'visceral mass' and, in some species, it produces the shell from a gland. This gland produces chitin, proteins and calcium carbonate to make the shell. The shell usually has an external layer made from proteins called the periostracum, with layers of calcium carbonate below that. Some molluscs then have a mother-of-pearl inner layer, or nacreous layer, which can be seen when the outer layers have eroded. This can often be observed in sea-worn top shells and is clearly visible on the underside of an ormer.

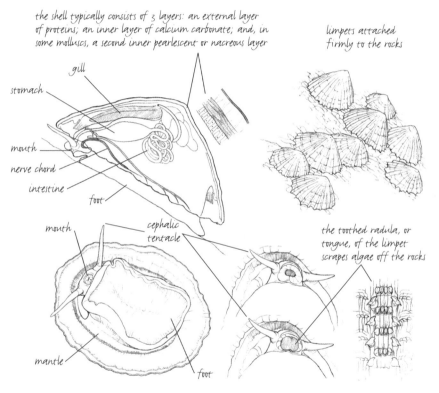

the shell typically consists of 3 layers: an external layer of proteins; an inner layer of calcium carbonate; and, in some molluscs, a second inner pearlescent or nacreous layer

limpets attached firmly to the rocks

gill

stomach

mouth

nerve chord

intestine

foot

mouth

cephalic tentacle

the toothed radula, or tongue, of the limpet scrapes algae off the rocks

mantle

foot

Limpets show some of the common features shared by many molluscs, such as a foot, mantle, shell and soft body.

The visceral mass is where the internal organs are found, including the gills (in most aquatic molluscs), a heart and a nervous system. Molluscan blood differs from the blood of vertebrates in that it uses haemocyanin rather than haemoglobin to carry oxygen around the body. This copper-based molecule is not as efficient as the iron in haemoglobin in carrying oxygen, which is why molluscs are so slowmoving.

As far as reproduction is concerned, most molluscs start their lives swimming as a planktonic larval stage before reaching maturity, although there are some that omit this stage, like the Dog Whelk (*Nucella lapillus*), which lays egg capsules. After a period of time, the whelks hatch in their fully developed form.

Certain molluscs use a radula to feed, which can be covered in teeth to help rasp algae off rocks, as is the case with limpets. With the use of an underwater microphone it is possible to hear the rasping action of limpets as they scour algae from rocks. Other molluscs have a radula that has adapted to bore holes into other molluscs, like the necklace shells and whelks. Bivalve molluscs do not have radulae at all and instead filter food from the water.

The huge diversity of eye types found in molluscs is an incredibly interesting aspect of their evolution. Primitive chitons use photoreceptive aesthetes, more evolved chitons use acelli, scallops have eyes around the edge of the scallop, and there are the more developed eyes of the gastropods and the highly evolved eyes of the squid and octopus. The more primitive molluscan eyes are used to detect light or dark and safe periods to graze, while molluscs with more advanced eye types, like the squid, rely on their eyes to detect prey.

Molluscs are the invertebrates you are most likely to find on seashores, and the sections that follow look at the various molluscs found on British shores. These includes the gastropods, which often have spiral-shaped shells, and the bivalves, which are found in beds, or buried in sediment, wood or even rock. There are also algae-grazing winkles, carnivorous predatory Dog Whelks (*Nucella lapillus*) and bioluminescent Common Piddocks (*Pholas dactylus*) that can bore into rock. The molluscan phylum represents extremely diverse species, from those with the most undeveloped of brains to the highly intelligent cephalopods.

Mussels feed on the high tide by filtering particles and plankton from the water.

Chitons

The eyes indicate the antiquity of the soul.

Ralph Waldo Emerson, *Essays and English Traits* 1914

Chitons may look like wood lice, but they are actually well-armoured primitive molluscs of the class Polyplacophora. Chitons have been proven, through fossil records, to have lived over 400 million years ago. Modern chitons are well camouflaged and can be found stuck securely to the undersides of rocks or shells by a strong muscular foot. Their oval, flattened bodies have eight overlapping plates that protect their soft undersides. The mantle forms a thick skirt around the plates called a 'girdle', which sometimes has spines. In between the foot and the mantle there is a visible groove called a pallial groove, which is where the gills are situated. A chiton does not undergo torsion like the gastropods, so the anus is at the posterior end, the mouth at the anterior. Both the gonads and the kidneys extend along the length of the chiton, producing gametes and processing waste respectively. All chitons are marine and have separate sexes.

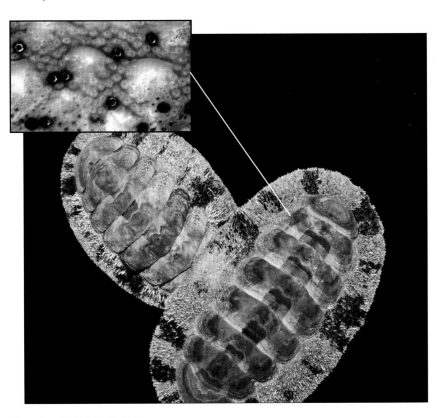

The ocelli or simple eyes of a chiton.

This class of polyplacophoran does not like direct sunlight or sudden (potentially predatory) shadows. Should you leave the stone or shell to which a chiton is attached overturned for a few minutes, you will see the chiton slowly make its way to the shaded side of the stone out of direct sunlight. It is thought that some chitons may use photoreceptive 'aesthetes' just below their shells to detect light. They have many aesthetes spread over their plates which are not visible with our own naked eye. An aesthete may act as a spread-out compound eye, although some research shows that the aesthetes also release material to repair the external layer of the shell, or periostracum.

There are some chitons with different types of eye called 'ocelli'. The ocelli are embedded in the shell and have a pigment layer, lens and retina. Research has shown that these more developed ocelli are able to detect changes in light through water and air, and perhaps even have spatial vision. This has obvious advantages for intertidal invertebrates. They have lots of ocelli so that they can detect as much light as possible in their nocturnal feeding. These ocelli have only been found in chitons from the last 10 million years of fossil records, so they are thought to be an advanced step in the evolution of chitons' eyes.

Underneath the shell of a chiton the head end is well hidden but, in fact, chitons have no defined head as such; instead they have a mouth at one end and an anus at the other. If we compare this to the molluscan squid head, which relies on the eyes and brain to capture prey, we can see how much evolutionary progress there has been in some molluscs. The chitons have no sensory tentacles to detect food. Instead they have a radula covered in teeth that are used to graze algae off rocks and also for feeding on ascidians. As a result of their dislike of direct sunlight chitons are often found under rocks, and a close examination of the undersides of boulders often reveals a well-camouflaged chiton clamped tightly to the rock. The chitons even go as far as to create home scars similar to those of their limpet relatives. They will return to the same point until gradually a depression or a home scar is created.

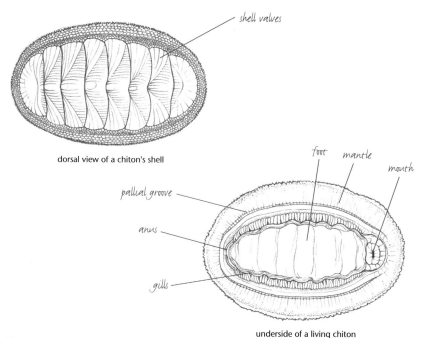

shell valves

dorsal view of a chiton's shell

foot mantle mouth

pallial groove

anus

gills

underside of a living chiton

The anatomy of a chiton.

Acanthochitona crinita

This conspicuous chiton is found mostly in the west and south-west of Britain, although its distribution is thought to extend into much of the British Isles, apart from the east coast of England. It occurs on the lower shore down into subtidal waters. The mantle skirt surrounding the plates has distinctive tufts of bristles, with nine or ten tufts on each side. The eight mottled plates vary in colour from white to green, and have a white V-shaped marking in their centre. This chiton is about 3.5cm long and, like the wood louse, will roll into a ball if disturbed and unattached.

LENGTH Up to 3.5cm
ZONE Lower shore to subtidal
DISTRIBUTION W and SW of British Isles
SIMILAR SPECIES *Acanthochitona fascicularis*

Grey Chiton *Lepidochitona cinerea*

The Grey Chiton is widespread around the shores of the British Isles, where it may be found on the mid to lower shore. It is mostly grey and very well camouflaged against rocky surfaces, although the colour can vary to include yellow, green and red patches. Grey Chitons have a smooth, flat appearance, with the plates covered in small granules. The edge of the mantle has very fine cylindrical, golden spines. The head valve or plate has eight notches, with other valves showing one or two notches.

LENGTH Up to 2.5cm
ZONE Mid to lower shore
DISTRIBUTION All of British Isles
SIMILAR SPECIES *Lepidochitona scabridus, Leptochiton asellus, Tonicella marmorea*

Gastropods

Their feet, you see, amidships, next the cuddy-hole abaft,
Drew in at once, and left their heads exposed to every shaft.
So Archi-mollusks dwindled, and the race was sinking fast,
When by the merest accident salvation came at last.
A fleet of fry turned out one day, eventful in the sequel,
Whose head-and-foot retractors on the two sides were unequal:
Their starboard halliards fixed astern ran only to the head,
While those aport were set abeam and served the foot instead.
Predaceous foes, still drifting by in numbers unabated,
Were baffled now by tactics which their dining plans frustrated.
Their prey upon alarm collapsed, but promptly turned about,
With tender morsel safe within and the horny foot without!

Walter Garstang, *The Ballad of the Veliger* 1928

The gastropods are the most diverse of the molluscs and there are in the region of 80,000
species worldwide. The only other invertebrates with more named species are the insects.
The gastropods and bivalves together represent 98% of the known living molluscs. Gastropods
include the limpets, top shells, cowries, sea hares and slugs. Some marine gastropod species, like
the Small Periwinkle (*Melarhaphe neritoides*), are well adapted to a life where submersion is only
limited to the short periods of high spring tides. Cowries, on the other hand, tend to be found

When in motion cowries extend a siphon, which is used to detect prey.

in lower shore regions where they do not have to deal with long periods out of the water. Each of these gastropods benefits from its calcareous exoskeleton, which protects it from predators, supports its soft body and shelters it from waves between the tides.

Gastropod translates as 'stomach-foot', but gastropods might perhaps be better described by the term 'bottom-head'. Gastropods all undergo 'torsion', which means that during development their visceral mass, or the area in which the organs are held, twists 180° to the head and foot. This results in the organs, including the anus, becoming situated over the head or anterior end. This potentially means that the anus and kidneys excrete waste over the head end, where the sensory organs are situated. To avoid this disadvantageous calamity, waste falls to the left or right of the anterior sensory organs with the aid of currents or slits. This torsion is thought to benefit the gastropod as the sensory organs are also situated at the anterior end, so that a gastropod can detect prey ahead rather than behind itself.

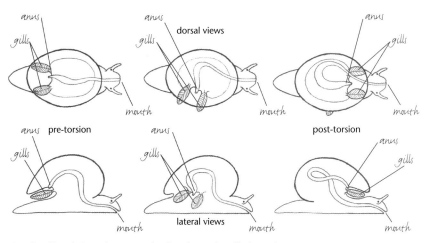

Dorsal and lateral views of a gastropod undergoing torsion of its internal organs.

A gastropod's basic anatomy is that of a foot with a well-defined head area. The head has a radula, which can consist of thousands of teeth for the rasping of algae off rocks (as in the case of limpets), a pair of jaws, eyes and sensory tentacles. The foot and head can be retracted into the shell often with the benefit of an 'operculum', which is a trapdoor-like structure that prevents predators from reaching a gastrpod's soft body and also stops it from drying out on the low tide. Gastropods have helical shells that are not always obvious or visible in the adult forms, for example in the cowries, limpets and sea hares. Some marine gastropods can breathe through a pair of ctenidia, which are gills, or use their body surface for gaseous exchange.

The eyes of gastropods are extremely varied to reflect their variety of diet and methods of predation. Some gastropods have eyes on the tips of retractable tentacles that they can withdraw into the shell for safety. There are others that have eyes at the bases of tentacles, and some which even have eyes at the head and 'tail' end. The eyes of gastropods are considerably more developed than the chitons' simple photoreceptive aesthetes, reflecting their different feeding habits and methods.

It is useful to become familiar with the shapes and names of structures of gastropods' shells as this will help with species identification. The height of a shell is measured from its base to its uppermost point, or apex. As the shell spirals to its apex it creates what are called 'whorls'. The whorls are often patterned and can have either longitudinal or spiral ridges.

The opening of a shell is called the aperture. Many gastropods withdraw their soft body structure into the aperture for safety, and some further close themselves into the shell with an operculum. In the centre of the bottom of the shell some gastropod shells have an umbilicus of varying shape and size, like the Flat Top Shell (*Gibbula umbilicalis*). The underside consists of the large locomotory foot, and tentacles and mouth at the head end that are often clearly visible.

Gastropods feed on algae and some are also carnivorous, employing aggressive forms of predation by boring holes into bivalves, crustaceans and other molluscs. The Dog Whelk (*Nucella lapillus*) secretes a calcium-dissolving enzyme to soften the shells of molluscs like limpets. Then, through the use of a boring organ, it drills a small hole in the shell, dissolves the flesh of the mollusc with an enzyme, and finally sucks up the shellfish soup through the hole it has laboriously bored.

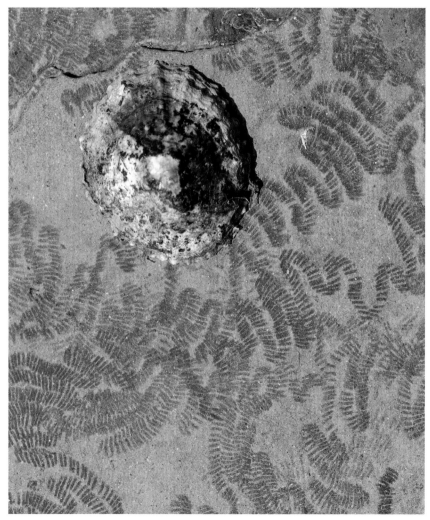

These markings are left by the grazing and rasping action of a limpet feeding on algae.

Both the rocky foreshore and the strandline are great places to find gastropods. Empty shells found on the strandline will give an indication of the species of living gastropod that might be found on neighbouring rocky shores, in the sediment between the high and low tides, and even in deeper water still. This means that the youngest of seashore explorers can find pleasure exploring the sandy shore for shells, while older, more capable rockpool visitors can explore the rocky shore for live specimens. Both will find powerful proof of the diversity and beauty of our seashore gastropods.

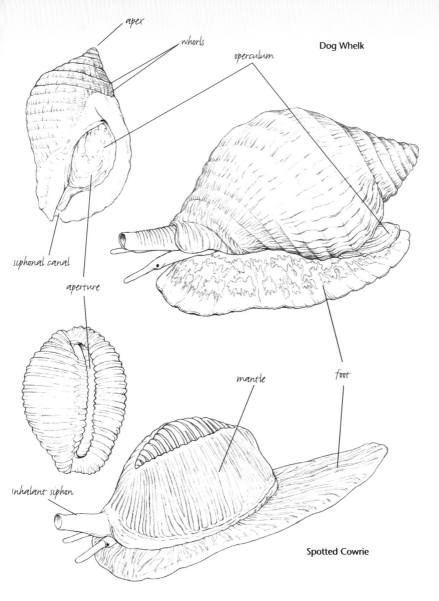

Some shared and unique features of the gastropods, illustrated in the Dog Whelk and the Spotted Cowrie (*Trivia monacha*).

Flat Top Shell   *Gibbula umbilicalis*

The Flat Top Shell is found on the seashore from the upper shore down to the subtidal of sheltered rocky shores. It occurs on the western coasts of the British Isles, including suitable rocky shores of Ireland. It has a characteristic hole close to the aperture, or opening, of the top shell. The shell is flat and round with a grey-green or cream background and purple striations that run diagonally down the shell whorls. It is often possible to see the nacreous or mother-of-pearl layer on the underside or on worn areas.

HEIGHT OF SHELL Up to 1.5cm
ZONE Upper to lower shore
DISTRIBUTION W coasts of British Isles
SIMILAR SPECIES *Gibbula cineraria, G. pennanti*

Thick Top Shell   *Osilinus lineatus*

The Thick Top Shell occurs on the south-west coasts of England and Wales. Found on the mid shore down to the subtidal, this is the largest of the top shells. It has a thick 'tooth' on the aperture, and the six whorls, of up to 3cm in height, can be grey, green or purple with purple stripes. The mother-of-pearl white is very obvious on the underside. A recent study showed how the reproductive phase of the Thick Top Shell has changed in the south-west over a nine-year period. The species used to reproduce in July, but is now found to reproduce all year round, a difference that is thought to be a consequence of climate change.

HEIGHT OF SHELL Up to 3cm
ZONE Upper to lower shore
DISTRIBUTION SW England and Wales
SIMILAR SPECIES *Gibbula cineraria, G. umbilicalis*

Grey Top Shell *Gibbula cineraria*

The Grey Top Shell is found all around the coasts of the British Isles, on lower rocky shores and in some higher shore pools. This top shell is small (1.5cm high) and has a hole on the underside as does the Flat Top Shell, but the hole is more oval in shape and less obvious and may even be absent in some Devonian specimens. It is grey to cream in colour with pale striations in brown or purple giving it an overall grey appearance. It has a blunt, conical spiral made up of five to six whorls. The species is not resilient to the pressures of the high tide, so is found grazing on the lower shore.

HEIGHT OF SHELL Up to 1.5cm
ZONE Lower shore to subtidal
DISTRIBUTION All of British Isles
SIMILAR SPECIES *Gibbula umbilicalis,*
G. pennanti, Osilinus lineatus

Painted Top Shell *Calliostoma zizyphinum*

This stunning top shell is found on coasts around the British Isles on the lower shore, as it cannot tolerate long periods of exposure. It has a conical shape with straight-sided whorls, and striations in pink, purple and red. There is also a white variety. The orange foot can be seen clinging to the rocks, while the top-heavy shell hangs down. It has an operculum but it is less robust-looking than on other top shells. The shell is wiped clean with its own mucus-covered foot, which prevents plants and animals from growing on the shell. The Painted Top Shell does not have a larval stage as do other top shells.

HEIGHT OF SHELL Up to 3cm
ZONE Lower shore
DISTRIBUTION All of British Isles
SIMILAR SPECIES *Gibbula magus*

Common Limpet   *Patella vulgata*

This common yellow-footed limpet is found all around the British Isles, on the rocky high shore down to the subtidal, and also in estuaries. Common Limpets are firmly attached to the rocks by their muscular foot. They return to the same spot or 'home scar' after grazing algae off the surrounding rocky surfaces with their tongue-like radula. They leave a slime trail which helps them find their way back to their home scar and also fertilizes new algae growth. The secure home scar helps them to avoid predation and withstand wave action, and keeps them cool on the low tides.

DIAMETER OF SHELL Up to 6cm
ZONE Upper to lower shore
DISTRIBUTION All of British Isles
SIMILAR SPECIES *Patella depressa, P. ulyssiponensis*

Black-footed Limpet   *Patella depressa*

The Black-footed Limpet is less well distributed than the Common Limpet, being found mostly on the south-west coasts of England and Wales. As the name suggests, the foot of the limpet is black, and the species is found on relatively exposed shores from the mid shore down to the subtidal. This limpet is smaller than the Common Limpet, reaching about 3cm across, and has a flatter shell with a squarer rear end. On the underside, tentacles can be found around the edge of the mantle. The Black-footed Limpet has not reached Ireland, but it is thought that it will spread northwards with climate change.

DIAMETER OF SHELL Up to 3cm
ZONE Mid shore to subtidal
DISTRIBUTION All of British Isles
SIMILAR SPECIES *Patella vulgata, P. ulyssiponensis*

Keyhole Limpet *Diodora graeca*

The Keyhole Limpet is found on the western shores of England and Ireland. It occurs on the lower shore, and is often associated with the Breadcrumb Sponge, on which it feeds. It has a characteristic hole at the top of the shell towards one end, from which extends a siphon that inhales water for respiration. The shell is up to 4cm across, grey with brown bands across it and ridges that run from the hole at the top of the shell down to the outer edge. This limpet does not have a larval stage; instead the juveniles hatch from egg capsules.

DIAMETER OF SHELL Up to 4cm
ZONE Lower shore
DISTRIBUTION W England, Ireland and Wales
SIMILAR SPECIES *Emarginula crassa*

Common Tortoiseshell Limpet *Tectura testudinalis*

The Common Tortoiseshell Limpet is a boreal (cooler water) species and it is found most commonly in the northern reaches of the British Isles, as far south as Liverpool and the Humber. As the sea temperatures increase this species appears to be slowly retreating northwards, and it is declining in its most southerly limits. It can be found on the mid shore and has an attractive smooth conical shell with very fine ridges. The shell is small, reaching up to 2.5cm across, with a cream and brown tortoiseshell pattern.

DIAMETER OF SHELL Up to 2.5cm
ZONE Mid shore
DISTRIBUTION Northern British Isles
SIMILAR SPECIES None

Blue-rayed Limpet *Patella pellucidum*

The Blue-rayed Limpet is found on algae-dominated seashores around the British Isles. This mollusc occurs commonly on the lower shore, attached to the kelps, False Irish Moss and the Toothed Wracks on which it feeds. Check for them on the blades of kelps on the low tide or amongst holdfasts on the strandline. Blue-rayed Limpet has a clear, pale brown shell, with iridescent blue lines running along its length, and is a small limpet, growing only to around 1.5cm. Small juvenile limpets are usually found on Irish Moss, and larger specimens on kelps.

DIAMETER OF SHELL Up to 1.5cm
ZONE Lower shore
DISTRIBUTION All of British Isles
SIMILAR SPECIES None

Green Ormer *Haliotis tuberculata*

Green Ormers are currently only found on the Channel Islands, on lower rocky shores where they can be found grazing on algae. They are also known as abalones, and have an ear-shaped shell about 9cm long with a flattened whorl at one end. There are five to seven holes on the upper surface of the shell. Green Ormers are edible and are collected in the Channel Islands, although in order to preserve stocks ormering is strictly controlled and permitted on only a few selected days. There is a minimum catch size of 9cm, and when harvesting Green Ormers, fishermen must be above the water and no wetsuits must be worn.

LENGTH OF SHELL Up to 12cm
ZONE Lower shore
DISTRIBUTION Channel Islands
SIMILAR SPECIES None

Pheasant Shell   *Tricolia pullus*

The Pheasant Shell is a southern species found along the west coasts of England and Wales, and on some Irish coasts. It can be seen grazing on red seaweeds on the lower shore. It can also be found empty and washed up on the shore by those with a keen eye. The spiral shell has five or six whorls, but is small, reaching only 9mm long. Pheasant Shells have a striking deep red, at times zigzag pattern on the shell that is well worth a look under a magnifying glass.

HEIGHT OF SHELL Up to 0.9cm
ZONE Lower shore
DISTRIBUTION W England, Wales and Ireland
SIMILAR SPECIES None

Spotted Cowrie   *Trivia monacha*

The Spotted Cowrie is commonly found around the British Isles, but mainly in western Britain and Ireland. It occurs on the low tide, when it may often be seen hanging from rocky walls, overhangs and rocky crevices close to ascidians like the Star Ascidian, on which it feeds. The shell is oval and up to 1.2cm long, with ridges running across it and three characteristic dark spots on the top. The aperture of the shell is a slit from which the foot emerges, and part of the mantle covers the shell, which can be red, yellow, orange or brown.

LENGTH OF SHELL Up to 1.2cm
ZONE Lower shore
DISTRIBUTION All of British Isles
SIMILAR SPECIES *Trivia arctica*

Arctic Cowrie   *Trivia arctica*

The Arctic Cowrie is a cold-water species, being more commonly found in the north of the British Isles, on the lower shore close to the ascidians on which it feeds. The Arctic Cowrie has no spots on its shell, but is a more uniform cream or pale brown in colour. It grows up to 1cm long, and the opening of the shell is a narrow slit from which the foot emerges. The underside of the shell is pale, as is the foot and mantle. As in the Spotted Cowrie, the siphon is visibly extended when in motion.

LENGTH OF SHELL Up to 1cm
ZONE Lower shore
DISTRIBUTION Northern British Isles
SIMILAR SPECIES *Trivia monacha*

Small Periwinkle   *Melarhaphe neritoides*

The Small Periwinkle is the first periwinkle you are likely to find on the shore. It can be found on most shores except in the east and south-east of England. Although marine, it occurs several metres above the high tide on exposed shores, where waves hit and create the salty splash zone. The small (up to 0.9cm in height), spiral, black shell is found in crevices in boulders. The periwinkles feed on detritus and the lichen *Verrucaria maura*. The Small Periwinkle releases egg capsules on the spring tides in late winter, which then release the larval stage.

HEIGHT OF SHELL Up to 0.9cm
ZONE Splash zone to upper shore
DISTRIBUTION All of British Isles except E and SE England
SIMILAR SPECIES None

Rough Periwinkle *Littorina saxatilis*

The Rough Periwinkle can be found on the upper shore, at times together with the Small Periwinkle. it is widely distributed around British coasts, but absent from the east and south-east of England. The shell is up to 2cm high and has striations along its three or four whorls. It can be found in crevices and also amongst the Channelled Wrack and Spiral Wrack on the upper shore, both in estuaries and saltmarsh, where it can tolerate the low salinities. Like all periwinkles it does not have a charcterisitic pearlescent layer that differentiates the periwinkles from the top shells.

HEIGHT OF SHELL Up to 2cm

ZONE Upper shore

DISTRIBUTION All of British Isles except E and SE England

SIMILAR SPECIES *Littorina littorea*

Common Periwinkle *Littorina littorea*

The Common Periwinkle is edible and can be found all around the British Isles, although it is rare in or absent from the Scilly Isles and the Channel Islands. As the largest periwinkle, it can reach a height of 5cm. The opening of the aperture is white, with no mother-of-pearl, and runs vertically in line with the apex of the spirals. The species is dark brown-black in colour and often congregates in great piles. This periwinkle reproduces all year round in the south of England, and in spring in Scotland, releasing egg capsules directly into the water.

HEIGHT OF SHELL Up to 5cm

ZONE Upper shore

DISTRIBUTION All of British Isles except Scilly Isles and Channel Islands

SIMILAR SPECIES *Littorina saxatilis, Osilinus lineatus*

Flat Periwinkle   *Littorina obtusata*

The Flat Periwinkle is common in all coastal regions around the British Isles. It can often be found on the Egg Wrack, Toothed Wrack and Bladder Wrack, on which it feeds. The colours of the Flat Periwinkle shell vary from white, green, yellow, orange and dark brown, to red or even striped. The colour depends on the habitat, with darker shells occurring on exposed shores and lighter ones on the more sheltered shores. The species lays egg cases from which perfectly formed juvenile Flat Periwinkles hatch. The body whorl is only slightly larger than the aperture, and the whorls are flattened to form a flat, squat shell with a small spire.

HEIGHT OF SHELL Up to 1.5cm
ZONE Mid to lower shore
DISTRIBUTION All of British Isles
SIMILAR SPECIES *Littorina mariae*

Necklace Shell   *Euspira catena*

This predatory mollusc is common on all shores around the British Isles, where it can be found on sandy bottoms. It is similar in shape to the terrestrial garden snail, with a large (up to 3cm high), round shell with flattened spirals and a broad, flattened foot. The aperture is oval and large, with a small hole or umbilical beside the opening. The shell is smooth with few markings, apart from a stripe close to the aperture. This is a boring shell, drilling holes in bivalves buried in the sediment and leaving characteristic holes in the bivalves. Egg capsules are laid in a characteristic open collar-shaped mass of jelly and sand grains.

HEIGHT OF SHELL Up to 3cm
ZONE Lower shore to subtidal
DISTRIBUTION All of British Isles
SIMILAR SPECIES *Polinices polianus*

Common Wentletrap   *Epitonium clathrus*

This carnivorous high-spired shell is the most widely distributed of the wentletraps, found on the south and west coasts of England. Wentletrap is the Dutch word for spiral staircase and this species' intricate geometric shape is reflective of its name. The Common Wentletrap is about 4cm high and has prominent longitudinal midribs running up the whorls. It can be found on the lowest of spring tides, sometimes feeding on anemones. In the spring it comes inshore to lay its triangular eggs, from which larvae hatch. Interestingly individuals change sex every year.

HEIGHT OF SHELL Up to 4cm
ZONE Lower shore to subtidal
DISTRIBUTION S and W of England
SIMILAR SPECIES *Bittium reticulatum,*
Turritella communis

Needle Whelk   *Bittium reticulatum*

The elongate Needle Whelk is found most commonly on the south and west coasts of England, on sandy and muddy shores, and on rocks and stones, often amongst Eelgrass. It is pale brown in colour, has a small aperture with 10–15 whorls and grows up to 1cm tall. Its rough and bumpy surface is covered in tubercles. It feeds on sponges and the eggs are laid in long coiled ribbons.

HEIGHT OF SHELL Up to 1cm
ZONE Lower shore to subtidal
DISTRIBUTION S and W of England
SIMILAR SPECIES *Epitonium clathrus,*
Turritella communis

Violet Snail *Janthina janthina*

The Violet Snail has been found washed up on the coasts of south-west Wales, England and Ireland. It is a dark violet, delicate shell with six flattened whorls. It follows the ocean's currents aboard a raft made from the bubbly mucus that is released from the foot of the snail. The eggs of the snail are fertilised inside the female after the male has released his gametes into the water. The eggs develop attached to the bubble raft. The snail is thought to be a hermaphrodite, changing sex during its lifetime. The Violet Snail will feed on *Velella velella*, hydroids that might be travelling on the same currents.

HEIGHT OF SHELL Up to 4cm
ZONE Strandline
DISTRIBUTION SW Wales, England and Ireland
SIMILAR SPECIES None

Common Pelican's Foot *Aporrhais pespelecani*

The Common Pelican's Foot is only found at depth, burrowed into soft sediment, but can occasionally be washed up onto British shores. It is the sole British representative of the Strombacea group, which are mostly found in tropical waters. The Victorians used its shells in rows to frame marine paintings. It has, as its name suggests, a shell that resembles the webbed foot of a bird. The tall spiral shell is made up of 10 whorls and can be up to 4.5cm tall and 3cm wide. Close to the aperture, the shell fans out with five defined ribs that are 'webbed'. The shell is cream in colour with ribs and knobs with a purplish tint.

HEIGHT OF SHELL Up to 4.5cm
ZONE Subtidal
DISTRIBUTION All of British Isles
SIMILAR SPECIES None

Slipper Limpet   *Crepidula fornicata*

The Slipper Limpet is a prolific invasive species that came to our shores in the late nineteenth century. It is now spread across the south, east and west coasts of England and Wales. The species can form great reefs of individuals and outcompetes other native species. It grows in towers, with the individuals attached to the rock being female and the upper limpets being males with a long tapering penis to fertilise the lower females. The males closest to the females are progressively more female, with the closest males eventually losing their penises once the females die.

HEIGHT OF SHELL Up to 5cm
ZONE Lower shore to subtidal
DISTRIBUTION S, E and W of England and Wales
SIMILAR SPECIES None

Dog Whelk   *Nucella lapillus*

The common Dog Whelk is found in abundance on the mid shore around the rocky shores of the British Isles. Its shell can vary in colour from white or yellow to brown, and it may be striped; it even varies in shell shape and thickness. This depends on the exposure to waves and storms on the beach, and also on feeding habits. The shell is thick, with the largest whorl being close to the aperture (opening) and a shortened spiral shape. The Dog Whelk is a carnivorous predator, boring holes into molluscs and devouring barnacles. It is gregarious and common amongst the barnacles and mussels on which it feeds.

HEIGHT OF SHELL Up to 4cm
ZONE Mid shore to subtidal
DISTRIBUTION All of British Isles
SIMILAR SPECIES *Littorina littorea*

Common Whelk *Buccinum undatum*

The Common Whelk is an important commercial gastropod found on all shores of the British Isles. It has a stout spiral shell, with a strong muscular foot. The whelks lay egg masses in the winter months, appearing like a ball of bubble wrap. Within each of the many capsules there are around 1,000 eggs. Many of these do not survive, being eaten by developing embryos, and only a few whelks hatch from each capsule. The empty cases are ultimately washed up on our shores as 'wash balls'. The whelks also produce a purple dye, 'purpurin', which immobilises their prey and has also been used historically to dye clothing.

HEIGHT OF SHELL Up to 10cm
ZONE Lower shore
DISTRIBUTION All of British Isles
SIMILAR SPECIES *Neptunea antiqua*

Netted Dog Whelk *Nassarius reticulatus*

The Netted Dog Whelk is found around British rocky shores on the lower tides. It is a small but relatively fast-moving whelk with a cream-coloured shell and whorls with a netted pattern. Netted Dog Whelks feed on dead and decaying matter, using their siphons to detect new sources of food. The aperture of the whelk is oval and in fully mature individuals has teeth on the outer edge. The shell has smooth-edged whorls, rather than definitive bumps as in the Common Whelk. The egg capsules appear as clear, spade-shaped capsules that are laid on algae and Eelgrass in early spring.

HEIGHT OF SHELL Up to 3cm
ZONE Lower shore
DISTRIBUTION All of British Isles
SIMILAR SPECIES *Nassarius incrassatus, Ocenebra erinacea*

Oyster Drill   *Ocenebra erinacea*

The Oyster Drill is mostly found on the west and south-west coasts of Britain. The shell is cream or yellow. It grows to approximately 4cm in height, with 8–10 whorls and ridges and grooves that give the shell a sculpted and robust appearance. The Oyster Drill lives exclusively by drilling holes into bivalves with a mechanical and chemical action, and is commonly associated with the oyster beds that it feeds on. In spring the Oyster Drill comes into shore to lay triangular-shaped egg capsules from which the young hatch as crawling individuals, omitting any larval stage.

HEIGHT OF SHELL Up to 4cm
ZONE Lower shore
DISTRIBUTION W and SW of British Isles
SIMILAR SPECIES *Urospalinx cinerea*

Sea Hare   *Aplysia punctata*

The Sea Hare is found around the British Isles in shallow water and on low spring tides. It has two pairs of tentacles on the head, the front two rhinophores resembling a hare's ears. The body has wing-like structures, and a hidden shell lies inside the body. The Sea Hare releases a purple cloud of sulphuric acid to deter predators. These hermaphrodites mate in pairs in spring, but also in chains of up to ten individuals. The individual at the front acts as a female, the one at the rear as a male and the individuals in between as both male and female, laying tangled egg masses on Wireweed and Eelgrass.

LENGTH OF BODY Up to 20cm
ZONE Lower shore to subtidal
DISTRIBUTION All of British Isles
SIMILAR SPECIES *Aplysia fasciata, A. depilans, Elysia viridi*

Grey Sea Slug   *Aeolidia papillosa*

The Grey Sea Slug is found all around the British Isles on the mid to lower shore. This gastropod is usually grey but as in many other intertidal species, the colour can vary. The Grey Sea Slug is large, growing up to 12cm long, with both tentacles and rhinophores. The upper dorsal surface is covered, apart from the mid-dorsal section, in tentacle-like appendages called cerata that have white tips. The species feeds on anemones and can reuse the stinging capacity of an anemone's tentacles within its own cerata. Here the nematocysts are stored in the tips, for self-defence against predators.

LENGTH OF BODY Up to 12cm
ZONE Mid to lower shore
DISTRIBUTION All of British Isles
SIMILAR SPECIES *Aeolidiella alderi, Favorinus blianus*

Sea Lemon   *Archidoris pseudoargus*

This most commonly found sea slug can be found all around the British Isles under boulders on the low tide. The oval body of the Sea Lemon is mottled, bumpy and yellow, closely resembling a lemon. On the rear end is a ring of feathery gills. These naked gills are an aspect of the nudibranchs, which literally translates as 'naked gills'. The species is sometimes found on or near the Breadcrumb Sponge, on which it feeds. It has no shell but is still classed as a gastropod. The eggs of the Sea Lemon are spiralled ribbons that can be found on rocky shores.

LENGTH OF BODY Up to 12cm
ZONE Lower shore
DISTRIBUTION All of British Isles
SIMILAR SPECIES *Berthella plumula, Geitodoris planata*

Scarlet Lady   *Coryphella browni*

The Scarlet Lady is found on the west coast of the British Isles, as far north as Orkney. It is another type of nudibranch gastropod. This striking sea slug can recycle stinging nematocysts from the hydroid *Tubularia indivisa* that it feeds on, and use them in its bright red cerata, which are red or chocolate-brown due to the presence of a digestive gland. Its body is white, translucent and 5cm long. The Scarlet Lady is perhaps one of the most attractive of the nudibranchs found on British shores in shallow water in spring and summer.

LENGTH OF BODY Up to 3cm
ZONE Lower shore to subtidal
DISTRIBUTION All of British Isles except E
SIMILAR SPECIES *Coryphella gracilis*

Celtic Sea Slug   *Onchidella celtica*

The Celtic Sea Slug is most common on shores in Devon and Cornwall, with some reports of individuals in Scotland. It can be found on exposed shores amongst barnacles and in crevices. It is grey, warty, only grows to around 1.3cm long and lacks any gills, unlike the nudibranchs. Instead the mantle cavity acts as a lung, and it is most closely related to terrestrial slugs and snails that also do not have gills. The head end is often not visible under the warty, fleshy body. It is thought that this pulmonate nudibranch will extend its distribution northwards with climate change.

LENGTH OF BODY Up to 1.3cm
ZONE Upper to lower shore
DISTRIBUTION SW of British Isles
SIMILAR SPECIES None

Bivalves

To what use does our pecten apply his numerous shining eyes? Is he a sage amongst mollusks, occupied in calmly contemplating the manners of bivalves in general, in order to establish some favourite hypothesis of a shellfish philosophy?

George Montagu, *Testacea Brittannica* 1803

The bivalves have two symmetrical shells, or valves, which are joined by a ligamentous hinge. They are mare commonly found burrowed into sandy shores and soft sediment than on rocky shores, although it is not unusual to find some bivalves on exposed and sheltered rocky surfaces and structures. It is even possible to find evidence of them washed up on the beaches in the form of their shells. Interestingly, when they die and the shells separate, due to beach hydrodynamics their left- and right-handed valves wash up at either end of the shore. Shells that have had the misfortune of being drilled by whelks or necklace shells wash up somewhere in between.

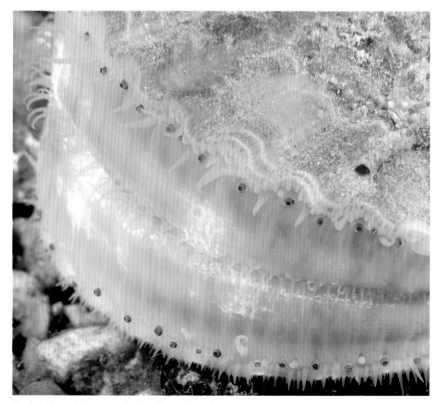

The dark blue pallial eyes are clearly visible on this scallop.

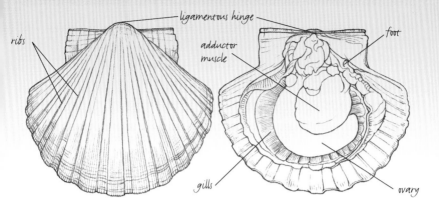

The anatomy of the Great Scallop (*Pecten maximus*).

The bivalves have lost the gastropods' radula, tentacles and other apparatus necessary for feeding and are instead filter feeders, often burrowing into soft sediment. A bivalve in the sediment, like a Gaper Clam (*Ensis ensis*), draws water into its shell with a siphon, extracts plankton and organic matter from the water, then expels it with waste materials. On the low tide this might be seen as a jet of water rising up to a metre into the air. You may also see holes in the sediment caused by the burrowing actions or the siphons of the bivalves. Not all bivalves burrow and some attach themselves to the surfaces of rock, wood and other materials. A mussel, for example, uses byssus threads to attach itself to sediment, pier legs and other individuals, forming mussel beds.

There are some bivalves, such as scallops, which even swim or propel themselves through the water. Using the powerful adductor muscle they slowly open, drawing in water, then very rapidly the valves snap shut. A jet of water is ejected at some force out of the back of the two valves, which creates a jerky swimming motion. The scallop shell has a flattened valve and also a cupped, concave valve. Inside the two valves the large white adductor muscle can be found holding the valves powerfully tight. The adductor muscle is the white scallop meat that we eat. The muscle is commonly eaten with the roe, which is the ovary of this hermaphroditic scallop. Alongside these edible parts are the gills and other internal organs. The shells show clear concentric growth rings, making it possible to age a scallop.

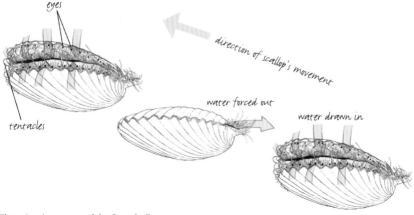

The swimming process of the Great Scallop.

Scallops have fascinating eyes. Looking at the edge of a slightly open scallop you can see blue dots along the edge of the mantle, which are relatively well-developed eyes. When eyes are situated along the mantle like this they are called pallial eyes. In a scallop the eyes along the edge of the mantle are numerous. They have a layer of mirror-like guanine crystals which line eye-reflecting images onto the scallop's eye retina. This retina has different photoreceptor cells, allowing the scallop to detect moving objects and to ascertain favourable spots in the water containing the most food. Other burrowing bivalves have little need for such numerous or well-developed eyes, as their lives are spent buried in sand. They may have eyes on just the extended peripherals of the bivalve which reach out of the sediment close to the siphons.

Some extraordinary bivalves, like the piddocks and shipworms, can burrow into stone and wood. The Common Piddock (*Pholas dactylus*) uses its foot, engorged with blood, to attach itself to a rocky surface with a sucker, then draws the valves of its shell against the rocks, mechanically scraping them. The shipworm uses a similar method that causes untold destruction to wooden structures. When these burrowing bivalves have created a safe niche they extend their siphons from the surface of the structure to filter feed.

The best-known bivalves are the commercially important ones, such as mussels, oysters, cockles and scallops. Commercial methods of extraction and aquaculture vary from growing bivalves in bags, and hand harvesting mussel and oyster beds directly from the sea bed, to the heavy mechanical trawling of sea beds for scallops that can prove destructive to important marine habitats. From a marine ecology perspective, the preferred method of harvesting bivalves is hand-diving for scallops as this has the least impact on other sedimentary species.

Though we might not often see the burrowing bivalves, we may find their empty shells on our shores. There are numerous bivalves and many can be difficult to identify. What follows is a small selection of some of the most common species that can be found in the intertidal zone and cast up on shores.

In oyster farms fingernail-sized oysters are placed in fine mesh bags in nutrient-rich water where they filter plankton and detritus. They grow to a marketable size in 2–4 years.

Common Mussel   *Mytilus edulis*

The Common Mussel can be found in great abundance in beds all around the British Isles from the mid shore in the shallow intertidal zone and below low tide. The mussel shell is oval and variable in size and thickness, depending on its situation and food availability. It has a grey to deep blue or purple colour and faint concentric growth rings. It attaches to rocks with byssus threads and even entraps potentially drilling whelks in the byssus threads to avoid predation. The mussels spawn in spring and autumn, then a larval stage develops; the larvae settle after a couple of months.

LENGTH OF SHELL Up to 10cm
ZONE Mid shore to subtidal
DISTRIBUTION All of British Isles
SIMILAR SPECIES *Mytilus galloprovincialis*

Native Oyster   *Ostrea edulis*

The Native Oyster can be found in the shallow intertidal zone around much of the British Isles, although more common in the south and west. This once abundant oyster has been historically harvested and is now depleted. Native Oysters have a rough surface and the two shells differ; the concave half, in which the meat sits, attaches to the rock or soft substrate. The shell is flatter and rounder than that of the Pacific Oyster and is smaller, growing up to 11cm long. It is grey with blue bands, but can appear grey or brown. In some areas the Native Oyster is being outcompeted by the invasive Slipper Limpet.

LENGTH OF SHELL Up to 11cm
ZONE Lower shore to subtidal
DISTRIBUTION All of British Isles
SIMILAR SPECIES *Crassotrea gigas*

Pacific Oyster   *Crassotrea gigas*

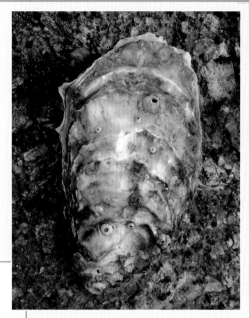

The Pacific Oyster has been found on rocky shores around the British Isles where larvae have settled, and here the oyster can be found attached to rocks and structures. The Pacific Oyster is a non-native and invasive species that was originally thought to be unable to reproduce in our cooler waters. It obviously can, and it has even formed beds in some estuaries. The left valve has a deeper cup shape, obvious radiating ribs and a more elongated shape than that of the Native Oyster, and it grows to 18cm in length. This oyster has been harvested in British waters since its introduction in the 1920s.

LENGTH OF SHELL Up to 18cm
ZONE Lower shore to subtidal
DISTRIBUTION All of British Isles
SIMILAR SPECIES *Ostrea edulis*

Saddle Oyster   *Anomia ephippium*

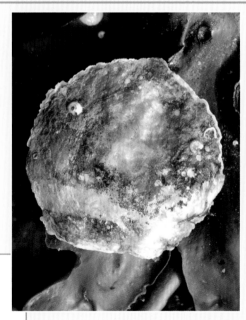

The Saddle Oyster grows up to 6cm long and can be found in the intertidal region of lower shores around the British Isles, attached to rocky surfaces. The valves are not symmetrical, with the right valve having a hole from which the byssus threads attach to the rock. The adductor mussel is much reduced and the left valve is quite flat. The shell is much thinner than that of the other true oysters, and the pale brown shells are sometimes found washed up on beaches.

LENGTH OF SHELL Up to 6cm
ZONE Lower shore to subtidal
DISTRIBUTION All of British Isles
SIMILAR SPECIES *Pododesmus striata, P. squama*

Great Scallop *Pecten maximus*

The Great Scallop is found all around the British Isles, but less commonly on the east coast of England. This shell can be found on very low spring tides in some estuarial and seashore regions. The species has blue pallial eyes surrounding the edge of the mantle. Making use of its powerful adductor muscle, it will move away from danger when necessary. It is the adductor muscle that we eat, whilst the gills, eyes and other organs are discarded. The brightly coloured, fan-shaped shell can be up to 16cm long, with distinct radiating ribs with a very flat dark brown or pink upper valve and a paler, cupped lower valve.

DIAMETER OF SHELL Up to 16cm
ZONE Lower shore to subtidal
DISTRIBUTION All of British Isles
SIMILAR SPECIES *Aequipecten opercularis, Chlamys varia*

Common Cockle *Cerastoderma edule*

The Common Cockle is found all around the British Isles in estuaries and sandy bays. It has very globular, thick shells with concentric growth rings. It uses its foot to burrow into the soft sediment to depths of up to 5cm. Common Cockles are filter feeders, extending siphons to extract sea water when burrowed. The cockles release their gametes into the water, where they fertilise. The larvae develop and a juvenile cockle metamorphoses and settles on the soft sediment. Remarkably, these cockles can leap to avoid predation by extending the foot and pushing off the sea floor.

DIAMETER OF SHELL Up to 5cm
ZONE Lower shore to subtidal
DISTRIBUTION All of British Isles
SIMILAR SPECIES *Acanthocardia aculeata*

Striped Venus Clam   *Chamelea gallina*

The Striped Venus Clam can be found all around the British Isles except for south-east England, buried in the sediment on the lower shore to depths of about 5cm. It has a triangular cream-coloured shell with concentric ridges and radiating red-brown stripes running from the hinge to the outer edge. These clams use their siphons to filter plankton from the water. The Striped Venus Clam has separate sexes and releases gametes into the water, which develop into the veliger larvae. These go through a planktonic phase before taking on the adult form.

LENGTH OF SHELL Up to 4cm
ZONE Lower shore to subtidal
DISTRIBUTION All of British Isles
SIMILAR SPECIES *Clausinella fasciata, Mercenaria mercenaria*

Thin Tellin   *Angulus tenuis*

The delicate and colourful shells of the Thin Tellin are abundant in fine sandy areas around the British Isles. The animals live just below the surface of the sand, where their siphons protrude from their burrows to feed. Flatfish nibble at the Thin Tellin's siphons, but the bivalves have evolved the useful ability to regenerate them. The shell is smooth and small, and up to 2.5cm long. It has concentric rings and occurs in delicate shades of pink, orange or white. This small bivalve can live for up to 10 years.

LENGTH OF SHELL Up to 2.5cm
ZONE Mid shore to subtidal
DISTRIBUTION All of British Isles
SIMILAR SPECIES *Arcopagia balaustina, Fabulina fabula, Macoma balthica*

Banded Wedge Shell   *Donax vittatus*

The Banded Wedge Shell is common on moderately exposed sandy shores around the British Isles. The shell has a characteristic wedge shape with an off-centre hinge. Banded Wedge Shells can be orange, yellow, purple or brown, with colour bands running across the shell. The species' powerful foot allows it to burrow under the surface of the sand. The siphon may be predated on by flatfish, but this wedge shell can survive the predation. It has separate sexes and goes through a larval stage.

LENGTH OF SHELL Up to 3.5cm
ZONE Mid to lower shore
DISTRIBUTION All of British Isles
SIMILAR SPECIES *Angulus squalidus*

Common Otter Shell   *Lutraria lutraria*

The Common Otter Shell is found from the lower shore to deeper waters, buried deep in the sediment all around the British Isles. It is a very large, smooth, pale shell of up to 12.5cm in length, with an off-centre hinge and concentric rings. The foot is small but it still manages to burrow down into the sediment to depths of up to 30cm, although this can take it some time. It has a long siphon with a tough sheath, similar to that of the gaper clams, which extends to the surface to filter nutrients from the water.

LENGTH OF SHELL Up to 12.5cm
ZONE Lower shore to subtidal
DISTRIBUTION All of British Isles
SIMILAR SPECIES *Lutraria angustior,*
L. magna, Mya arenaria

Razor Clam *Ensis ensis*

The Razor Clam or Razor Shell is widely distributed around the British Isles on the very lowest of spring tides into the shallow sublittoral. Shaped like a cut-throat razor, this is an efficient burrower that will burrow deep when disturbed, including by the vibration of feet. As it burrows a spout of water is ejected, and it leaves a recognisable keyhole shape on the surface of the sediment from the fused siphons that filter feed from the water. The shell is pale cream in colour, growing up to 12.5cm long. The ends of the two valves gape rather than meet.

LENGTH OF SHELL Up to 12.5cm
ZONE Lower shore to subtidal
DISTRIBUTION All of British Isles
SIMILAR SPECIES *Ensis arcuatus, E. siliqua, Pharus legumen*

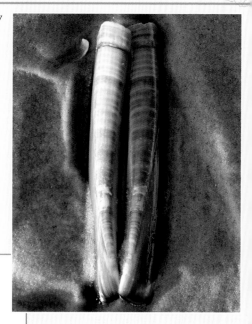

Common Piddock *Pholas dactylus*

The Common Piddock is a lusitanian (warmer water) species found in the south and west of Britain. It can occasionally be located on the lower shore, boring into soft rock. It has a rectangular shell with ridges and spines that help to grind rock away. The shell gapes at both ends, with the foot and its sucker-like apparatus coming from the anterior end to aid boring. This boring piddock is also bioluminescent, emitting a green light. Pliny once stated of this edible Roman delicacy that they 'glitter both in the mouths of those masticating them and in their hands'.

LENGTH OF SHELL Up to 12cm
ZONE Lower shore to subtidal
DISTRIBUTION S and W of British Isles
SIMILAR SPECIES None

Blunt Gaper Clam   *Mya truncata*

The burrowing Blunt Gaper Clam is found all around the British Isles in muddy sand. It occurs at some depth, from the mid shore down to the lower shore. As its name suggests, the Blunt Gaper Clam has a large open gape at the posterior end. The valves are quite large (up to 7.5cm) and have concentric shells with blunt, squared ends. The siphons of the Blunt Gaper Clam are enclosed within a tough, leathery sheath that extends out of the burrow to feed.

LENGTH OF SHELL Up to 7.5cm
ZONE Mid to lower shore
DISTRIBUTION All of British Isles
SIMILAR SPECIES *Lutraria lutraria, Mya arenaria*

Fan Mussel   *Atrina fragilis*

The largest bivalve species found on British shores, though only a few Fan Mussels live within the intertidal region in the south-west of England. They are more commonly found in deeper waters, although their numbers have been depleted by scallop dredging. The lower, pointed part of the shell is buried in the sediment, whilst the upper, exposed, broader part is agape so that it can filter feed nutrients from the water. Other species grow on the exposed end of the fan-shaped shell. These mussels produce golden byssus threads that keep them attached to the sediment. The threads were once used to make expensive gloves and stockings.

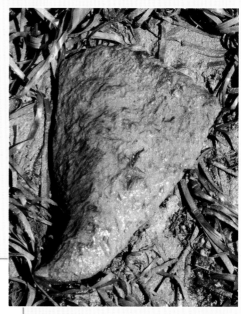

LENGTH OF SHELL Up to 48cm
ZONE Lower shore to subtidal
DISTRIBUTION SW England
SIMILAR SPECIES None

CRUSTACEANS

...when I took my pocket-handkerchief to wipe my nose, I found it smelt exactly as if it had wrapped up a lobster. On my imparting this discovery in confidence to Peggotty, she informed me that her brother dealt in lobsters, crabs, and crawfish; and I afterwards found that a heap of these creatures, in a state of wonderful conglomeration with one another... were usually to be found in a little wooden outhouse where the pots and kettles were kept.

Charles Dickens, *David Copperfield* 1850

Crustaceans are the subphylum of the arthropods, to which belong the commercially valuable crabs and lobsters that many a young (and more mature) seashore visitor has been delighted to discover. However, many other fascinating and perhaps surprising species are also classed as crustaceans. They vary from the smallest pelagic plankton and encrusting barnacles, and sandhoppers that fizz on the surface of the sand on retreating tides as they hop from their sandy burrows, to the larger Edible Crabs (*Cancer pagurus*) and Common Lobsters (*Homarus gammarus*). Crustaceans are found in the deepest parts of the seas and oceans, free-floating during their larval stages, and concealed within the crevices of rocks on coasts in vast varieties of form and appearance as adults.

This Spider Crab and the barnacles encrusted on its shell are both crustaceans.

Like the bodies of all crustaceans, the body of a lobster has three defined regions – a head, thorax and abdomen – and clearly jointed legs. This key common feature of jointed appendages, or athropoda, is what leads crustaceans to being part of the arthropod phylum. As anyone who has eaten a lobster can testify, it has a tough semi-rigid exoskeleton that protects it from predators. Lobsters also have an area of toughened exoskeleton surrounding the main thoracic region. This is what is called the carapace, and it serves to protect crustaceans from coming to harm from predators.

A toughened exoskeleton could prove to prevent growth, so a lobster undergoes ecdysis, or moult, in order to grow. Similar to how a snake sheds its skin, crabs, shrimps and lobsters moult their shells, including even the most detailed parts of their heads. A crustacean's head has many appendages, including two characteristic pairs of antennae, a pair of mandibles and two 'maxillae'. By using these appendages in different ways, crustaceans have the ability to feed in a variety of ways.

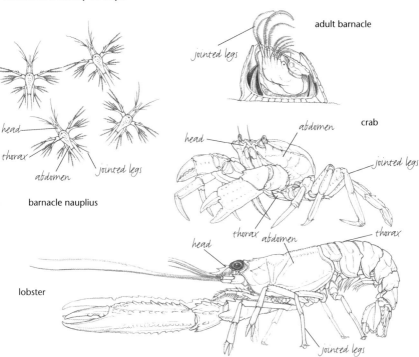

Despite looking quite different from each other, barnacles, crabs and lobsters are all crustaceans. They all share (at some stage in their life cycle) the common features of a head, thorax, abdomen and jointed legs.

These appendages are not always obvious in the vastly different crustacean forms. A barnacle's paired legs and divided body parts are well concealed within its adult form. Indeed, barnacles were only relatively recently recognised to be crustaceans and are not, as was previously thought, molluscs.

Crustaceans mostly have separate sexes, with males and females of individual species being readily identifiable, in the crabs for example, and crustaceans commonly undergo a larval stage before taking on adult form. They also demonstrate a nauplius larval stage. The soup of plankton found in our coastal waters is not restricted to marine algae or species that remain plankton their whole lives, but also contains the larval stages of many of the species found in the intertidal zones. The nauplius stage of crustaceans is characterised by the use of antennae on the head for swimming and the presence of a single naupliar eye. The nauplius develops into the adult crustacean form through successive moults. The stages may include a zoea stage, where the appendages on the thoracic region are used to swim. This develops into the nauplius, which uses the appendages on the tail section for swimming, as is more familiarly seen in the adult forms of lobsters and prawns.

Crustaceans such as prawns, shrimps, crabs and lobsters have been and continue to be an important source of protein for humans, and the ways in which we catch or cultivate crustaceans have altered dramatically over the years. Fishing for crabs and lobsters has changed from a time when small fishing boats would lay willow pots, to an era when an abundance of more robust lobster pots made from metal and rubber is laid from much bigger fishing vessels. The pressure of these plentiful, larger and more efficient fishing vessels on the crab and lobster fishing industry has resulted in the development of new guidelines designed to help maintain stocks. These include not catching berried (laden with eggs) female crabs and lobsters, and setting minimum catch sizes. Such bylaws have been created to help ensure that crabs and lobsters can reach maturity and reproduce successfully.

Fishermen work closely with fisheries managers to protect egg-bearing female and undersized crabs to help safeguard crab stocks.

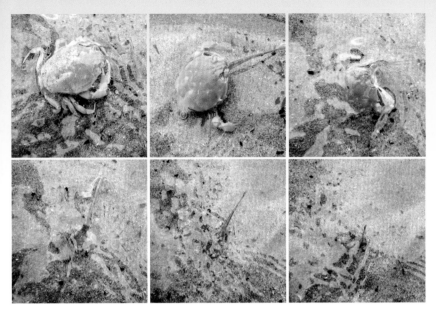

This sequence of photos shows a Masked Crab (*Corystes cassivelaunus*) burrowing into sand.

The first crustaceans you are likely to find on the seashore are barnacles encrusted on the rocks. You may also notice signs of a Masked Crab burrowed beneath the surface of the sand, or spot juvenile crabs on the upper shore. Larger Edible Crabs conceal and confine themselves in crevices in the rocks on the low tide, and while it is tempting to try to remove an Edible Crab from its protective nook, its claws are powerful and its grip is strong. If you want a close look at some crabs it is sensible to start your search by looking for smaller individuals under rocks and boulders.

You may find a complete and lifeless-looking moult of a crab washed up on the seashore. If you do, with a bit of careful and gentle exploration nearby, there is a chance that you could find the soft-shelled, freshly moulted crab itself concealed in relative safety under a rock or in a crevice. Indeed, an entire tidal cycle can be spent looking solely for our various crustacean coastal inhabitants.

A berried lobster returned to the sea helps to secure the next generation of lobsters.

Barnacles

The prosbosciformed penis is wonderfully developed... when fully extended it must equal between eight and nine times the entire length of the animal!

Charles Darwin, *Living Cirripedia* 1852

The barnacles belong to the infraclass **Cirripedia** and are, rather surprisingly, relatives of crabs and lobsters, though often they are mistaken for relatives of limpets or as a form of mollusc. It was not until the nineteenth century that these small, encrusting species were confirmed as crustaceans, when planktonic crustacean larvae were witnessed to settle and develop into barnacles. On close examination of the life cycles of barnacles it became clear that they share characteristics with the crustaceans.

As the majority of barnacles are stuck on rocks in one place (sessile), they have to face the challenge of how to fertilise their neighbours. One individual may possess both male and female gonads, but will still cross-fertilise with other individuals to ensure genetic variety. In order to reach neighbouring barnacles, the animals have developed an incredibly useful, extendible penis. Relative to body size, it is thought to be the largest penis in the Animal Kingdom. Using hydrostatic pressure the penis can reach towards an individual and fertilize the female eggs within. A fertilised gamete then develops into the nauplius stage. This is released to swim as a free-floating planktonic phase.

The nauplius then develops into a cyprid. At this stage the cyprid does not feed, but looks for a suitable place to settle for its adult life stage. Using its antennules, it senses for a suitable location. Then, using a cement-like substance, it attaches the antennules to the surface of choice and rotates so that its appendages are now facing upwards. The barnacle then moults into the final adult stage, secreting defensive plates that create a protective 'home' for it. Once the barnacle is in place it uses its cirri, or curled feet, to project from its stony, volcano-like structure, and fan out and catch food. When the tide is low and the chances of drying out or being eaten increase, to assist in their survival barnacles use a trapdoor-like structure – they withdraw their feeding appendages, then close the 'door'.

The 'prosbosciformed penis' of a barnacle is thought to be the largest relative to body size in the Animal Kingdom.

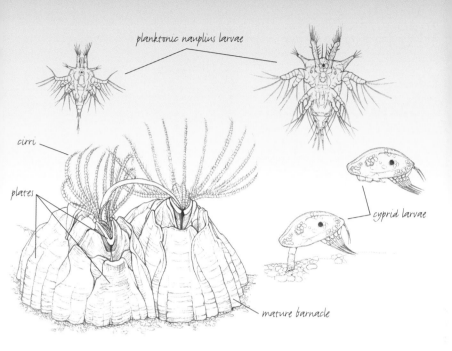

planktonic nauplius larvae

cirri

plates

cyprid larvae

mature barnacle

Hermaphroditic mature barnacles cross-fertilise, producing nauplius larvae that metamorphose into cyprid larvae and settle on rocks, ultimately developing into mature barnacles.

Barnacles are not restricted to natural surfaces. They often 'foul' the surfaces of boat keels, oil rigs and other structures, thereby offering surfaces on which other marine invertebrates may grow. The fouling slows the speed of boats, alters the integrity of structures and encourages further fouling by other organisms. A lot of research is being carried out into ways of preventing the fouling, and into developing anti-fouling methods designed to avoid the encrusting of organisms where it is not wanted. Historically, preventing fouling has included using paint with tributyltin as the active agent. This was found to cause imposex in dog whelks as, ultimately, female whelks grew penises and lost their reproductive abilities. Methods of anti-fouling have improved since and should no longer have such adverse reactions on wildlife. There is even now research into using many marine organisms, including sea sponges, to source a critical compound that may help prevent fouling.

Charles Darwin was an expert in the field of barnacles and was a source of much of our understanding of the cirripedes. He concentrated many years of research on the barnacles, which had only relatively recently in his lifetime been recognised as crustaceans rather than molluscs. Darwin set himself the challenge of identifying and organising the barnacles into some order, with the aim of further clarifying scientific understanding of both their evolution and their zoology. What he imagined might take a year in fact took him eight years. While he dealt with his own personal health problems (of palpitations and probable gout-related flatulence), he closely examined hundreds of specimens of barnacle sent to him by other naturalists. He categorically proved that they were crustaceans, that not all barnacles were hermaphrodites and that barnacles did indeed support his theory of evolution and show vast variability. Ultimately, Darwin proved that he was a naturalist of great talent and ability. If you try to identify just the few species listed in the following pages, you will see what an incredibly difficult task he set himself.

Acorn Barnacle   *Semibalanus balanoides*

The Acorn Barnacle is common on all
shores around the British Isles and is
the most abundant of the barnacles.
It is found in the mid to low shore
region, usually below or overlapping
the range of Montagu's Barnacle. The
opening region of the barnacle is
roughly kite shaped, with the wall of
the barnacle consisting of six plates.
The barnacle can grow to 1.5cm across,
and below the aperture the tissue is
cream/pink in colour. The barnacles
use their extended cirri, or fan-like
projections, to feed on zooplankton.

DIAMETER Up to 1.5cm
ZONE Mid to lower shore
DISTRIBUTION All of British Isles
SIMILAR SPECIES *Balanus crenatus,
Chthalamus montagui, Elimnius modestus*

Montagu's Barnacle   *Chthamalus montagui*

The Montagu's Barnacle is found on
the upper to mid shore, overlapping
or above the Acorn Barnacle. This is a
warm-water species that occurs around
the west coasts of the British Isles,
but it is absent from the Isle of Wight
around to the east coasts of England
and Scotland. It has a kite-shaped
opening with six plates. The plates are
concave and cross over, so that the
cross is approximately a third of the
way down the plates. The barnacle
grows to a maximum diameter of
1.4cm. The tissue below the aperture
is usually blue.

DIAMETER Up to 1.4cm
ZONE Upper to mid shore
DISTRIBUTION W coasts of British Isles
SIMILAR SPECIES *Balanus crenatus,
Elimnius modestus, Semibalanus balanoides*

Volcano Barnacle   *Balanus perforatus*

This large barnacle, of up to 5cm in diameter and 3cm in height, can be found on the south-west English and Welsh coasts. It has a distinctly volcano-shaped appearance, with striations towards the aperture. The aperture is oval and the tissue inside is bright pink, blue and purple. The tergum and scutum of the operculum are noticeably beak shaped and sunken within the aperture. The Volcano Barnacle can be found from the mid shore to the sublittoral region, on the hulls of ships and on other structures.

DIAMETER Up to 5cm
ZONE Mid shore to subtidal
DISTRIBUTION SW England and Wales
SIMILAR SPECIES *Balanus crenatus*

Goose-necked Barnacle   *Pollicipes pollicipes*

This is a stalked barnacle that has a goose-like 'neck' which attaches to rocks or floating objects. The species is also commonly known as 'percerbes' in Portugal, where it is harvested for food. The Goose-necked Barnacle is uncommon on British shores but has been found attached to objects that have washed up in the south-west of England. The stalk, or peduncle, is brown, and at the end of it a capitulum holds the feeding tentacles safely. The capitulum has many white triangular plates,= and is short and broad.

LENGTH Up to 10cm
ZONE Upper to lower shore
DISTRIBUTION SW England
SIMILAR SPECIES *Lepas anatifera, Scalpellum scalpellum*

Isopods and amphipods

It seems to revel in those malodorous conditions that would be fatal to any other of the denizens of the deep.

Joseph Sinel, *An Outline of the Natural History of Our Shores* 1906

The isopods that we find on the seashore are related to the terrestrial woodlice seen under rocks and boulders on land. They can be found on the highest mark of the tide, including in coastal defence structures and harbour walls, to the deepest marine trenches. The largest, found in the trenches, is the Giant Isopod (*Bathynomus giganteus*) which can be as much as 30cm in length.

An isopods has three sections, typical of crustaceans, which are technically called the head, pereon (thorax) and pleon (abdomen), and which are dorso-ventrally flattened. The head has two pairs of antennae with prominent eyes, and the seven pairs of appendages on the seven sections of the thorax are generally equally sized. The abdomen is different in each species, but in the case of the Sea Slater (*Ligia oceanica*) the telson has very long, paired uropods, which in a lobster develop into a fan-shaped tail. An isopods has no carapace but has a cephalothorax that fuses the head to the first of the eight thoracic segments.

This Giant Isopod from the deep sea clearly shows the common feature of isopods – its dorso-lateral flattening.

Amphipods can often be seen on the seashore. In the evenings, as the tide drops, Sand Hoppers (*Talitrus saltator*) emerge from their burrows (which can be as deep as 30cm) and the surface of the sand becomes alive with them erratically hopping around. The strandline is also an excellent place to find an abundance of fly larvae and insects feeding on the rotting algae. To navigate around the beach the Sand Hopper curls its tail underneath itself, then rapidly unfurls it, a technique that enables it to jump to considerable heights.

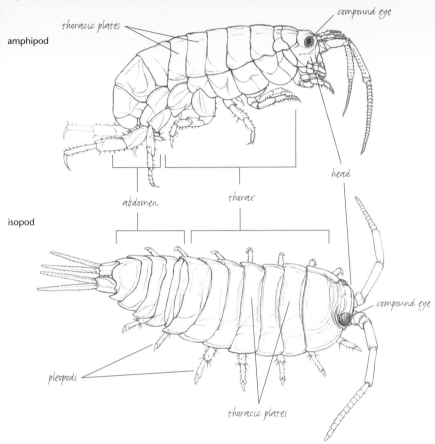

The anatomies of an amphipod Sand Hopper showing its extended thoracic plates and of a laterally flattened isopod Sea Slater.

Like isopods, amphipods do not have carapaces, but unlike isopods they are laterally flattened so appear to be lying on their side. Their thoracic plates extend down the side of the body, and this is another feature that separates them from the isopods. As in the case of the amphipods, there are also Giant Isopods (*Alicella gigantea*), which can be found in the deep sea and can be over 30cm long.

An amphipods also has three typically crustacean sections, of a head, thorax and abdomen. The head has two pairs of antennae, while the thorax has seven pairs of pereopods, or jointed appendages, which are of different sizes; the first two pairs are pincer-like and used for feeding. The first four pairs of appendages face forwards, while the last three of the pereopods of the thorax face backwards. The first section of the abdomen has swimming legs, or pleopods, and the second section has uropods and also a telson, or tail-like structure.

The humble Sand Hopper amphipod has the ability to navigate using the position of the sun and moon and also by beach morphology. Incredibly, it uses both a circadian clock, which follows a 24-hour cycle, and a circatidal clock, which follows a 12.4-hour tidal cycle. This abillity has obvious benefits in a tidal environment where the high and low tides present such contrasting conditions, each providing different pressures and opportunities.

Circatidal rhythms in marine organisms are rarely mentioned, but are a fascinating aspect of coastal ecology. Amphipods and isopods both benefit from a circatidal clock, as do other marine species like the Shore Crab (*Carcinus maenas*). Just as our rockpooling trip might be controlled by the tides and the rhythms of the lunar cycles, so too are many biological functions of marine and coastal organisms on a tidal rhythm. For species that live on the coast and in our estuaries, tidal rhythms will reflect food availability and also the best times to release planktonic larvae.

Amphipods even continue to follow the tidal rhythms when removed from their natural environments. In a laboratory the speckled Speckled Sea Louse (*Eurydice pulchra*) in effect remembers the tidal cycle. Despite constant conditions, it will actively swim around at the time of the high tide on the beach from which they came. As if in a celebration of the new and full moons, even in a laboratory it swims the most on a night-time spring high tide. Quite how it does this is still being clarified and it is a fascinating area of research. It is always interesting, therefore, to explore the seashore at different phases of the lunar tidal cycle to see what might be more or less active during different periods of the tide and the changing phases of the moon.

While the chances of ever finding Giant Isopods or Giant Amphipods on the seashore are minute, opportunities to locate their considerably smaller relatives are much higher. In fact, you would be hard pushed to walk onto a beach and not unwittingly be standing very close to an amphipod or isopod. They might even be worthy of your own experimentation. Why not take your notebook and record how active Sand Hoppers and Sea Slaters are? If you note the tidal and weather conditions, and time of day and lunar cycle, it is very possible that you will also find evidence of these remarkable rhythms of nature.

Some of the features of amphipods, such as lateral flattening and extended thoracic plates, can be seen on this Giant Amphipod.

Sea Slater *Ligia oceanica*

The Sea Slater can be found on all
rocky coastlines around the British
Isles. This grey isopod has the
characteristic seven paired legs and
an oval, flattened body like that of a
wood louse, with equally paired legs
on its thorax. It can be found under
rocks and in crevices during the day. At
night it comes out to feed on seaweed
and detritus. It has two appendages on
its rear end, called uropods, which are
used for defence and sensory purposes.
It also has large, compound eyes.

LENGTH Up to 3cm
ZONE Upper to lower shore
DISTRIBUTION All of British Isles
SIMILAR SPECIES *Idotea* species

Sand Hopper *Talitrus saltator*

The Sand Hopper is an amphipod
that occurs all around the coasts of
the British Isles. It is often found
under rotting piles of seaweed on the
strandline, or hiding in burrows in the
sand, feeding on detritus. It is about
2cm long, pale cream in colour and
has a laterally flattened body. The
antennae are obvious and one is longer
than the other. Sand Hoppers are an
important source of food for animals
that feed off the strandline, including
bats, hedgehogs and other small
mammals. In male Sand Hoppers, the
second feeding limb of the thorax is
often large and claw-like.

LENGTH Up to 2cm
ZONE Strandline
DISTRIBUTION All of British Isles
SIMILAR SPECIES *Bathyporeia elegans,*
Gammarus locusta

Shrimps and prawns

It is amusing to see how rapidly and cleverly the shrimp takes its place in the sand.

Philip H. Gosse, *A Year at the Shore* 1865

Defining shrimps and prawns can be very confusing. Many people use the term shrimp to describe the smaller edible species and call the larger variety prawns, although this usage is reversed in some English-speaking countries. There is also some debate over the scientific differences between the terms shrimp and prawn. The illustration opposite aims to clarify some of the anatomical differences between the Common Prawn (*Palaemon serratus*) and Brown Shrimp (*Crangon crangon*).

Prawns typically have three pairs of claws on the first three walking legs or pereopods. However the Common Prawn has two pairs of clawed pereopods, with the second pereopods being larger than the first. The Common Prawn also has equally sized segments on the abdomen and a curved overall shape from head to tail. The Brown Shrimp has an angular body with two pairs of clawed pereopods. Prawns and shrimps are also thought to differ on the second abdominal segment. In prawns it overlaps both the first and third segments, whereas in shrimps it overlaps only the third segment. Both prawns and shrimps use the pincers on their front legs to scavenge and collect food, and their appendages and tail make them both great swimmers, allowing them to dart rapidly backwards into a safe spot away from predators.

The Common Prawn showing its serrated rostrum.

The life cycles of shrimps and prawns have various stages of metamorphosis, like those of other crustaceans. It is often possible to find a female shrimp which has eggs held between the legs of the abdominal section. Prior to the eggs being laid, a male shrimp or prawn lays his spermatophores between the female's legs, which then fertilise the eggs as she releases them. A shrimp or prawn will lay up to one million eggs, which hatch into planktonic nauplii. Inside the body of a nauplius is a yolk on which the nauplius feeds. After moulting, the nauplius develops into the zoea stage, at which point it can feed on algae, and then it develops into a mysis, which looks like a small shrimp. After successive moults from the nauplius stage, the animals take the form of their final post-larvae phase.

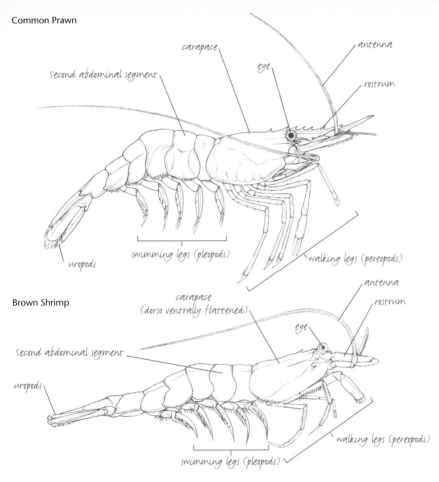

The anatomies of the Common Prawn (top) and Brown Shrimp (bottom).

As far back as the fifteenth century we had developed means of farming shrimps and prawns. However, as the demands of our population have grown, so too have the scale and impact of shrimp and prawn farms. Coastal habitats can be lost due to farms being constructed in areas where, for example, mangroves were previously grown. The farms also have problems associated with the feed, which contains fertilisers that can result in the eutrophication of ponds and neighbouring waters due to the diffusion of excess nutrients. The high stocking

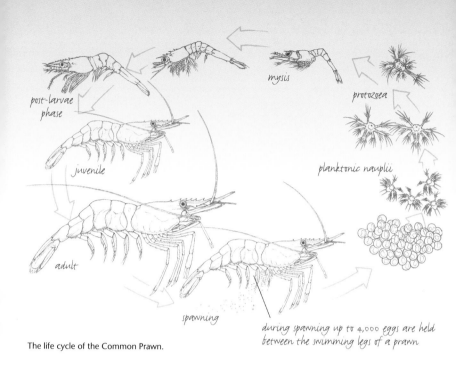

mysis

protozoea

post-larvae
phase

planktonic nauplii

juvenile

adult

spawning

during spawning up to 4,000 eggs are held
between the swimming legs of a prawn

The life cycle of the Common Prawn.

density of one species can also lead to disease. Better practise and guidelines have improved farming techniques in recent years on some farms. However, fished prawns and shrimps can also damage natural marine ecosystems when they have been caught by trawling nets. Sadly, these nets also catch many other species that are then discarded and discarded stocks can constitute a vast proportion of the haul.

Prawns and shrimps are great scavengers and if you stand still with your bare feet in a rockpool they will dutifully perform a 'prawn pedicure' and remove unwanted dead skin from your feet.

An egg-laden Pistol Shrimp (*Alpheus macrocheles*).

Common Prawn   *Palaemon serratus*

The Common Prawn can be found on all coasts around the British Isles, although less frequently on the east coasts. It may be spotted by the keen-eyed rockpooler darting into rocky crevices and seaweeds in rockpools on the low tide and also in subtidal areas. It can grow to a sizeable 11cm in length, and has a transparent body with brown lines marking the body and legs. The front two legs have claws and the rostrum above the eyes is characteristically curved upwards. Common Prawns breed from November, when the female carries up to 4,000 eggs for up to four months.

LENGTH Up to 11cm
ZONE Lower shore to subtidal
DISTRIBUTION All of British Isles
SIMILAR SPECIES *Palaemon elegans*

Chameleon Prawn   *Hippolyte varians*

The Chameleon Prawn, as you might expect, changes its colour from green to red to brown, sometimes with a mottled appearance, depending on the habitat in which it lives. It can be found all around the British Isles on the shore, and down to considerable depths. At night it changes colour to avoid predation, becoming a well-camouflaged transparent blue. This is a relatively small prawn, growing to around 3cm, with a spine above each eye. The rostrum and carapace are very straight.

LENGTH Up to 3cm
ZONE Mid shore to subtidal
DISTRIBUTION All of British Isles
SIMILAR SPECIES None

Brown Shrimp   *Crangon crangon*

The Brown Shrimp can be found all around the British Isles. This crustacean commonly burrows into muddy and sandy bottoms. It has a flattened rostrum and grows up to 8cm long. The tail is fan shaped and the antennae are as long as the body. It is often hard to see this species because of its ability to camouflage itself against its habitat, but it may be spotted darting rapidly in the water. At night time beside an estuary it is often possible to see the reflective eyes of the Brown Shrimp in torchlight.

LENGTH Up to 8cm
ZONE Mid shore to subtidal
DISTRIBUTION All of British Isles
SIMILAR SPECIES *Crangon almanii*

Snakelocks Shrimp   *Periclimenes sagittifer*

The Snakelocks Shrimp is most commonly found living within the tentacles of the Snakelocks Anemone, with which it has a symbiotic relationship. It also lives with other anemones on the mid to lower shore. It has been found in only a limited number of locations on the Channel Islands, and specifically below Swanage Pier in Dorset. This small shrimp, just 3cm long, is transparent with attractive blue and red markings on the body, and blue stripy legs and pincers. The distribution of the Snakelocks Shrimp may change as sea temperatures increase.

LENGTH Up to 3cm
ZONE Mid shore to subtidal
DISTRIBUTION Channel Islands and Dorset
SIMILAR SPECIES *Periclimenes aegylios*

Mantis Shrimp   *Rissoides desmaresti*

The Mantis Shrimp is not in the same order as prawns and shrimps. It is in a separate order called Stomatopoda. Confusingly, in spite of their common name Mantis Shrimps are also not mantids. They are, however, attractive but rare crustaceans. They can be found in burrows in gravelly bottoms in a few isolated spots on the south of England and also in North Wales. The claws are large, like that of a mantis, and they use them to stun their prey with considerable force. They have been nicknamed 'thumb splitters', which gives some indication of the ferocity of their blow.

LENGTH Up to 10cm
ZONE Lower shore to subtidal
DISTRIBUTION S England and N Wales
SIMILAR SPECIES *Platysquilla eusebia*

Pistol Shrimp   *Alpheus macrocheles*

This Pistol Shrimp can occasionally be found around the south and west of England. It is a stunning small shrimp of 3.5cm length. Despite its small size it has an incredible weapon which it uses to capture prey. Through the rapid snapping of its largest claw it creates an implosion of a bubble of such force that it can stun or even kill its prey. The Pistol Shrimp is orange-red and has relatively large claws of uneven size, with a short rostrum.

LENGTH Up to 3.5cm
ZONE Lower shore
DISTRIBUTION S and W England and Ireland
SIMILAR SPECIES *Alpheus glaber*

Crabs

And now his wandering feet can reach
The rugged tracks of the desolate beach;
Creeping about like a Triton imp,
To find the haunts of the crab and shrimp.

Eliza Cook, *The Sea Child* 1838

The growth process for humans is relatively painless and gradual; as we grow our skin grows with us to accommodate our expanding frame. But for a crab, with its hard exoskeleton, if its shell expanded as the crab grew the shell would simply break. So how do crabs grow? It is possible that you may have inadvertently come across a 'dead crab' on the shoreline – a crab that is anatomically perfect, with the eye sockets, the carapace, four pairs of legs and a pair of claws that make it a ten-legged decapod. However, if you take a closer look you may find you can lift the carapace and see the 'dead man's fingers', or gills, of the 'crab'. If it was actually dead this would be abundantly clear by the smell alone. What you have actually discovered is the moult of a crab.

This soft-shelled Edible Crab (*Cancer pagurus*) has just emerged from its moult, which can be seen at the top of the photo.

When moulting a crab performs the most remarkable of feats: it crawls out of the lifted carapace backwards, leaving the entirety of its form behind, including the gills. The crab that emerges is soft bodied and in a perfect state to continue swelling with water, increasing its original size by approximately 20%. Whilst soft-bodied, when it is known as a 'peeler crab', it is very vulnerable to predators, so it conceals itself in the safety of rocks and boulders until its shell is once again hard and protective. In a harsh environment of aggressive waves and predators, perhaps the biggest benefit of the crab's ability to moult is that with successive moults it can regenerate lost limbs. Crabs moult less as they get larger, and you may find old and large crabs and lobsters that have become encrusted with barnacles, seaweeds and other organisms.

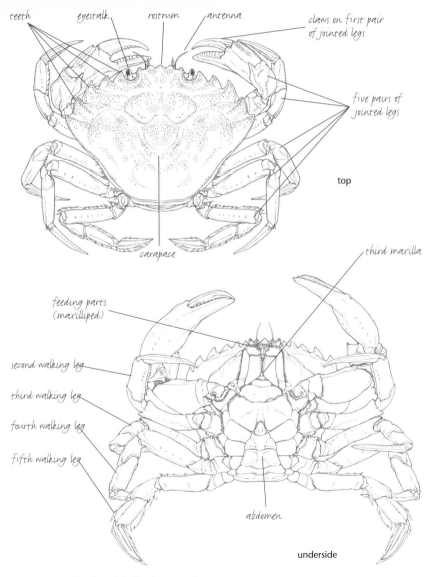

The anatomy of the Shore Crab (*Carcinus maenas*).

When picking up a crab it is advisable to do so by placing thumb and finger at either side of the broadest width of the carapace with the claws facing away from you. You can then carefully look at the underside of the crab to sex it and also check whether it is with eggs or 'berried'.

When a female crab has moulted and is still soft, she attracts the male with enticing smelling pheromones. Crabs engage in copulation through an embrace in which their abdomens, which are folded underneath the body, are lifted. Copulation takes place through the male's 'pleopods'. Once the female has been fertilised the eggs grow on the female's underside in what looks like an orange fungal growth. The hundreds of thousands of eggs are cared for under the female for up to four months before they are released into the water in their larval stage as zoeae. What we recognise as a juvenile crab settles on the shore after several successive moults and after its 'megalopa' phase.

You can find many types of crab on shores, ranging from the hermit crabs, which make use of abandoned shells for protection, to the true crabs, which have their abdomens neatly

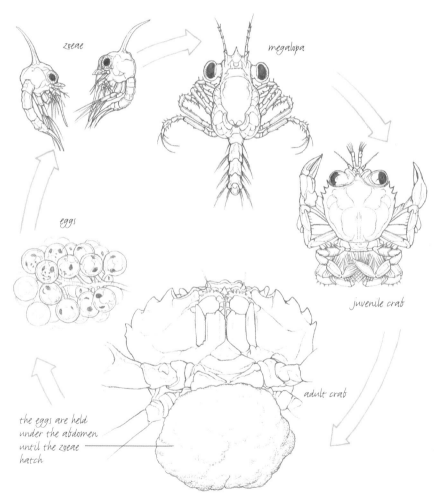

zoeae

megalopa

eggs

juvenile crab

adult crab

the eggs are held under the abdomen until the zoeae hatch

The life cycle of the Shore Crab (*Carcinus maenas*).

folded under their tails. Like all crabs, the true crabs have ten paired limbs (including the claws) with the last four being of relatively equal size. There are some true crabs with a flattened final pair of legs, which they use like oars to swim through the water, and others whose last pair of legs are hard to see because they are so small. Trying to find as many different species of crab as you can on the seashore is a proven way to entertain young children. It can also help you to understand the crabs' morphological differences.

As well as being morphologically different from each other, crabs also appear to have varying temperaments, and different species exhibit differing levels of aggression when they feel under threat. Hermit Crabs (*Pagurus bernhardus*) are best watched from the side of a pool; here, once they feel safe from danger, they scurry across the rocks making them easily distinguishable from slow-moving periwinkles. However, when under threat, they rapidly retreat into their borrowed shells.

The Shore Crab is quite easy to find. It tends to hide beneath rocks on the lower tide and becomes more active on the high tide. Shore Crabs can be aggressive but can still be handled carefully. Edible Crabs are rarely seen out of the hard-to-reach crevices in which they shelter on the low tide. When picked up they tend to stay bunched up in defensive balls, with the claws and legs held tightly to the body. The same is often true for Montagu's Crab (*Xantho hydrophilus*), though it will hold its claws out wide and broad at times. On the other hand the Velvet Swimming Crab (*Necora puber*), is quick to go into a great attack display. It will move rapidly, holding its claws tall and wide above its head attacking, anything that dares to come close.

If you happen across soft peeler crabs, they have minimal defence, as their soft claws are hardly able to open, let alone inflict any damage. They must be handled with real care to avoid damaging their soft, unprotected bodies with your own pincer-like grip. To avoid doing any harm to crabs, when returning one to its place beneath a boulder it is wise to turn the rock over and let the crab find its own way back underneath.

The male Shore Crab (left) has a pointed abdomen consisting of five sections, while the female (right) Shore Crab's abdomen is clearly more rounded with seven sections.

Shore Crab   *Carcinus maenas*

The Shore Crab is very commonly found in large numbers on all shores and estuaries around the British Isles. The small juveniles can be seen on the high shore, and can be white, green and mottled. The adults are mostly green with an orange-red coloration, depending on their life stage, and can grow to 8cm across. They have five 'teeth' on either side of the eyes at the front of the carapace. The Shore Crab reproduces all year round in the warmer southern reaches of the British Isles and during the spring in cooler Scottish waters.

CARAPACE WIDTH Up to 8cm
ZONE Upper shore to subtidal
DISTRIBUTION All of British Isles
SIMILAR SPECIES *Pachygrapsus marmoratus*

Hermit Crab   *Pagurus bernhardus*

Hermit Crabs can be found around all of the British Isles, on all tidal heights and below low tide. They most commonly adopt the spiral shells of gastropods. When competing for a shell, a crab raps on another shell containing a Hermit Crab. If a Hermit Crab has a powerful, rigorous rap showing good stamina, the defending crab, recognising its own weakness and to avoid fighting, will vacate the shell for the more powerful crab to take up residence. The crab itself is orange or red. Its claws have a gnarly surface with pointed lumps covering them.

CARAPACE WIDTH Up to 3.5cm
ZONE Upper shore to subtidal
DISTRIBUTION All of British Isles
SIMILAR SPECIES *Pagurus cuanensis, P. prideaux*

Velvet Swimming Crab   *Necora puber*

The Velvet Swimming Crab is most commonly found on sheltered shores, under rocks and boulders, around the British Isles. This beautiful blue-mottled crab has had a variety of names over the years. The name Velvet Swimming Crab describes its soft and velvety carapace and its flattened back legs, which help it to swim and burrow. More recently, the name Devil Crab appears to have stuck, as a result of its aggressive mentality and devilish red eyes. Under attack it lives up to this name by holding its pincers out high and waving them around, and it is very difficult to handle.

CARAPACE WIDTH Up to 8cm high
ZONE Mid shore to subtidal
DISTRIBUTION All of British Isles
SIMILAR SPECIES *Callinectes sapidus, Liocarcinus marmoreus*

Masked Crab   *Corystes cassivelaunus*

The Masked Crab lives on the sandy lower shore and down to the subtidal region and is widely distributed around the British Isles. It spends most of its daylight hours submerged beneath the sand. Its antennae protrude from the sand's surface and are used to channel water to the gills. The carapace of the shell is pale orange and longer (up to 4cm) than it is wide (up to 3cm). This burrowing crab has straight antennae, which exceed the length of its carapace, and slender claws. The males' claws are twice the length of its carapace, while the females' are considerably shorter.

CARAPACE WIDTH 3cm
ZONE Lower shore to subtidal
DISTRIBUTION All of British Isles
SIMILAR SPECIES *Goneplax rhomboides*

Edible Crab   *Cancer pagurus*

The Edible Crab is, as the name suggests, the crab we most commonly eat in our crab sandwiches. It is common on the shores and in seas all around the British Isles. It is possible to find juvenile Edible Crabs under rocks and boulders, but larger crabs hide in crevices on the low tide. In deeper waters the Edible Crab can grow up to 30cm across. It has a characteristic 'pie-crust' edge to the front of the carapace and is a rusty red colour. The Edible Crab's claws have black tips and are very powerful, capable of crushing other crabs and molluscs for food.

CARAPACE WIDTH Up to 30cm
ZONE Lower shore to subtidal
DISTRIBUTION All of British Isles
SIMILAR SPECIES None

Broad-clawed Porcelain Crab   *Porcellana platycheles*

The Broad-clawed Porcelain Crab is a master of disguise and can easily be missed, as it attaches itself to the undersides of rocks on the low tide around all British coastlines. It is well camouflaged, being pale brown and held tightly against the rock. The claws are flat and hairy, and when adjacent to the carapace almost indistinguishable from it. The Broad-clawed Porcelain Crab is small, only growing to 1.5cm, and its last pair of legs is small and easily missed. The female crab carries eggs under her abdomen from her second year in spring and summer.

CARAPACE WIDTH Up to 1.5cm
ZONE Lower shore
DISTRIBUTION All of British Isles
SIMILAR SPECIES *Pisidia longicornis*

Long-clawed Porcelain Crab   *Pisidia longicornis*

This small, delicate crab can be found all around the British coast in the intertidal zone. It is about 1cm wide, with two long, slender claws, and the last pair of legs is very small and at times hidden. The three walking pairs of legs are often mottled in appearance. When you lift a rock and discover a Long-clawed Porcelain Crab, it will scamper away with its claws held out in front, one claw noticeably longer than the other. It is readily distinguishable from other crabs although it is often found in the same areas as Broad-clawed Porcelain Crabs, and also at times at depth amongst bryozoans.

CARAPACE WIDTH Up to 1cm
ZONE Upper to lower shore
DISTRIBUTION All of British Isles
SIMILAR SPECIES *Porcellana platycheles*

Montagu's Crab   *Xantho hydrophilus*

Montagu's Crab is named after the Devon-based nineteenth-century naturalist George Montagu. This robust-looking crab is found on the south and west coasts of Britain and Ireland. It has a 'muscly' appearance, with a broad carapace up to 6cm wide. The surface of the carapace is furrowed, giving this crab its alternative common name of 'Furrowed Crab'. It eats Dog Whelks and other crabs. It differs from Risso's Crab, which has far hairier legs. The eggs of Montagu's Crab are deep purple.

CARAPACE WIDTH Up to 6cm
ZONE Lower shore to subtidal
DISTRIBUTION S and W of Britain and Ireland
SIMILAR SPECIES *Xantho pilipes*

Risso's Crab   *Xantho pilipes*

Risso's Crab has a broader distribution than Montagu's Crab. It can be found on the coasts of Ireland and most English and Scottish coasts, apart from parts of eastern England and Scotland. It has a less furrowed carapace and hairier legs than Montagu's Crab, and also has hairs on its carapace. The carapace can grow to 7cm across and about 3cm long. Risso's Crab also has brown tips to its claws, while Montagu's Crab has black tips.

CARAPACE WIDTH Up to 7cm
ZONE Lower shore to subtidal
DISTRIBUTION All of British Isles
SIMILAR SPECIES *Xantho hydrophilus*

Hairy Crab   *Pilumnus hirtellus*

The Hairy Crab can be found on the lower tidal regions of the rocky shore all around the British Isles. This crustacean, or Bristly Crab as it is also known, has a much rounder body than many other crabs. It is very small, with a carapace length of about 1.5cm. The Hairy Crab has very unequal pincers, with one being noticeably larger than the other and smooth, while the other, smaller pincer is covered in bristly spines. The Hairy Crab, true to its name, has hairs all over its body, including the legs and carapace.

CARAPACE WIDTH Up to 1.5cm
ZONE Lower shore
DISTRIBUTION All of British Isles
SIMILAR SPECIES *Porcellana platycheles*

Spider Crab   *Maja squinado*

The Spider Crab may occasionally be found in lower shore tidal pools, although it is more commonly found in deeper waters. In the early summer months it moves closer to shore and is found on the west and south-west coasts of the British Isles. The Spider Crab is red-orange and its carapace and legs are covered in short spines. The carapace is rounded and comes to a point around the eyes. There are spines around the edge of the carapace. This crab can grow very large, up to 20cm across its carapace. Its claws are long and large, with male crabs having larger claws than females.

CARAPACE WIDTH Up to 20cm
ZONE Lower shore to subtidal
DISTRIBUTION W and SW of British Isles
SIMILAR SPECIES *Hyas araneus*

Chinese Mitten Crab   *Eriocheir sinensis*

The Chinese Mitten Crab is an invasive species that arrived on our shores in the early twentieth century. It makes burrows in mud walls and riverbanks, making them vulnerable to collapse. These crabs can travel vast distances across land and reproduce quickly – these abilities will ultimately facilitate their spread across the British Isles. They are easily recognised by the fluffy-looking 'mittens' that cover their claws. The carapace is as deep as it is wide, with four pointed 'teeth' on either side of the eyes. If you find this crab do report your findings to help scientists better understand the distribution of the species.

CARAPACE WIDTH Up to 6cm
ZONE Mid shore
DISTRIBUTION Estuaries in British Isles
SIMILAR SPECIES None

Lobsters

For all the ingenious men, and all the scientific men, and all the fanciful men, in the world, with all the German bogey-painters into the bargain, could never invent, if all their wits were boiled into one, anything so curious and so ridiculous, as a lobster.

Charles Kingsley, *The Water-Babies* 1863

Lobsters have adaptations that can appear rather extraterrestrial to us on land, yet they are extremely well suited to their aquatic life. They are very similar to their crustacean relatives, the crabs, and share many adaptations and life stories. Unlike in the crabs, however, a lobster's abdomen is held straight out behind it rather than curled under its carapace and thorax. Lobsters reproduce in a similar way to crabs, when the female is soft from moulting. She is attracted to the male by the smell of his urine and pheromones, which offer an indication of a male's dominance and suitability to mate. The female retreats with him into his cave or rocky shelter, where he protects her and breeds with her during her vulnerable soft-bodied stage.

The fertilised eggs are held under the female's body, where she nurtures them until they hatch, releasing larvae into the water in great numbers. Lobster larvae are tasty food for other zooplankton, so a large number are released (thousands) to ensure the survival of

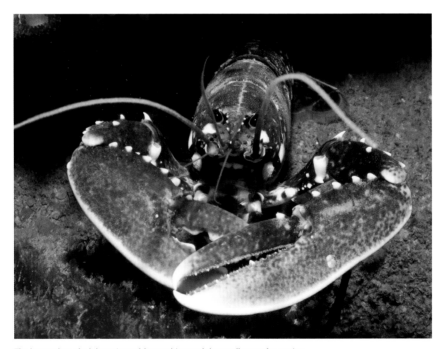

The larger claw of a lobster is used for crushing and the smaller one for cutting.

at least some progeny. A lobster takes on its adult appearance through a succession of moults. By the time it has reached maturity it may have gone through the moulting process 25 times. As larger adult lobsters moult less than younger ones, they can become more encrusted with keel worms, barnacles and other organisms.

Lobsters moult their shells in a very similar way to crabs. As a lobster's body expands with water its shell splits and it crawls out its shell backwards, leaving behind a perfectly formed, empty replica of itself. Weakened by the moulting process, the lobster will lie on its side, with its limbs too soft to support its own weight until its shell hardens once more. To grow a new shell a lobster requires considerable amounts of calcium, and it often eats its own moult for the essential minerals it provides, which encourage new shell growth.

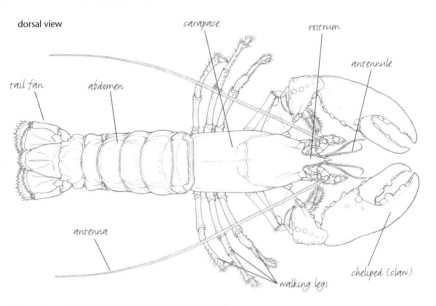

The anatomy of the Common Lobster (*Homarus gammarus*).

A lobster has two front claws of different sizes and functions: one is a powerful crushing claw; the other a fast-snipping, cutting claw, which uses different muscles that allow for a faster snip. It also has claws on the second and third pairs of legs. The claws help it prey and feed on a variety of foods. It discovers food using its sensory antennules and legs, and its diet can include fish, crustaceans, molluscs and even other lobsters. Although it may be an aggressive fighter, a lobster is also capable of hasty retreat and escape from predators. Its stalked eyes give it good vision, and it uses the eyes and its sensitive antennules to detect predators. If it senses a predator it retreats into a protective nook or cranny of a rocky wall, defending itself with its powerful claws.

The next page describes two lobster species you may see on the seashore. One species belongs to the Nephropidae, or clawed lobster family – which have well-extended abdomens and striking fan-shaped tails – the other to the Galatheoidae, or squat lobster family. Squat lobsters are much more commonly found in the intertidal zone than are Common Lobsters. Its form shares more with the Common Lobster than it does with any of the true crabs. The abdomen of a squat lobster is held underneath the body until the animal is disturbed, when it will violently flap its abdomen and swim away.

Common Lobster *Homarus gammarus*

The Common Lobster can be found all around the British Isles. Small, pale juvenile lobsters may be seen in crevices of rockpools on the low tide. This crustacean is brilliant blue, with some white spots. On very rare occasions albino versions have also been found, and even a pale blue variety. The sensory antennules are long and red. The largest recorded lobsters have grown to a metre long, but more commonly they are about 50cm in length.

LENGTH Up to 50cm
ZONE Lower shore to subtidal
DISTRIBUTION All of British Isles
SIMILAR SPECIES None

Squat Lobster *Galathea squamifera*

This common species of squat lobster is found around British rocky shores on the low tide. This crustacean tends to be nocturnal in habit, so usually found under rocks and boulders in the daytime. It has a brown body with a greenish hue. The claws are spineless, but the appendage closest to the body of the pincered legs is spiny. The body is flattened and the tail or abdomen is tucked beneath the main body or thoracic region. If you place one in a tray of water you may see it flick its tail, rapidly propelling itself backwards.

LENGTH Up to 6.5cm
ZONE Lower shore to subtidal
DISTRIBUTION All of British Isles
SIMILAR SPECIES *Galathea strigosa*

SEA SPIDERS

There is a minute marine spider...which seems,
from its lack of centralization,
to realize our infantile ideas of Mr. No-body.

Philip H. Gosse, *Tenby: A Sea-Side Holiday* 1856

It is still unclear, and remains under dispute, whether the sea spiders are more closely related to the crustaceans or to the true spiders, as they share characteristic features of both. What is clear is that the alternate name for this order, Pantapoda, which means 'all legs', is a true and clear depiction of these curious species with very long legs and no apparent body. The pycnogonids are well camouflaged and often very small, making them hard to find. The body of a sea spider is so small that many of its organs spread into its legs. Sea spiders have a number of intriguing anatomical qualities that make them unique.

The body forms of sea spiders differ amongst the many species found around the world. Sea spiders have a number of paired appendages with different functions. They usually have four 'walking' appendages. *Nymphon gracile* has four pairs of spindly legs, which it can also use for swimming. It also benefits from chelifores, claw-like appendages at the front that are used to

The ovigers or legs of a sea spider are where the egg sacs are carried.

bring food to the mouth. It is thought that the next appendages on the head, the palps, may also help bring food to the mouth, as well as possibly having a sensory function. A sea spider does not have any gaseous exchange organs, like gills or lungs; instead it diffuses gases and even waste across the surface of its skin and gut system.

Nymphon gracile has ovigerous, or egg-carrying, legs in both the male and female, while many other sea spiders, including *Pycnogonum littorale*, only have ovigerous legs in the male. The egg-carrying legs have dual functions, acting as a tool for cleaning the appendages and as a place for the males to store the fertilised egg sacs. For cleaning, a sea spider uses its jointed ovigerous limbs to lightly grip a leg and wipe any detritus away. To reproduce, a male fertilises the eggs by releasing his gametes from gonophores at the bases of the walking legs (as if from his armpits). The developing larvae have a parasitic phase when they live attached to a host, feeding and growing until adulthood.

While some species, including *Nymphon gracile*, use their front appendages (chelifores) like many crustaceans use their claws, to tear and manipulate their food, others do not possess these appendages and instead their proboscis is moveable and can easily graze algae and byrozoans; this is the case with *Pycnogonum littorale*. The shape and structure of the proboscis is therefore often key in the identification of species of sea spider.

These sea spiders use their large proboscises to pierce soft-bodied invertebrates like anemones, tunicates and sponges, then draw up their food through the proboscis as if it were using a straw to suck up the juices. Teeth at the base of the proboscis are capable of reducing the food to small digestible particles. Although this may sound like a vicious predatory tactic, sea spiders are so small that the considerably larger invertebrates they feed on can go on to live another day relatively unscathed.

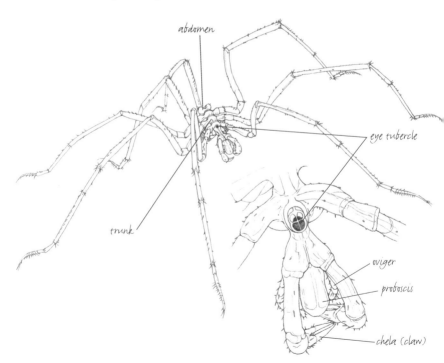

The anatomy of a sea spider (*Nymphon gracile*) with a close-up of its feeding parts.

Nymphon gracile

This sea spider is found all around the British Isles, although it is less common in the east. It is a delicate sea spider with very long legs, about three or four times longer than its body. Its body is translucent and longer than it is broad, and both sexes have ovigers with teeth to help them clean their appendages. It has visible pincer-like appendages with claws on their tips, and palps for feeding as well as a proboscis, which is longer than it is wide. It may be possible to see males in March and April, when they carry the egg sacs on their ovigers to the intertidal area.

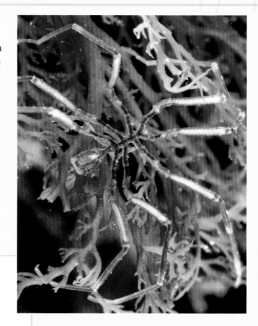

LENGTH OF BODY Up to 1cm
ZONE Upper to lower shore
DISTRIBUTION All of British Isles
SIMILAR SPECIES *Endeis spinosa, Nymphon brevistore, N. hirtum*

Pycnogonum littorale

This species of sea spider can be found on shores all around the British Isles. It is a relatively stocky species, 0.5cm long, with a short proboscis, short legs and no chelicera or palps. Its colour can vary and the male tends to be a darker brown than the more cream-coloured female. The male has ovigerous legs, while the female does not. During spring to autumn when reproducing, the male and female can sometimes be found attached to each other, staying like that for as long as five weeks.

LENGTH OF BODY Up to 0.5cm
ZONE Upper to lower shore
DISTRIBUTION All of British Isles
SIMILAR SPECIES *Achelia echinata, A. hispida, A. longipes*

BRYOZOANS

Down to the worm, thence to the zoophyte,
that link which bonds Prometheus to his rock.
The living fibre to insensate matter.

James Montgomery, *Pelican Island* 1828

The Bryozoa – **also known as Ectoprocta or Polyzoa**, and commonly as moss animals – are colonies of individual zooids that can collectively appear branching, leaf-like or mat-forming, and which are often mistaken for seaweeds and algae. These might initially appear to be rather basic species, but when studied in close detail under a microscope their anatomy and how they survive and feed is revealed to be both interesting and astonishing.

The first zooid to settle onto the substrate has the rather impressive title of an 'ancestrula'. From the ancestrula the rest of the colony develops by budding. Some zooids are responsible for attaching to the substrate, while others help keep the bryozoan clean.

Sea Chervil (*Alyconidium diaphanum*) can cause an irritating rash known to fisherman as 'Dogger Bank itch'.

The avicularia are cleaning zooids and some are shaped like birds' heads; the 'beak' of an avicularium appears to move up and down like an oil derrick to remove any larvae that might settle. This prevents bryozoans from acquiring unwanted 'epiphytic' species that might try to grow on their surfaces. The vibraculum is another type of cleaning zooid on the surface of some bryozoan species. It uses a whip-like structure to clean debris from the bryozoan's surface.

The bryozoan colony of zooids feeds with the use of lophophores, which look similar to the tentacles of feeding cnidarians. However, the lophophores are ciliated, meaning that they have hair-like structures which help the flow of water into the alimentary canal. The lophopore comes out of an opening, which may have an operculum (like a trapdoor) to close off the structure with the aid of contracting muscles. Bryozoans use their lophophores to help capture bacteria and diatoms that they feed on.

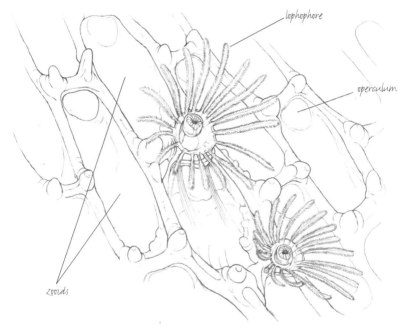

Bryozoans consist of colonies of zooids that capture food with polyp-like lophophores, which are protected by an operculum when not emerged.

Each bryozoan colony tends to have both male and female parts, so is classed as hermaphroditic. Some bryozoans may contain both males and females within the same individual zooid, or the sexes may be separate within a colony. In most species the eggs are kept within a chamber from which the larvae are released. From there they go on to a pelagic larval stage before the ancestrulas settle. Through a process of budding a bryozoan colony grows and takes shape, becoming the species we might find washed up on a seashore.

There is a wide variety of bryozoans: the Hornwrack (*Flustra foliacea*) smells of lemon and the Sea Chervil can cause a nasty skin irritation; both of these species are relatively easy to identify. However, many of the finer bryozoans are very difficult to identify and there is still confusion and debate amongst scientists over the identification and classification of certain species. The examples that follow are a small sample of the relatively common bryozoans that can be washed up on beaches or found within the intertidal region.

Sea Chervil   *Alyconidium diaphanum*

Sea Chervil can be found all around the British Isles on the very low shore, or subtidally. It is often washed up on the shore. If encountered, care should be taken as it can cause skin irritation, known to fishermen as 'Dogger Bank itch'. Sea Chervil is also poisonous to dogs so they should not be allowed to eat it. It is an upright, fleshy, gelatinous and branched bryozoan that is found attached to rocks, shells and seaweeds. It forms an erect colony that can grow up to 50cm long, but is more usually around 15cm in length. Its colour can vary from grey or brown to red, and it may even be transparent.

LENGTH Up to 15cm

ZONE Strandline or lower shore to subtidal

DISTRIBUTION All of British Isles

SIMILAR SPECIES *Alcyonidium hirsutum, A. parasiticum*

Sea Mat   *Electra pilosa*

The Sea Mat can be found commonly around the British Isles, usually encrusting toothed wracks, kelps and other seaweeds and invertebrates. It can be seen from the midshore down to the subtidal, and washed up on detached seaweeds and shells. A seaweed with a Sea Mat attached to it appears to have a white to silver, fine, flat mesh covering parts of its surface and if held horizontally at eye level, the spines protruding from the surface of the bryozoan can be seen with the naked eye.

FLATTENED COLONY

ZONE Mid shore to subtidal

DISTRIBUTION All of British Isles

SIMILAR SPECIES *Electra crustulenta, Membranipora membranacea*

Hornwrack *Flustra foliacea*

The Hornwrack is widely distributed around the British Isles. It can be found growing subtidally, but also gets washed up on shores after heavy storms. Due to its flattened branching shape, it can understandably be mistaken for a seaweed, but on closer inspection it is possible to see individual zooids. When fresh it smells of lemons. In its first year it is an encrusting bryozoan, but after the second year it starts to grow upright and branch. It does not grow in winter so it is possible to age it by its visible growth rings.

LENGTH Up to 20cm
ZONE Strandline and subtidal
DISTRIBUTION All of British Isles
SIMILAR SPECIES *Chartella papyracea, Securiflustra securifrons, Sertella septentrionalis*

Ross *Pentapora fascialis*

This bryozoan grows in the south and south-west of England, and on the coasts of western Ireland and Wales. It grows subtidally, although it can sometimes be found washed ashore or into low-shore rockpools. It is also known as Ross Coral because it has a coral-like appearance, and has undulating burnt-orange sheets that grow in convoluted and irregular domed shapes resembling a coral head. It can grow to a substantial size, measuring up to 30cm in diameter.

DIAMETER Up to 30cm
ZONE Strandline and subtidal
DISTRIBUTION S and W of British Isles
SIMILAR SPECIES None

ECHINODERMS

We put some stranded starfish carefully back into the water—
I hardly know enough of the race at this moment to be quite
certain whether they had reason to feel obliged to us for doing so,
or the reverse.

Charles Dickens, *David Copperfield* 1850

Echinoderm translates as 'spiny skin' and this is certainly a characteristic feature of most of the echinoderms we find on the seashore. Unlike in the crustaceans, within this phylum the skeleton of calcareous plates is found under the skin rather than on it. The plates all have different spines, grains and other projections. The echinoderms we may discover on British shores include the brittlestars, urchins and sea cucumbers, and this section focuses on these. However, this phylum also includes the beautifully delicate feather-stars and sea-lilies which are not covered in this handbook.

Heavy storms can cause mass mortalities of starfish, which dehydrate rapidly when cast ashore.

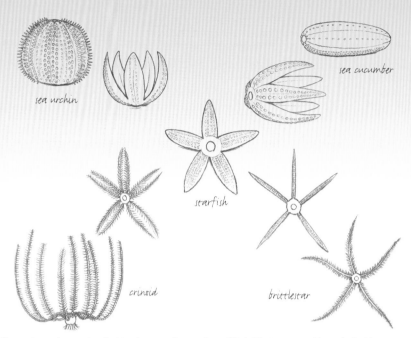

The pentameral symmetry of echinoderms can be seen in starfish, brittlestars, sea urchins and crinoids.

The echinoderms are also characterised by their pentameral symmetry – a radial symmetry that is divisible by five. There is evidence of this in every species of echinoderm, although it may not be immediately obvious in all of them or even at all in their adult forms. If you look at both starfish and brittlestars, you will see that the majority have five arms. This symmetry is also clearly seen on the naked test of an urchin, that is on its hardened exoskeleton. The test looks as if the arms of a starfish have raised up, curled into a sphere and fused with an obvious radial symmetry of five.

Echinoderms' hardened exoskeletons are often sold in coastal souvenir shops, having been unsustainably sourced. Starfish dehydrate rapidly out of water, so it is important not to remove them from pools for extended periods to prevent them from drying out and dying. Historically the tests of sea urchins have also been made into lamps. The fragile nature of the paper-thin test of the Heart Urchin (*Echinocardium cordatum*) has perhaps saved it from the fate of the souvenir shop.

Many of the echinoderms have an ingenious water vascular system that is used for feeding, locomotion and respiration. If you spend some time examining the surface of a starfish you may notice a small scar or spot. This is the inlet valve of the starfish, called the 'madreporite'. When starfish want to move, water passes through their madreporite into a series of radial and lateral canals and into their sucker-shaped 'podia', or tube feet. Through the hydrostatic pressure of filling and emptying of water, starfish are able to extend and use their tube feet to stick to rocky surfaces and seemingly glide over the surfaces of rocks. The tube feet run along the length of the arms in ambulacral grooves.

Living in the sea can be a challenge. One such challenge is how to avoid the larval stages of species that settle on any available space, including on other organisms, which can make life much more cumbersome. Some echinoderms have 'pedicellaria', which are like tube feet but have a pincer-like apparatus on the end of the structure. The pedicellaria are thought

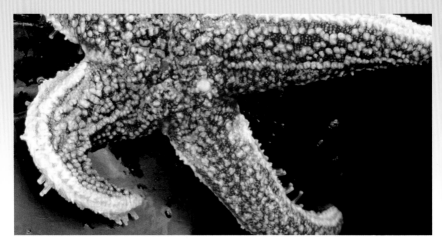

The light spot on the upper surface of this starfish is the 'madreporite' which acts as an inlet valve for water.

to remove unwanted material and larvae from the animal and can also allow it to defend itself against predators, although the specific function of the pedicellaria in different species remains unclear. If you look under a microscope at sea urchins extending their projections, you can see both tube feet and the pedicellaria. You can also experience the pedicellaria first-hand by placing a large starfish upside down on your arm. The pincer-like pedicellaria will grab hold of the hairs on your arm.

There are echinoderms that graze algae off rocks, like the urchins, and some that are more carnivorous, like the mussel-eating starfish. Many echinoderms are brightly coloured, and they add both texture and colour to our stunning seashore spectra. Look carefully under boulders and rocky overhangs for these spiny-skinned marine species.

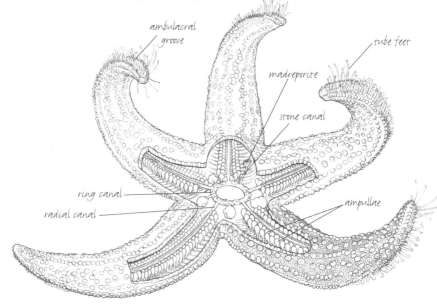

A starfish's water vascular system provides water pressure to control its tube feet.

Starfish

The asteroids, as they are also known (from the name of their class, Asteroidea), are the true stars of the seashore for intertidal explorers. They can prove tricky to find, but the pleasure of finding one always makes the time and effort taken worthwhile. In the intertidal zone the Cushion Star (*Asterina gibbosa*) is the easiest to locate on a sheltered rocky shore, attached to Coral Weeds in deep pools or to the underside of rocks. Cushion Stars provide a great opportunity to examine a starfish's incredible anatomy a little closer. If you place one in a transparent shallow tray or a bucket of water you will be able to clearly watch how it moves.

Looking at the underside, right in the middle of a starfish's central disc you will see the mouth. The central disc is fused with the arms, which is characteristic of the starfish. On the underside you will see grooves running along the length of the arms, with small tube feet protruding from the ambulacral grooves. The mouth is connected to not one but two stomachs – the cardiac stomach and the pyloric stomach. In some species the cardiac stomach can be everted from the mouth and body to eat prey.

The Common Starfish (*Asterias rubens*) is a carnivorous predator and eats mussels. It uses its tube feet, which run along the length of its five arms, to hold a mussel as though in a passionate embrace. It then uses its hydrostatic tube feet to grip the two valves of the mussel shell and prize it part by a few millimetres. Its cardiac stomach then passes out of its mouth into the mussel, and the mussel is ingested into this stomach whilst still out of the starfish's

The tube feet of starfish are used for both locomotion and passing food to the mouth.

body. The food is then passed to the pyloric stomach, which is connected to pyloric glands that have the necessary enzymes to digest prey. Waste is passed out of the anus, which lies on the upper surface of most starfish, and currents flush the waste away.

Interestingly, a starfish can lose its cardiac stomach and regenerate a new one. This is not the only power of regeneration starfish have. They also have the ability to regenerate lost limbs. It is not uncommon to find starfish with unevenly sized limbs or a very short stump in the place of one arm. In the harsh intertidal environment, of predators and extreme wave actions, the ability to regenerate can prove extremely beneficial. Should a starfish lose a limb (or even limbs) to a crab, it may be able to regrow it. If one arm is sufficiently attached to the central disc, the starfish can even grow four new arms.

Starfish get oxygen through the inlet of water from the madreporite, through the tube feet and through small 'papillae' on the surface of the skin. Their well-developed water vascular system consists of radial and lateral canals that stretch into the arms to help distribute the oxygen. In order to see, albeit in a rather primitive way, the tube feet at the ends of the arms are light sensitive, and starfish also have light receptors over the surfaces of their bodies. Pedicellarea can also be found on starfish. These small, pincer-like cleaning appendages (also found in bryozoans) keep the surface of a starfish free from settling larvae.

Most starfish species have individual males and females, though in some species individuals are hermaphroditic. The gonads of a starfish run the length of its arms, and the gametes are released from between the arms. Starfish often aggregate at times of spawning to make sure fertilisation takes place. Should this congregating coincide with storms, mass mortalities of starfish can be observed on beaches. If starfish are saved from this fate and reproduce successfully, their life cycle will include a planktonic larval stage before they settle in their adult form.

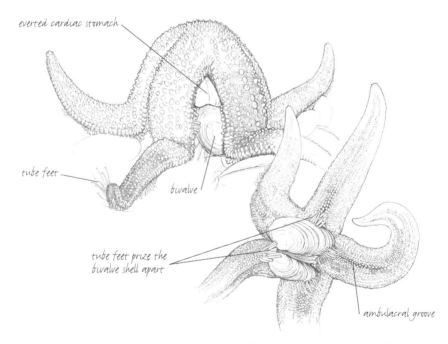

everted cardiac stomach

tube feet

bivalve

tube feet prize the bivalve shell apart

ambulacral groove

The Common Starfish will engulf bivalves. It separates their shells with its tube feet before the starfish everts one of its stomachs and consumes the bivalve's flesh.

Cushion Star *Asterina gibbosa*

The Cushion Star is an abundant starfish found in rockpools on the low shore of the south and south-west coasts of Britain. This is a small starfish, growing to about 6cm in diameter, with short arms and a domed surface. The Cushion Star changes sex during its life, initially maturing as a male, then changing to a female at about four years old. If an individual is larger than 2cm it is most probably a female. The Cushion Star is a scavenger, feeding on dead and decaying algae and invertebrates. The female lays eggs in rocky crevices in May, from which hatch small starfish.

DIAMETER Up to 6cm
ZONE Lower shore
DISTRIBUTION S and SW British Isles
SIMILAR SPECIES *Anseropoda placenta, Asterina phylactica, Porania pulvillus*

Asterina phylactica

This cushion star is a southerly species that is at its most northern limit, which is potentially spreading northwards with climate change. It can be found around the south and south-west coasts of Britain and Ireland. It was first discovered around Britain in 1979. It is very similar to the Cushion Star, but is smaller, only growing to 1.5cm across, and has a dark star shape in the centre of the body on its upper, spinier surface. It aggregates in May, when individuals gather together to spawn. They stay together after the eggs are fertilised, protecting them until they hatch.

DIAMETER Up to 1.5cm
ZONE Lower shore
DISTRIBUTION S and SW British Isles
SIMILAR SPECIES *Asterina gibbosa, Anseropoda placenta, Porania pulvillus*

Common Starfish   *Asterias rubens*

The Common Starfish is common on British shores and can be found on low tides and occasionally washed up onto the seashore. It usually has five long, rounded arms, and individuals can grow up to 30cm in diameter. The Common Starfish normally has a brown to red upper surface with white spines that are especially obvious down the centres of the arms. These starfish are often found on mussel and oyster beds as this is what they primarily feed on. In spring they migrate to shallower water, where they feed and spawn, undergoing a swimming larval stage as plankton before they settle.

DIAMETER Up to 30cm
ZONE Lower shore to subtidal
DISTRIBUTION All of British Isles
SIMILAR SPECIES *Crossaster papposus*

Spiny Starfish   *Marthasterias glacialis*

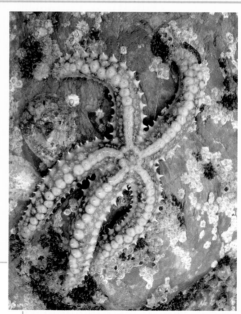

The Spiny Starfish can be found on very low spring tides in rockpools and crevices, but it is most commonly found below the low-tide mark. This is the largest starfish occurring in the British Isles, measuring up to 70cm in diameter. Its long arms are covered in large and very obvious spines, which have a cushion-like appearance at their bases and also have cleaning pedicellariae. Spiny Starfish are often pale blue-grey, but can also be yellow or orange. Relative to their overall size their central disc is quite small. Spiny Starfish can be male or female and they congregate in summer, when spawning takes place.

DIAMETER Up to 70cm
ZONE Lower shore to subtidal
DISTRIBUTION All of British Isles
SIMILAR SPECIES None

Bloody Henry   *Henricia oculata*

The Bloody Henry is a colourful starfish
that can be found around the British
Isles, but is most common in the south
and south-west. Its arms are slender
and smooth in appearance, but feel
rough to the touch, and they have
upturned tips. The Bloody Henry does
not have any cleaning pedicellariae.
This starfish grows up to 12cm across,
and varies in colour – it is often dark
purple or red, but can occasionally be
yellow. It is a suspension feeder that
uses its extended arms and mucus
to trap food matter. It also feeds on
sponges and hydroids by everting its
stomach, as do other asteroids.

DIAMETER Up to 12cm
ZONE Lower shore to subtidal
DISTRIBUTION All of British Isles
SIMILAR SPECIES *Henricia sanguinolenta,
Solaster endeca*

Common Sunstar   *Crossaster papposus*

The Common Sunstar is a northern
species, with the British Isles being its
most southerly limit. It is less common
in southern waters, but can occasionally
be found on the very low tides around
the British Isles. It is a beautiful starfish
with many arms (8–14). It grows to
20cm in diameter and has a large
central disc relative to its arm length.
The Common Sunstar feeds on a
variety of food, including the Common
Starfish and other echinoderms. It can
also be found amongst aggregations
of brittlestars, on which it feeds. It is
orange to red with concentric white
rings and a spiny upper surface.

DIAMETER Up to 20cm
ZONE Lower shore to subtidal
DISTRIBUTION Northern British Isles
SIMILAR SPECIES *Asterias rubens,
Solaster endeca*

Seven-armed Starfish *Luidia ciliaris*

The aptly named Seven-armed Starfish can be found on gravelly and sandy bottoms in the lower tide and sublittoral regions around the British Isles, although it is absent from the east of England coast. Its seven arms are often uneven in size as these starfish lose limbs easily. It grows up to 60cm across, although smaller specimens are more likely to be found in rockpools. The arms are slender, and red or orange, with spines around the internal edges. The tube feet lack suckers but are very long, and this starfish can move quickly compared to others.

DIAMETER Up to 60cm
ZONE Lower shore to subtidal
DISTRIBUTION All of British Isles except E England
SIMILAR SPECIES *Luidia sarsi, Solaster endeca*

Sand Star *Astropecten irregularis*

The Sand Star is commonly found around the British Isles, in the subtidal region and on the very low tide on sandy beaches or washed ashore. It has a flattened stiff body that can grow to 20cm across. Stiff, pointed spines fringe the length of its arms, which are held out firmly when it is well and healthy. It uses pedicellareae to clean between its spines. The upper surface is often sandy or pale pink in colour, with pretty purple tips to its arms. The Sand Star burrows into the sand, where it feeds on young bivalves, worms and crustaceans, using its pointed tube feet to pass food to its mouth.

DIAMETER Up to 20cm
ZONE Lower shore to subtidal
DISTRIBUTION All of British Isles
SIMILAR SPECIES None

Brittlestars

Like the haddock, the cod also is a great naturalist;
and he, too, carries his devotion to our dear science so far as to
die for its sake with a new species in its stomach…and doubtless
his knowledge of the Ophiurae* exceeds that of any biped.
He has great taste for that tribe.

Edward Forbes, *History of British Starfish and other Animals of the Class Echinodermata* 1841

*Ophiurae is more familiarly known today as Ophiuroidea

The brittlestars are so delicate that even with the gentlest of handling they can lose their limbs. Fortunately, like many of the echinoderms, they can regenerate lost limbs, a useful tactic in the presence of predators and aggressive intertidal conditions. There are even species of brittlestar that can spontaneously split into two and reproduce asexually by fission, eventually becoming whole again.

The brittlestars can be found under boulders and rocks, or on the surfaces of rocks and seaweeds on the lower shore. It can be tricky to see these fine and often small echinoderms amongst the gravel and sediment. However, once you have found one, and have the spatial recognition imprinted within, you will be able to go on to find many more. In deeper waters brittlestars can be found in more obvious and vast aggregations.

An aggregation of the Black Brittlestar (*Ophiolomina nigra*) on the eggs of a Common Whelk (*Buccinum undatum*).

Brittlestar's five slender arms are joined together by a central button-like disc, from which the arms are clearly defined. Unlike the starfish, brittlestars do not use their tube feet for locomotion, but for feeding. Their arms are articulated, with small plates allowing a brittlestar to move its arms in a sinusoidal movement and 'snake' its way across the seashore, at quite some speed compared to the starfish. The brittlestars' class name (Ophiuroidea) is derived from the Greek for snake and refers to their snake-like limbs. They use one arm as a leading arm, while the other four arms are used more actively for pushing against the substrate. The plates on the arms are also often covered in spines giving a brittlestar a particularly hairy appearance.

A brittlestar's central disc contains all of its reproductive and digestive organs, and its organs do not run into the arms as in the Asteroidea starfish. A brittlestar has no eyes to sense food, but instead has nerves in its skin, that can detect chemicals in the water, and receptors in its skin and tube feet, which may be able to detect light.

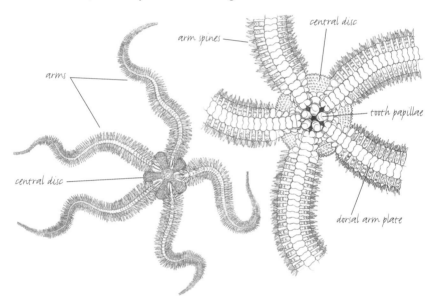

The anatomy of the Common Brittlestar (*Ophiothrix fragilis*), including a close-up of the underside of its central disc.

So how do these delicate echinoderms feed and survive? Some brittlestars secrete a sticky mucus from their arms. This then traps any suspended matter, which in turn passes to the mouth, on the underside of the disc, via currents created by either the tube feet or by the mouth. In other species food is passed to the mouth using the tube feet, which have no suckers, to the simple stomach. Cleaning pedicellarea are also absent in brittlestars. Waste is passed out of the mouth, which acts as an anus. To reproduce the brittlestars will, like sea spiders and starfish, often release their gametes from between their arms. It is also common for them to look after their young in special brooding sacs, or bursa. They then release larval brittlestars into the water.

When you lift a boulder on the lower shore, take a close look at what might appear to be bare, empty sediment. If you take a moment to focus on the gravel the delicate structure of a brittlestar might appear before your eyes. Once you have found one, your trained eye will start to see quite a few lurking in the soft sediment and under boulders. They can be difficult to identify to species level without the use of a hand lens, but nonetheless are still a delightful find and are great to observe snaking across the sediment.

Common Brittlestar   *Ophiothrix fragilis*

The Common Brittlestar can be found in large numbers around the British Isles on the lower shore. It can grow to a considerable size, with the disc alone reaching 2cm in diameter. However, individuals found on the seashore tend to be quite small. The disc of this brittlestar has radial lines from the centre, and the arms are incredibly brittle and fragile. They extend to five times the diameter of the disc, and have a hairy appearance due to the density of the spines on the arm plates. In deeper waters these brittlestars can be seen congregating in great piles, arms extended to gather food from the water.

DIAMETER OF DISC Up to 2cm
ZONE Lower shore to subtidal
DISTRIBUTION All of British Isles
SIMILAR SPECIES *Ophiura ophiura, O. albida*

Black Brittlestar   *Ophiocomina nigra*

The Black Brittlestar is common on most of the British Isles coasts, but is absent from the east coast of England. Like the Common Brittlestar, it is found on the lower shore under rocks and boulders, and also forms aggregations in deeper waters. However, unlike Common Brittlestars, Black Brittlestar seem to keep one another at arm's length, with individuals rarely touching. The body is of a similar size to that of the Common Brittlestar when fully grown, but with more distinct, smooth, spaced out spines. As its name suggests, this brittlestar is usually black or very dark brown.

DIAMETER OF DISC Up to 2.5cm
ZONE Lower shore to subtidal
DISTRIBUTION All of British Isles except E England
SIMILAR SPECIES *Ophiopsila aranea*

Sea and heart urchins

*Now if you have the empty box of an urchin…hold it up to the light,
and look into the cavity…light streams through a multitude of holes…
as smooth and regular as if drilled with a fairy's wimble;*

Rev John G Wood, *The Common Objects of the Sea Shore* 1857

The sea and heart urchins are characterised by a 'test'. This is a calcium-based structure made up of fused skeletal plates and covered in a thin skin. The true urchins have very spherical tests, while those of heart urchins are more irregularly rounded; sand dollars, found outside the British Isles, are flatter still. The word 'urchin' comes from an old English word for hedgehog and reflects the spines that cover the surface of a test. These spiny species have even ended up lending themselves to a French phrase for a man who is never happy, '*Il a des oursins dans la poche!*' It is no wonder that a man might be unsettled with urchins in his pockets!

When a sea urchin has died and only the test remains, it is possible to see pentameral symmetry from the lines radiating from the uppermost point of the globe along the five fused ambulacral plates. These lines have pores running along their length from which the tube feet emerge. A sea urchin also has spines covering the body which are attached to the test by an articulated joint, allowing an urchin to use the spines for locomotion. When the spines are removed the white bumps remain. Whilst still alive, in between the spines are different types of small pedicellariae. The pedicellariae are small, stalked projections which, in some cases, have vicious-looking jaws capable of releasing a toxin. The globelliferous pedicellariae protect urchins from predation, whilst differently shaped pedicellariae keep urchins clean and even grasp food.

An empty test of a Green Sea Urchin (*Psammechinus miliaris*) denuded of spines.

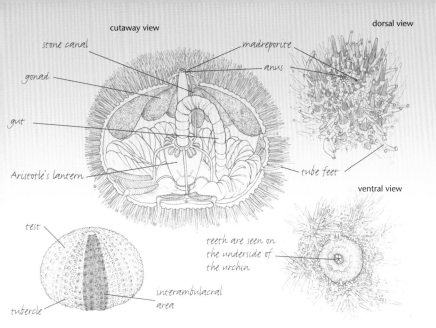

cutaway view

dorsal view

stone canal

madreporite

anus

gonad

gut

Aristotle's lantern

tube feet

ventral view

test

teeth are seen on
the underside of
the urchin

interambulacral
area

tubercle

The anatomy of the Green Sea Urchin (*Psammechinus miliaris*).

The uppermost apex of the test is also the point at which the anus and madreporite are located. Just as in the starfish, the madreporite acts as the inlet valve for water to get drawn in for the vascular system, to give the tube feet the hydraulic pressure needed to work. The mouth, however, is situated on the underside of the urchin. Here you will find the dental apparatus, which is an intricate and exquisite testament to anatomical evolution. These echinoids use their well-adapted teeth to graze on algae, barnacles and other invertebrates.

In large public aquariums, it is possible to see urchins attached to the acrylic of the tank. If you look closely at the underside of an attached urchin, you can see the concentric teeth or jaws open and close, grazing algae from the acrylic. The five teeth extend up into the cavity and interlink to create an amazing structure capable of scraping algae and invertebrates

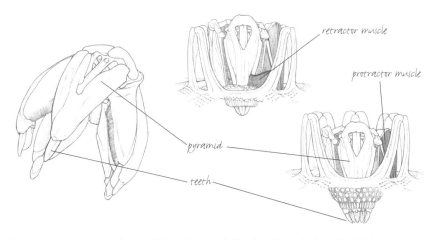

retractor muscle

protractor muscle

pyramid

teeth

Protractor and retractor mussels control the opening and closing of the five teeth of the Aristotle's lantern, thereby allowing the urchin to graze.

off rocks, and to even scour the rock itself. The jaws are controlled by 60 muscles, which cause the powerful opening and closing of the teeth. These incredible teeth are even self-sharpening. This is thought to be due to the way in which the calcite crystals of the teeth are laid down, which means that, when the teeth are chipped, a sharp edge remains. This feat of natural engineering has been used to research technology for our own benefit to create self-sharpening tools.

Urchins like starfish, move with the use of their long tube feet that run in five double lines of pores radiating from the apex of the test. However, they also use their jointed spines to push themselves along the surfaces of the rocks or substrate. The spines additionally protect them from predators, which is particularly important when the speed and size of an urchin is considered.

Sea urchins reproduce by releasing gametes into the water, the male releasing the sperm and the female releasing the eggs, spawning simultaneously. They are broadly broadcast into the sea, where they fertilise and the cells divide. Shortly after, a microscopic planktonic pluteus is produced that bears a loose resemblance to an adult urchin, with a mouth, through gut and anus and long oral arms. A month or so later, the pluteus metamorphoses to produce a perfectly formed miniature adult. This settles on a rock and grows over time.

If you compare the sea urchins with heart urchins, it becomes very clear that the anatomy of heart urchins serves a different role. As heart urchins burrow into the sediment they no longer feed on encrusting invertebrates, but instead filter food from the water. The anus has migrated to the underside of the body, and the spines have become much more numerous and finer, face in one direction and have spade-like tips. The spines are used less for ambulatory locomotion; instead they are better suited to burrowing and creating the currents needed to bring food in rich water to the mouth.

To find sea urchins on the seashore you will need to look carefully under rocks and be aware that some may be camouflaged and covered in pieces of seaweed or gravel. There is also a good chance of finding the paper-thin heart urchins washed up on the shore after storms, on sandy beaches and in estuaries.

The tube feet and spines of a sea urchin work together, allowing it to move across rocky bedrock.

Green Sea Urchin   *Psammechinus miliaris*

The Green Sea Urchin is common on low-tide rocky shores all around the British Isles. Its test is up to 5cm across, green in colour and flattened. It is about half as high as it is broad. The spines are short and green with purple tips. This small urchin can be found under rocks and in crevices with seaweed and gravel often stuck to its spines. It feeds on seaweeds and invertebrates such as bryozoans and barnacles. These small echinoderms release gametes into the water which, once fertilised, undergo a planktonic pluteus phase before settling.

DIAMETER Up to 5cm
ZONE Lower shore
DISTRIBUTION All of British Isles
SIMILAR SPECIES *Paracentrotus lividus*

Edible Sea Urchin   *Echinus esculentus*

The Edible Sea Urchin is common in much of Britain, except the east and south-east of England. It is often found in deeper waters, although it also occurs on the lower shore. The test of the Edible Sea Urchin is very round and can vary in colour from the usual pinkish-red to green or purple. It grows up to 16cm in diameter. This urchin is seen as a delicacy, the well-established gonads, or roe, being the parts that are eaten. The gametes of the urchin are released into the water by the separate sexes. They fertilise and go through a planktonic larval stage before settling.

DIAMETER Up to 16cm
ZONE Lower shore to subtidal
DISTRIBUTION All of British Isles
SIMILAR SPECIES *Echinus acutus*

Purple Sea Urchin *Paracentrotus lividus*

The Purple Sea Urchin is at its most northerly distribution in the British Isles. Occasionally it has been found in the south and south-west of England, but it is more common on the west coast of Ireland and the Channel Islands. The test is a flattened globe measuring up to 7cm across, with long spines. The spines are deep purple, brown or green, sharp and have a dense covering compared with those of the Green and Edible Sea Urchins. It is thought that climate change will result in a change in the distribution of this species, with more individuals being found around the south of England.

DIAMETER Up to 7cm
ZONE Lower shore to subtidal
DISTRIBUTION S and SW of British Isles
SIMILAR SPECIES *Psammechinus miliaris*

Heart Urchin *Echinocardium cordatum*

The delicate Heart Urchin, or Sea Potato, can be found all around the British Isles. It is classed as an irregular urchin as it does not share certain key characteristics of some of the sea urchins. After a storm, or on low tides, the 9cm-long, paper-thin test remains of a dead urchin may be found. Live individuals are covered in large, fine spines that face backwards. Heart Urchins have no need of an Aristotle's lantern, but they have a simple mouth that is not central on the underside of the test. They live in permanent burrows in sandy sediments, and use their tube feet to pass food to the mouth.

LENGTH Up to 9cm
ZONE Mid shore to subtidal
DISTRIBUTION All of British Isles
SIMILAR SPECIES *Echinocardium flavescens, Brissopsis lyrifera*

Sea cucumbers

I see the glorious sea cucumber…a magnificent coronet of plumes
wherewith the headless king is adorned.

Philip H. Gosse, *A Year at the Shore* 1865

The sea cucumbers are generally found in deep waters, although sporadically they may be discovered on very low spring tides on the rocky shore. Despite their worm-like appearance, they are in fact echinoderms of the class Holothurioideae. They are long, cylinder-shaped animals with a mouth at one end and an anus at the other. Despite their rounded appearance, some have a walking edge to the body with three rows of tube feet running down their length and, on the upper surface, there are two rows of tube feet. From this arrangement of tube feet it is possible to recognise the pentameral symmetry – albeit rather distorted in the sea cucumbers – that is so representative of the echinoderms.

Whilst sea cucumbers do have spiny skins, this characteristic is not as obvious as it is in starfish and urchins. The skin is rough and consists of calcium spicules, which are often used to identify different species of sea cucumber. The various spicules of the sea cucumbers are called tables, buttons and baskets to describe their different shapes. There are sea cucumbers that burrow into the sediment and others that may be found on the surfaces of rocks or in mussel beds. A few sea cucumbers use a toxin called holothurin, which they release from their body walls as a method of defence.

The Cotton Spinner (*Holothuria forskali*) ejects cotton-like threads from its anus to deter predators.

Other sea cucumbers have a quite shocking means of defence, very different from the hardened, spiky exteriors of their cousins. The Cotton Spinner is so called because, when startled, it has a habit of spewing sticky, cotton-like threads out of its anus, causing the rupture of internal tissue due to the power of the expulsion. This is where the regenerative powers of echinoderms come into their own within the sea cucumbers. The threads are in fact the Cuverian organs. These organs lengthen by up to 20 times and only become sticky after they have been discharged. The tubules are left entangling the predator and the sea cucumber is able to move off to recover. It can take sea cucumbers five weeks to regenerate their tubules, in the case of the Cotton Spinner, and so this method is used only when it is most needed.

The holothurians feed in different ways although many of them have a net-like arrangement of retractable tentacles at their mouth end. These are actually modified tube feet and are often covered in mucus, helping them to trap food such as 'marine snow', the dead phytoplankton that fall to deeper waters. It is here in the dark, deep waters that sea cucumbers can most commonly be found. Burrowing sea cucumbers swallow sediment, extracting nutrients as they burrow.

Many of the sea cucumbers have separate sexes and release their gametes into the water, where they develop into a planktonic larval stage before settling in their miniature adult form. If you do discover a sea cucumber it is best not to touch it, as handling could prevent it from discharging its tubules and make it vulnerable to predators.

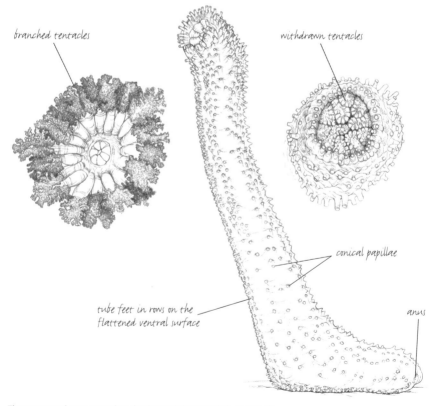

The anatomy of a sea cucumber, the Cotton Spinner (*Holothuria forskali*).

Cotton Spinner   *Holothuria forskali*

The curious-looking Cotton Spinner is found on the south and south-west coasts of Britain, on very low spring tides or subtidally. It is dark brown with 20 stumpy tentacles around its mouth, and can grow up to 25cm in length. The skin of the Cotton Spinner is dark brown, thick and warty. The underside of this sea cucumber tends to be yellow, and has three rows of tube feet. When disturbed, the Cotton Spinner is able to eject its cuverian tubules from its anus to entrap predators.

LENGTH Up to 25cm
ZONE Lower shore to subtidal
DISTRIBUTION S and SW British Isles
SIMILAR SPECIES *Cucumaria frondosa*

Sea Gherkin   *Pawsonia saxicola*

The Sea Gherkin is found around the south and south-west of England and Ireland, on the low rocky shore and on mussel beds. The body of this holothurian is about 15cm long, cylindrical and pale in colour, but it goes dark on exposure to sunlight. The Sea Gherkin has five rows of tube feet that run down its length, three on the underside with cylindrical tube feet, and two on the upper surface with conical tube feet. It has ten dark branching tentacles around its mouth, which it uses to feed.

LENGTH Up to 15cm
ZONE Lower shore to subtidal
DISTRIBUTION S and SW England and Ireland
SIMILAR SPECIES *Aslia lefevrei*

SEA SQUIRTS

The ascidians alone give us a whole chapter in Darwinism.

Arthur Willey, *Convergence in Evolution* 1911

The sea squirts, tunicates, ascidians or sea porks, as they are variably called, belong to the class Ascidiacea and appear to be relatively simple invertebrates that might perhaps be assumed to be closely related to the sponges or cnidarians, such as the anemones. However, they are chordates, as are fish, reptiles, amphibians and even mammals, including us. The key features of a chordate are the presence of a notochord and a post anal-tail at some stage of development. The notochord is a stiff, rod-like structure that is found in the embryos of all chordates. It acts as the main axis of an embryo and, if it continues into adulthood, it becomes the main support and eventually the vertebral column. So, though a sea squirt looks like a very simple organism, it actually shares common evolutionary ancestry with humans, demonstrating the beginnings of a backbone.

The sea squirts are mostly sessile, meaning that they attach as larvae to suitable substrates like rocky crevices, cliffs, seaweed and man-made structures, and there they stay. The Light Bulb Sea Squirt (*Clavelina lepadiformis*), for example, is sessile and occurs in clumps of individual sea squirts. Each sea squirt generally has an inhalant oral siphon that draws in water and an exhalant atrial siphon from which water flows out, so there are two open pores per individual, as on a pig's nose, but in sea squirts these openings are usually at right angles to one other. The bodies of these ascidians are gelatinous and transparent, like those of many ascidians, although there are some colour-variable species and some more opaque species too. A leathery tunic covers each individual, hence the name tunicate.

This sea squirt, *Ciona intestinalis*, can be found under pontoons as well as on rocky surfaces.

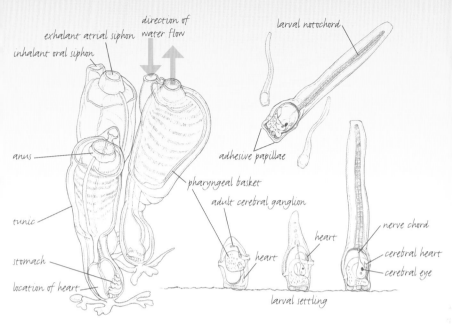

The anatomy and larval settling (bottom right) of the Light Bulb Sea Squirt.

So how do our primitive relatives feed when they have such an apparently basic structure? Through some specialised cilia, or hair-like structures, water is drawn in through the oral siphon, then enters into the pharynx through pores, where nutrients (in the form of plankton and detritus) are removed from the water, and waste is expelled via the anus, which is close to the exhalant siphon.

Compound ascidians are also tunicates, but are of quite different appearance. They are found in patches on the undersides of rocks. They often look and feel like smooth pieces of colourful glass, decorated with colourful ornamental flowers. Within each 'petal' of the 'flower' there is an inhalant siphon, and at the centre of the 'flower' the exhalant siphons are joined together to form a single cloaca, or opening, from which the water is expelled.

The ascidians can be difficult to identify on the seashore. The best place to find sea squirts in considerable numbers is on structures in harbours that are mostly submerged in fast-flowing, nutrient-rich water and in the shade. Pontoons and jetties are great places in which to find them and if you (carefully) look underneath them you may be repaid with the sight of some striking tunicate specimens, our very own distant relatives.

The flower-like Star Ascidian (*Botryllus schlosseri*) is classed as a compound ascidian.

Star Ascidian   *Botryllus schlosseri*

This compound ascidian can be found on the lower shore around all of the British Isles, attached to rocks and the stipe of kelps. It varies a lot in appearance, with some deeper-water examples being thicker than the lower shore, flattened specimens. It forms a flower or star shape, which is made up of 3 to 12 exhalant openings. The Star Ascidian can be up to 15cm across, and its colour can vary from blue to yellow or brown. Its eggs are kept in the atrium until they develop into larvae, at which point they are released from the atrial siphon. These tunicates can also reproduce by budding.

ENCRUSTING Up to 15cm in diameter
ZONE Lower shore
DISTRIBUTION All of British Isles
SIMILAR SPECIES *Aplidium nordmanni, Botryllus leachi, Sidnyum elegans*

Light Bulb Sea Squirt   *Clavelina lepadiformis*

The Light Bulb Sea Squirt is commonly found around the British Isles, on lower rocky shores attached to seaweeds, rocks and stones. This sea squirt has a few individuals attached by a 'stolon' at its base. The individuals are transparent and have visible pale lines within the tunicate, making it resemble the element in a light bulb. The eggs are self-fertilised in the atrium, then the larvae are released. After just a few hours the larvae settle to create a new colony. The species can also create new offspring by budding in spring.

HEIGHT Up to 2cm
ZONE Lower shore to subtidal
DISTRIBUTION All of British Isles
SIMILAR SPECIES *Ciona intestinalis*

Ciona intestinalis

Ciona intestinalis is a commonly found tunicate on both rocky surfaces, and within harbours on pontoons and other man-made structures on all British coasts. It occurs from low tide down into the subtidal region. This is a solitary sea squirt that grows up to 15cm long, with a transparent body and a yellow rim around the two siphons. Despite being solitary, it is often found in clumps of individuals.

LENGTH Up to 15cm
ZONE Lower shore to subtidal (pontoons)
DISTRIBUTION All of British Isles
SIMILAR SPECIES *Clavelina lepadiformis*

Baked Bean Sea Squirt   *Dendrodoa grossularia*

The Baked Bean Sea Squirt can be found around the British Isles, but is most common in the south and west. It occurs on low tides and at depth, either as solitary individuals or in clusters. The clusters are bumpy, often orange to red in colour and, true to their name, they do resemble baked beans, and measure about 2cm in height. The siphons are visible and as in many of the sea squirts the fertilised eggs are held in the atrium, from which the larvae are released.
The young larvae often settle on mature colonies.

ENCRUSTING Up to 2cm high projections
ZONE Lower shore to subtidal
DISTRIBUTION All of British Isles
SIMILAR SPECIES *Distomus variolosus*

Leathery Sea Squirt *Styela clava*

This introduced species is now found in numerous locations around the south and west of England, and even in some areas of Scotland and Ireland. It occurs on hard surfaces in the lower shore, especially on pontoons and jetties, and in harbours and oyster beds. It was first introduced with young oysters that were brought to the British Isles for cultivation. It is a solitary sea squirt that is attached to the substrate by a stalk, from which hangs a cylindrical body of up to 12cm in length. Living up to its name, it has a leathery texture, and obvious siphons.

LENGTH Up to 12cm
ZONE Lower shore to subtidal
DISTRIBUTION S and W England
SIMILAR SPECIES *Styela coriacea, S. spartita*

Didemnum vexillum

This fast-growing, highly invasive species can unfortunately be found in some marinas in England, Wales and around the coasts of Ireland, from the intertidal region down into deeper waters. It has the potential to completely and rapidly smother fishing pots and gear, and affect the diversity and economy of coastal regions. This colonial sea squirt can carpet structures and also create rope-like colonies. It is pale cream to white and fairly smooth. It forms spongy carpets over structures, as well as in rockpools.

ENCRUSTING
ZONE Mid shore to subtidal
DISTRIBUTION Sporadic reports around British Isles
SIMILAR SPECIES None

SEASHORE FISH

The stickleback is fearless in
The way he loves his wife.
Every minute of the day
He guards her with his life.

Ted Hughes, *Stickleback* from *The Cat and The Cuckoo* 1987

The seashore fish that spend their time between the tides are well adapted to this aggressive and mobile habitat dictated by tidal cycles and weather systems and their effects. Most 'pelagic' or deeper water fish, like cod, have quite different anatomies, and a clear and visible lateral line running the length of the body. This lateral line is used for sensing vibrations and pressure changes, and is very useful in the open sea for detecting predators and other sources of potential harm. However, if intertidal fish possessed such a characteristic, they would be awash with sensory overload from the changing tides and vibrations in the rockpools. Instead they have developed other astonishing adaptations to suit their hostile and changeable environment.

The Tompot Blenny (*Parablennius gattorugine*) is well camouflaged in and amongst crevices in lower tidal pools.

In order to describe and identify intertidal fish it is helpful to be familiar with basic fish anatomy. The position and number of fins often offer a good way of identifying species. The intertidal fish tend not to be torpedo shaped – a characteristic that is better suited to fast pelagic swimmers like mackerel – but are often flattened looking and less streamlined. This allows them to retreat into rocky crevices and under rocks to protect themselves from predators. As a result the dorsal and tail fins are not typically shaped like those of fast-swimming fish. The arrangement and shapes of the fins on a fish give a real indication of its speed and lifestyle. In rockpool species there are instances where the pelvic fins have evolved and fused into suckers, as seen in Montagu's Sea Snail (*Liparis montagui*), to prevent these fish from being washed away by waves and tides.

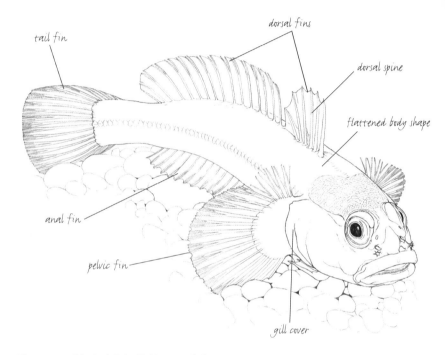

dorsal fins

dorsal spine

tail fin

flattened body shape

anal fin

pelvic fin

gill cover

The anatomy of the Rock Goby (*Gobius paganellus*)

Unlike most pelagic fish, intertidal fish also have a much smaller swim bladder, or even lack one. As they live in shallow water this buoyancy device has become redundant. Being regularly exposed on the low tide, they often have the ability to survive and breathe out of water, so when a pipefish is found in a 'dry' area there is no need to return it to a deeper pool. Many intertidal fish benefit from powerful, thick-lipped mouths, which help them crush mollusc and crustacean invertebrates like barnacles.

Many fish found on the rocky shore build nests to help ensure the survival of their offspring. While pelagic fish adopt a reproductive process commonly referred to as 'squirt and hope' by scientists, intertidal fish often undergo courtship rituals and lay eggs in nests, rather than releasing their eggs and sperm into the water as do deeper water fish. There can be more than one female laying eggs in a carefully constructed nest, with a single male fertilising the eggs and protecting them. As a result, the male also ensures that there is a variety of genes in his offspring, thereby offering an enhanced chance of survival.

To find fish at the seashore you have to look in every nook and cranny. Inside a deep rocky crevice it may be possible to see the decorated face of the Butterfly Blenny (*Blennius ocellaris*) staring back at you. You may find a clingfish under rocks and boulders, see gobies darting under seaweed as you approach a pool, or you can even find some more pelagic fish stranded in lower tidal pools. These include juveniles our most colourful wrasse, the Ballan Wrasse (*Labrus bergylta*). The wrasse are relatives of the tropical parrotfish found in coral reefs and are no less bright or striking. On the high tide there are other coastal fish which feed in the intertidal zone, like bass, and some of the flatfish such as plaice, dab and flounder. Many juvenile fish use the protection of coastal and estuarine waters to grow.

There are even fish lurking buried in the sand within the shallow intertidal zone on sandy beaches. These may include Lesser Sandeels (*Ammodytes tobianus*) almost completely buried in the sand, and the Lesser Weever Fish (*Echiithys vipera*), which buries itself in the surface of the sand so only its eyes are visible. Should you stand on a Lesser Weever Fish it can inject you with a small quantity of poison through its dorsal fin, which can cause considerable pain. The poison is 'thermo reactive', so to ease the pain you should carefully place your foot in water as hot as is comfortable. This will denature the poison and stop it from working. While it is fairly unlikely to happen, in order to avoid stepping on the weever it is useful to shuffle your feet in the sand. This also gives the fish the opportunity to avoid the possibly unpleasant experience of being trodden on.

To take a closer look at an intertidal fish, it is best to have a bucket (preferably transparent) and scoop the fish into it. This gives you a great chance to see it in its full glory without causing it any harm.

The Corkwing Wrasse (*Crenalibus melops*) builds nests from seaweed.

Shore Rockling   *Gaidropsarus mediterraneus*

The Shore Rockling can be found predominantly on the rocky shores of the south and west coasts of the British Isles as far north as Orkney. The rocklings have sensory barbels for detecting prey around their mouths, and the Shore Rockling has three such barbels. It has a uniform dark brown skin with two dorsal fins, although the fin close to the head is reduced to just a single ray followed by other rays that lie in a groove. The second dorsal fin and lower pectoral run along much of the length of the body to the tail. The Shore Rockling can grow to 25cm long.

LENGTH Up to 25cm
ZONE Lower shore to subtidal
DISTRIBUTION S and W of British Isles
SIMILAR SPECIES *Ciliata mustela, Gaidropsarus vulgaris, Raniceps raninus*

Five-bearded Rockling   *Ciliata mustela*

The Five-bearded Rockling is common on coasts all around the British Isles. It can be found on both rocky and sandy shores, where it feeds on invertebrates. To detect food sources the rockling flutters its dorsal fin to waft water towards its five whisker-like sensory barbels, one under the chin and four above the nostrils. It is a long, smooth, slender dark brown fish growing up to 25cm long with two dorsal fins and one anal fin. The first dorsal fin is reduced to one upright ray with further rays lying in a groove behind that, followed by the longer second dorsal fin. The rocklings release their gametes offshore.

LENGTH Up to 25cm
ZONE Lower shore to subtidal
DISTRIBUTION All of British Isles
SIMILAR SPECIES *Gaidropsarus mediterraneus, G. vulgaris*

Rock Goby   *Gobius paganellus*

The Rock Goby can be found on rocky shores around the British Isles. Like all gobies, it has two dorsal fins, and the pelvic fins are fused to create a weak sucker. This helps the gobies to stick to surfaces if disturbed by swell and wave action. The first of the dorsal fins has six spines, with one spine on the last dorsal fin closer to the tail. The species is well camouflaged with a brown mottled coloration, and grows up to 15cm long. When the female is ready to lay her eggs she acquires a bright blue protruding lump on her ventral side. The eggs are laid on rocks and other suitable surfaces in spring and summer.

LENGTH Up to 15cm
ZONE Lower shore to subtidal
DISTRIBUTION All of British Isles
SIMILAR SPECIES *Gobius cobitis, G. niger*

Common Goby   *Pomatoschistus microps*

The Common Goby is common in estuaries and on seashores around the British Isles. It has two separate dorsal fins and fused pelvic fins capable of loosely sticking to the substrate. It is well camouflaged with a brown mottled skin, and has large eyes positioned close to the top of the head. The male builds a simple nest, often from an upturned shell, under which a depression is made where the eggs are laid by the female. The male fertilises and oxygenates the eggs by fanning his progeny with his tail, and then protects them.

LENGTH Up to 6cm
ZONE Lower shore to subtidal
DISTRIBUTION All of British Isles
SIMILAR SPECIES *Pomatoschistus minutus*

Tompot Blenny *Parablennius gattorugine*

The Tompot Blenny is a spectacular seashore fish that can be found around all of the British Isles except for the east coast of England. It lives in crevices on the lower shore. It has a large, bulbous head (common to all blennies) and one continuous dorsal fin with an indentation. The Tompot Blenny has thick lips and two finely branched tentacles above the eyes. The male releases pheromones from his anal gland, darkens his skin and builds a nest when ready to spawn. The most successful males have a larger crown of tentacles. The male looks after his fertilised eggs until they hatch.

LENGTH Up to 30cm
ZONE Lower shore to subtidal
DISTRIBUTION All of British Isles
SIMILAR SPECIES *Blennius occelaris, Parablennius ruber*

Montagu's Blenny *Coryphoblennius galerita*

This blenny, named after the great nineteenth-century natural historian George Montagu, is found on the rocky shores around the south-west of Britain and the west of Ireland. It commonly occurs amongst coral weed, and likes to eat the curled feeding apparatus, or cirra, of barnacles. It has a long dorsal fin and light blue spots on the head and body. It also has a small crown, like an individual spike, above its eyes, which are fringed with short tentacles. The male protects his fertilised eggs, which are laid in rocky crevices by the female in the summer months.

LENGTH Up to 8.5cm
ZONE Mid to lower shore
DISTRIBUTION SW British Isles
SIMILAR SPECIES *Liphophrys pholis*

Butterfly Blenny *Blennius ocellaris*

The beautiful Butterfly Blenny is most commonly found in the English Channel and Irish Sea. It is a very attractive blenny, with two tentacles above its eyes and a dorsal fin like a butterfly's wing running the length of the body. The head or anterior end of the dorsal fin is considerably taller than the tail end. It has a characteristic dark spot with a white outline between the sixth and seventh rays. The Butterfly Blenny can grow as long as 20cm and tapers from the bulbous head to the tail.

LENGTH Up to 20cm
ZONE Lower shore to subtidal
DISTRIBUTION S and W British Isles
SIMILAR SPECIES *Parablennius gattorugine*

Shanny *Lipophrys pholis*

The Shanny is a common blenny found in rockpools around the British Isles, but less commonly on the east coast of England. It has the characteristic blunt head and tapering body shape of a blenny. The dorsal fin runs the length of the body, with a shallow indentation. The species can be green, brown or yellow, and has no tentacles on its head. It is often territorial and stays mostly in the same rockpool, although it does explore other areas. Its eggs encrust the rocks like spherical jewels. The eggs are protected by the male, who oxygenates them by fanning his tail over them.

LENGTH Up to 16cm
ZONE Lower shore
DISTRIBUTION All of British Isles
SIMILAR SPECIES *Coryphoblennius galerita*

Montagu's Sea Snail *Liparis montagui*

This erroneously named sea snail is most commonly seen in the northern reaches of the British Isles. There it can be found on the rocky lower shore, attached to kelps or rocks by a sucker on its lower ventral surface. It has a large bulbous head and upper body, with a tapering, thin tail and the body shape of a large tadpole. A single dorsal fin runs along most of its length, with the tail end being far taller than the anterior end. It can feed on crustaceans and grows to 6cm in length. The eggs of Montagu's Sea Snail are laid in spring and take about one month to hatch.

LENGTH Up to 6cm
ZONE Lower shore
DISTRIBUTION Northern British Isles
SIMILAR SPECIES *Liparis liparis*

Long-spined Sea Scorpion *Taurulus bubalis*

The Long-spined Sea Scorpion can be found all around the rocky shores of the British Isles. It has a visible lateral line that has short spines running along the length of its 18cm-long body, and three spines on the gill cover. It has a broad head and large eyes with two separate dorsal fins, and is well camouflaged, adopting the colours of the rocks and seaweeds. It has an extendible mouth allowing it to eat large fish and other invertebrates, and a fleshy tentacle hanging from its mouth. The species usually lays its orange eggs in early spring.

LENGTH Up to 18cm
ZONE Mid shore to subtidal
DISTRIBUTION All of British Isles
SIMILAR SPECIES *Myoxocephalus scorpius, Scorpaena porcus*

Shore Clingfish   *Lepadogaster purpurea*

The Shore Clingfish can be found all around the south-west of England, Wales and Ireland, often on the lower shore under boulders. This species of clingfish has two distinct blue spots on the dorsal surface close to the eyes at its broadest point. It has a well-adapted sucker, which has evolved from the pelvic fins; the sucker can cling tightly to surfaces. The mouth is shaped like a duck's bill. Shore Clingfish lay their eggs under, and where either the male or female protects the eggs.

LENGTH Up to 8cm

ZONE Lower shore

DISTRIBUTION SW England, Wales and Ireland

SIMILAR SPECIES *Lepadogaster candollei, L. lapadogaster*

Fifteen-spined Stickleback   *Spinachia spinachia*

The Fifteen-spined Stickleback is found in low-tide rockpools and shallow seas around the British Isles. Both Fifteen- and Three-spined Stickleback (*Gasterosteus aculeatus*) can be found in marine and brackish estuarial waters. This species has a long, slender body with usually 15 spines in front of a small dorsal fin, which lies opposite a short pelvic fin. The long tail section ends in a short caudal tail. The stickleback can grow up to 15cm long. The male constructs a nest of seaweeds made with sticky slime produced by his kidneys. Once the eggs are fertilised he protects the nest with his life.

LENGTH Up to 15cm

ZONE Lower shore to subtidal

DISTRIBUTION All of British Isles

SIMILAR SPECIES *Gasterosteus aculeatus*

Worm Pipefish   *Nerophis lumbriciformis*

The Worm Pipefish is most common on the south-west coasts of Britain and Ireland. It can be found under rocks and seaweed on the low tide, but is difficult to see as it so closely resembles a thin strand of brown seaweed. It can grow up to 15cm long and has a long, smooth brown body with only one dorsal fin and no tail, pectoral or anal fins. The pipefish are in the same family as seahorses and have a similar feeding apparatus, using a straw-shaped snout to suck up copepods on which they feed. The female lays her eggs in a groove on the underside of the male. He then fertilises and carries the eggs around.

LENGTH Up to 15cm
ZONE Lower shore
DISTRIBUTION SW Britain and Ireland
SIMILAR SPECIES None

Great Pipefish   *Syngnathus acus*

The Great Pipefish is a large pipefish growing up to 46cm long, which can be found on the south and west coasts of England, Wales and Scotland, and the south and east of Ireland. It has pectoral, dorsal, anal and tail fins, unlike the Worm Pipefish. The snout is twice the length of the head with a bump after the eyes and before the main body. The species has around 60 clearly visible body rings. It feeds on crustaceans and also small fish. The female deposits her eggs in the male's brood pouch, from which the perfectly formed juveniles hatch after five weeks.

LENGTH Up to 46cm
ZONE Lower shore to subtidal
DISTRIBUTION S and W British Isles
SIMILAR SPECIES *Syngnathus typhle,
S. rostellatus*

Nilson's Pipefish   *Syngnathus rostellatus*

Nilson's Pipefish is found in the south and west of the British Isles, on the lower shore and also in estuaries. It has pectoral, anal and tail fins which help it keep position and swim. It is a medium-sized pipefish, measuring up to 17cm long. Nilson's Pipefish has been found to make good use of the floating strandline of detached seaweeds, which it uses as an alternative habitat to the sea bed, thereby increasing its chance of survival. The male carries the fertilised eggs in a brood pouch close to his tail.

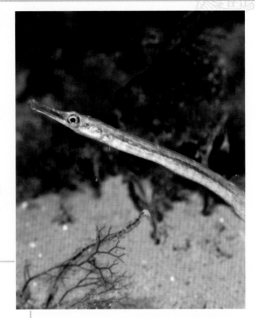

LENGTH Up to 17cm
ZONE Lower shore to subtidal
DISTRIBUTION S and W British Isles
SIMILAR SPECIES *Syngnathus acus*

Short-snouted Seahorse   *Hippocampus hippocampus*

The enigmatic Short-snouted Seahorse is one of only two British seahorse species. It can be found around the south of England and Ireland. The seahorse uses its prehensile tail to hold tight onto seaweed and seagrass. When swimming it flutters its dorsal and pectoral fins to swim upright through the water. The head is at an angle to the body, and the straw-like snout is a third of the length of the head and is used to suck prey from the water. The Short-snouted Seahorse also has two spikes above its eyes. The male seahorse broods the fertilised eggs in his pouch until they are ready to be released.

HEIGHT Up to 13cm high
ZONE Subtidal
DISTRIBUTION S England and Ireland
SIMILAR SPECIES *Hippocampus guttulatus*

Spiny Seahorse   *Hippocampus guttulatus*

The Spiny Seahorse has a wider distribution than the Short-snouted Seahorse, and can be found from the south of England, Ireland and Wales, to as far north as Orkney and Shetland. It has distinctive spine-like protrusions around its head down to its dorsal fin. In both British seahorse species, the male and female undergo an intricate courtship dance, after which the female lays her eggs in the brood pouch of the male, where he fertilises them. After some convulsive bending of his body the perfectly formed miniature seahorses burst out of the pouch.

HEIGHT Up to 18cm
ZONE Subtidal
DISTRIBUTION S England, Ireland and Wales
SIMILAR SPECIES *Hippocampus hippocampus*

Butterfish   *Pholis gunnellus*

The Butterfish is an eel-like fish found all around the British Isles, from the mid shore down to deeper subtidal waters. It has a distinctive long, thin, flattened body with 12 dark circles edged in white running along the length on the upper surface near the dorsal fin. The dorsal fin runs along most of the length of the fish, while the anal fin is approximately half the length and the pelvic fins are barely visible as small rays below the pectoral fins. As its name might suggest, it is very slimy. Unusually for an intertidal fish, both male and female Butterfish guard their developing eggs.

LENGTH Up to 25cm
ZONE Mid shore to subtidal
DISTRIBUTION All of British Isles
SIMILAR SPECIES *Zoarces viviparus*

Lesser Weever Fish *Echiichthys vipera*

The Lesser Weever Fish can be found (and occasionally painfully felt) on sandy beaches all around the British Isles, but most commonly on the south and west coasts. It has a short body, around 14cm long, which is often buried in the sand with only the eyes, which are positioned on the upper surface, protruding from the surface. The Lesser Weever Fish has a dark dorsal fin with spines, and an operculum that also has a spine capable of injecting a poisonous sting. It has a distinctly downturned mouth and a golden, mottled upper surface with a paler ventral, or lower, surface.

LENGTH Up to 14cm
ZONE Lower shore to subtidal
DISTRIBUTION All of British Isles
SIMILAR SPECIES *Trachinus dracho*

Lesser Sandeel *Ammodytes tobianus*

The Lesser Sandeel can occasionally be seen stranded in rockpools or in schools in shallow waters of estuaries and coastal waters around the British Isles. It is a long, silver, eel-like fish with a long dorsal fin running along most of its length, a shorter anal fin, and a forked tail for fast movement to avoid predatory fish such as mackerel and bass. The lower jaw is longer than the upper jaw and has an extendible mouth for feeding on planktonic larvae and eggs. Lesser Sandeels often bury themselves in the sand, and they can be seen swimming in schools, their silver sides catching the light as they swim.

LENGTH Up to 20cm
ZONE Lower shore to subtidal
DISTRIBUTION All of British Isles
SIMILAR SPECIES *Ammodytes marinus, Hyperoplus immaculatus, H. lanceolatus*

Corkwing Wrasse *Crenilabrus melops*

The Corkwing Wrasse can be found all around the British Isles in deep, large pools on the low tide. This wrasse has a characteristic black spot at the base of the tail fin, and a dark marking just behind the eye. It has a single dorsal fin with up to 17 spines and an anal fin that has three spines. The colour of the wrasse varies, with females tending to be brown, while the males are greener when young, maturing to become more reddish-brown with blue lines around the head. The male Corkwing Wrasse builds a nest in which the female lays her eggs, which the male then protects and aerates with his tail.

LENGTH Up to 25cm
ZONE Lower shore to subtidal
DISTRIBUTION All of British Isles
SIMILAR SPECIES *Labrus bergylta, L. mixtus*

Ballan Wrasse *Labrus bergylta*

The Ballan Wrasse is another brightly coloured fish found in the intertidal region on the high tide around the British Isles. It has a similar distribution of spines and rays to that of the Corkwing Wrasse. In the water it can be identified by its size, with the Ballan Wrasse being up to 60cm long, considerably larger than the Corkwing Wrasse. This fish always matures as a female, but can then undergo a sex change to become male. The male makes a small depression in which the female lays her eggs, which are a colourful range of greens, reds and browns.

LENGTH Up to 60cm
ZONE Upper shore to subtidal
DISTRIBUTION All of British Isles
SIMILAR SPECIES *Labrus mixtus,
Crenilabrus melops*

THE STRANDLINE

What is life? –'tis a delicate shell
Thrown up by the eternity's flow,
On time's bank of quicksand to dwell,
And a moment its loveliness show.
Gone back to its element grand,
To the billow that brought it on shore,
See, another is washing the land,
And the beautiful shell is no more!

James Montgomery, *What is Life?* 1828

The strandline is the area just above high tide where man-made and natural objects from the sea are left by the crashing waves and receding tides. The strandline is not a static environment and can be seen to migrate up and down the shore. This is due to the high spring tides and lower neap tides, which result in the location of the strandline migrating several metres up and down the shore over a lunar cycle

The strandline is a treasure chest of marine and human debris, some washed up from local shores and some that has travelled great distances.

The strandline is often made up of piles of seaweeds that become detached during storms and heavy swell. Before landing on a beach, the floating seaweed forms important islands of safety and protection for juvenile fish. Young Lumpsuckers, Five-bearded Rocklings, Nilson's Pipefish and Atlantic Horse Mackerel are all fish that have been observed to benefit from floating seaweeds. They may feed on the small invertebrates found amongst the algae, or use it as protection from prey, as a passive means of transportation and as a reference point for the formation of shoals.

As spring tides turn to neap tides there is little chance of the upper strandline material making its way back to sea until the next spring tide cycle. This gives the strandline a good chance to rot and decay. The warm, rotting seaweeds become ideal habitats for flies to lay their eggs in and are fruity feeding grounds for an array of insects and invertebrates. These in turn become food for other surprising strandline visitors.

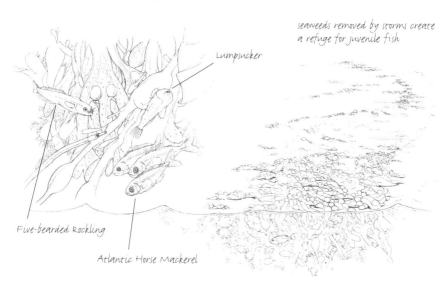

seaweeds removed by storms create a refuge for juvenile fish

Lumpsucker

Five-bearded Rockling

Atlantic Horse Mackerel

Seaweeds loosened into the sea by storms provide floating islands offering protection, breeding and feeding opportunities for juvenile fish. These eventually wash up onto the shore forming the strandline.

The strandline is not a solely marine habitat and is representative of the hazy area where land and sea merge. There are birds, shrews, bats and other small mammals that will head to the shore to feed on the rich buffet of invertebrates. In turn, foxes and otters will also come to the seashore to feed on all that is on offer at the rich, rotting mass of opportunity. The strandline remains a fairly unstudied area of research and may yet prove to be important to the health of the seashore ecosystem in other ways.

The unpleasant smell at the strandline may make some visitors feel that this region is an unnecessary assault on the senses. This can result in mechanical cleaning and removal of this rich and diverse part of the seashore ecology. This removes feeding grounds for small seashore mammals and eliminates the chances of finding marine treasures that may have travelled across the oceans to reach our shores.

The strandline has enormous potential for discovery. Items to be found include anything ranging from historical artefacts, to shells, skeletal remains of marine animals and birds, and modern human artefacts. The strandline has changed over the last few centuries and is an indicator of our impact on the marine environment.

Before the era of plastic, glass bottles and wooden pieces of ships and various cargo frequently washed up on our shores. These are now more commonly replaced with plastics and human-derived waste and litter. The persistence of plastics poses an inherent risk to marine wildlife. It also has the potential impact on the coastal economy from any associated loss in tourism. Plastics may have pollutants adhered to their surfaces, which once ingested by marine creatures, may work up the food chain and in turn affect our health too.

However, some beautiful and fascinating marine-related objects that can be found on every daily tidal cycle. The strandline demonstrates what can be found living around the immediate seashore, and the power of winds, currents and tides to carry flotsam and jetsam for thousands of kilometres. Some species that usually follow oceanic currents occasionally get blown ashore, such as the Portuguese Man o'War (*Physalia physalis*), the By-the-wind Sailor (*Velella velella*) and rather alien-looking Sea Gooseberries (*Pleurobrachia pileus*).

When exploring the strandline it is worth visiting different areas of it. A very high spring tide strandline might be host to lighter, smaller objects, such as mermaid's tears, compared with a lower neap strandline. If you look carefully you may even discover that the two halves of bivalve shells that have been drilled by a predatory whelk will have been deposited at opposite ends of the beach due to the hydrodynamics of the drilled shells.

The probability of discovering unusual and foreign, historical and modern, natural and man-made objects is vast. The chances of finding them are increased if you aim to be the first to wander the receding strandline. It is best to protect yourself by wearing gloves, and you should avoid handling any unsanitary or sharp objects. Time spent scouring the strandline also provides a good opportunity to collect and remove any human-derived plastic waste, so take a spare bag with you and discard rubbish safely after your visit. You can also join or organise beach cleans set up by local community groups or charitable organisations.

Sometimes the sea deposits unusual finds like this log covered in Common Goose Barnacles (*Lepas anatifera*).

By-the-wind Sailor   *Velella velella*

As its name suggests, the By-the-wind Sailor is an ocean drifter carried by oceanic wind and swell. This small blue disc floats on the surface of the sea. The tentacles hang from the disc, and there is a sail on the upper surface. Depending on the individual the sail can face in one of two directions, so that it will blow either left or right of the prevailing winds. Although more commonly found in warmer seas and oceans, this species can get blown onto our shores in vast numbers, often turning the strandline blue because of its vivid blue colour.

DIAMETER Up to 10cm, usually 3cm
ZONE Strandline
DISTRIBUTION Mostly S British Isles
SIMILAR SPECIES *Physalia physalis*

Mermaid's purse

A mermaid's purse is a dark, leathery-looking egg case with long tendrils running from the corners of a square or rectangular case. It can vary in shape, size and length depending on which shark or ray it comes from. Small, rectangular capsules are from Lesser Spotted Catsharks (previously named dogfish). Squarer capsules are from rays. Inside the case life begins with a very large yolk and a small embryonic shark or ray. The embryo feeds on the yolk, growing in the safety of the case. The developed juvenile then breaks free from one end of the egg case.

LENGTH Varied
ZONE Strandline
DISTRIBUTION All of British Isles
SIMILAR SPECIES Different species of catshark and ray produce different cases.

Cuttlefish bone

The delicate white bones of cuttlefish can often be found washed up on the strandline and onto our shores. A cuttlefish bone is in fact the internal structure of a cuttlefish, which helps it control its buoyancy. Examining the internal structure of the bone you can see that there are small chambers within. These fill with gas or water, allowing the cuttlefish to rise or sink in the water column. This chambered quality of the bone makes it an ideal material for silversmiths to use to make casts for jewellery. Its high levels of calcium also make it a great source of minerals for pet birds, snails and reptiles.

LENGTH Up to 15cm
ZONE Strandline
DISTRIBUTION All of British Isles
SIMILAR SPECIES None

Sea wash ball

This white or cream ball, which looks like bubble-wrap packaging, is often found on the strandline. It consists of the egg capsules of the Common Whelk. The eggs are laid on structures in the winter months and from each sac minute whelks hatch. The young whelks are cannibalistic, eating their siblings in the capsule. Once the whelks have hatched the sea wash balls break away, and are washed from their attached positions and tossed onto the shore. They can be seen attached to jetties on low tides during the winter months, as well as empty on the strandline. In times gone by sailors would used the balls to wash themselves.

DIAMETER up to 20cm
ZONE Strandline
DISTRIBUTION All of British Isles
SIMILAR SPECIES None

Sea Gooseberries *Pleurobracchia pileus*

Sea Gooseberries look like clear pearls of jelly and are about 2cm across. They can be washed up onto our shores in large numbers. They are in fact ctenophores, or comb jellies, which when viewed closely can be seen to have two long tentacles that they use to feed. They will capture planktonic copepods, for example, and bring the food to the mouth from their tentacles. They also have hundreds of hair-like structures called cilia, which are used for locomotion. When in water, the cilia catch the light and a rainbow of colours oscillates along their length.

DIAMETER Up to 2.5cm
ZONE Strandline
DISTRIBUTION All of British Isles
SIMILAR SPECIES None

Mermaid's tears

Mermaid's tear (or nurdles or plastic pellets, as they are also known) are of human origin. They appear as small, spherical eggs and can be mistaken as such by feeding birds or fish. Plastic is transported in the form of nurdles before it is melted and moulded into our recognisable everyday objects. They can be found on every beach on the strandline around the world, having leaked from factories and during transportation, and make their way into waterways and seas. They absorb pollutants on to their surface, and they have the potential to be absorbed into the flesh of animals that consume them.

DIAMETER Approximately 3mm
ZONE Strandline
DISTRIBUTION All of British Isles
SIMILAR SPECIES None

Heart Urchin test *Echinocardium cordatum*

The Heart Urchin test can be found denuded of its spines, leaving a pale, brittle, papery, heart-shaped test. The mouth or aperture can be seen on the underside of the test, and on the top surface the star shape indicating where the tube feet would have once extended is visible. If the spines are still attached, they will be facing mostly in one direction. The Heart Urchin is normally found buried just below the surface on sandy beaches. However, on low tides you may find a Heart Urchin that has been washed out of the sand by waves or storms.

DIAMETER Up to 6cm
ZONE Strandline
DISTRIBUTION All of British Isles
SIMILAR SPECIES None

Common Goose Barnacle *Lepas anatifera*

Sometimes the currents and tides deposit these unusual drifters onto our shores, usually around the south-west coast of the British Isles. The Goose Barnacle grows attached to any floating object, whether that be a log or a plastic bottle. It has a long neck that attaches to the floating object, and an egg-shaped, white 'capitulum'. From this structure a branched 'foot' extends to filter food from the water. Historically the Goose Barnacle was thought to be the egg of the Barnacle Goose as this species was never seen to lay eggs.

LENGTH Up to 60cm (including stalk)
ZONE Strandline
DISTRIBUTION W and S coasts of British Isles
SIMILAR SPECIES *Dosima fascicularis, Pollicipes pollicipes, Scalpellum scalpellum*

Buoy Barnacle   *Dosima fascicularis*

The Buoy Barnacle is named after its ability to float like a buoy on the surface of the sea, although it may be found attached to objects as a juvenile. From a gland this crustacean secretes a cement that is very light and similar to polystyrene in texture. The Buoy Barnacle is able to then float with its curled feet hanging down from its flotation device to collect food. In this way it can float on the currents, feeding as it travels. The Buoy Barnacle can also aggregate with other individuals, creating a raft of a few individuals stuck together.

LENGTH Up to 6cm
ZONE Strandline
DISTRIBUTION W and S coasts of British Isles
SIMILAR SPECIES *Lepas anatifera, Pollicipes pollicipes, Scalpellum scalpellum*

Bollan Cross

The Bollan Cross is an unusual but exciting find for the superstitious. It is a T-shaped piece of flattened bone, with rounded molar teeth covering one surface. It is in fact the pharyngeal teeth of the Ballan Wrasse. The Bollan Cross is boiled and worn as a good-luck talisman by seafarers, particularly on the Isle of Man. The 'cross' is positioned in the throat of the Ballan Wrasse to help it crush the crustaceans and molluscs it feeds on. If you find a Bollan Cross be sure to keep it in a safe place – according to Celtic tradition if you do so it is thought that 'you'll never lose your way'.

DIAMETER Up to 7cm
ZONE Strandline
DISTRIBUTION All of British Isles
SIMILAR SPECIES None

Sea Fan   *Eunicella verrucosa*

Sea Fans are found in deep water, attached to the sea bed, where the colony of miniature anemone-like polyps feeds on passing food. When washed up onto the shore they look like small trees, but while still alive the polyps emerge to feed and they are clearly animals. Mostly they grow very slowly, only about 10mm per year, so are very vulnerable to damage. They often become entangled in fishing lines, so are removed from the sea floor. Once this happens, it is very difficult for them to recolonise. The Pink Sea Fan is listed as a nationally important feature.

DIAMETER Up to 100cm (often less)
ZONE Strandline
DISTRIBUTION All of British Isles
SIMILAR SPECIES None

Sea beans

Sea beans are the seeds and fruit of trees and vines that have made their way from tropical locations on to British shores. Air can be trapped inside the hard casing of a sea bean, which helps it to travel hundreds of miles across the seas and oceans. The Hamburger Sea Bean (illustrated in the photograph) is from the Macuna vine found in Africa and South America, and travels to the British coast by oceanic currents. It is a hallucinogenic and toxic bean, which was historically carried by sailors as a good-luck talisman.

DIAMETER Varies
ZONE Strandline
DISTRIBUTION W and S British Isles
SIMILAR SPECIES None

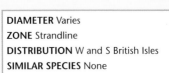

Squid eggs

Despite looking like an abandoned gelatinous wig of dreadlocked hair, or perhaps a string mop, this curious discovery is in fact a collection of squid eggs. They are likely to have been laid on kelps or seaweeds by the Common Squid (*Loligo vulgaris*). The eggs are laid (most commonly) in summer and autumn, with females laying up to 20,000 eggs within each of the gelatinous tubes. A small but perfectly formed squid hatches approximately one month later from each egg. At times the eggs are dislodged from the kelps on which they were laid, and wash up onto shores to baffle many a seashore explorer.

DIAMETER OF MASS Up to 30cm
ZONE Strandline
DISTRIBUTION All of British Isles
SIMILAR SPECIES None

Cetaceans

Sadly there are times when dolphins and whales get stranded on our shores. On page 28 there is information on what to do should you discover a stranding. Cetaceans can be washed up for many reasons, for example as a result of natural causes, starvation or illness, or due to collision with vessels or entanglement in fishing nets. If a dead stranding is found it is important to report it quickly as this offers the best chance of identifying the cause of death, thereby increasing our understanding of the health of the population. Occasionally cetaceans are stranded alive and, with expert help, may be shepherded back to the sea.

SIZE Various
ZONE Strandline
DISTRIBUTION All of British Isles
SIMILAR SPECIES None

Glossary

Acrorhagi The ring of wart-like bumps at the top of the column and below the tentacles of a sea anemone.

Aesthetes The simple photoreceptive eye of chitons.

Alginate A thick gum produced by brown seaweeds which keeps a seaweed supple and is important commercially for foods and beauty products.

Ambulacral groove The groove that runs along the length of the arm from the centre of a starfish to the tip.

Ancestrula The first zooid of a bryozoan to settle, from which a colony develops.

Antennule A small antenna – especially of crustaceans.

Anthozoa The class of cnidarian that includes the sea anemones and corals.

Aperture A hole or opening, for example in a gastropod.

Apex The tip or uppermost point of the spire or shell of an urchin or gastropod.

Aristotle's lantern The dental apparatus of the sea urchins.

Ascidian A term for sea squirts or tunicates.

Asexual Being able to reproduce without another individual's genetic material.

Asteroidea The name of the class for starfish.

Athecate A form of bryozoan that always has a polyp stage without a protective perisarc.

Avicularum An individual zooid that is capable of cleaning a bryozoan.

Ballast water The water carried by ships to maintain balance.

Berried A term used to describe a female crab or lobster with eggs under the abdomen.

Biradial symmetry A symmetry that creates a mirror image down one plane.

Biodiversity The variation of all life forms on the planet or within a smaller ecosystem or habitat.

Bivalve A mollusc that has two valves, as in the cockles, oysters and clams.

Bladders The swollen air bubbles in some seaweeds, which help keep them upright to maximise their exposure to sunlight.

Blade The flattened leaf-like area of a seaweed.

Bloom Term used to describe plankton blooms in nutrient-rich waters, where plankton multiply rapidly and have a high density.

Boreal/boreo-arctic species Species that originate in the cooler, northern boreo-arctic regions.

Bryozoans Colonies of zooid invertebrates such as Sea Mats.

Barbel A whisker-like sensory tendril around the mouth of a fish.

Byssus The threads of mussels, used as an anchor to each other and the substrate.

Capitulum The white shell-like part on the end of the crustacean Goose Barnacle.

Carapace The upper section of the shell covering the body of a crab, lobster or turtle.

Cephalopods The marine molluscs that include squid, octopus, cuttlefish and nautilus.

Cerata The tentacle-like structure of the sea slugs, which can regenerate the stings of the anemones on which sea slugs feed.

Cetacean Of the order Cetacea, which comprises whales, dolphins and porpoises.

Chela The pincer-like claw of a crustacean.

Choanocyte A cell that lines the structure of and draws water into a sponge.

Chlorophyta The green algae or seaweeds, such as the Sea Lettuce.

Circadian rhythm A natural rhythm that follows a 24-hour cycle.

Cloaca An opening for the evacuation of waste; also sometimes used in reproduction (e.g. birds).

Cnidocyte The cell used by cnidarians to sting predators or prey.

Colony An interconnected group of polyps or individual zooids that live together as one.

Crustaceans A group of arthropods that includes lobsters, crabs, barnacles and amphipods.

Cyprid A stage of the barnacle metamorphosis.

Dessication The state of drying out.

Dichotomous Where the axis is divided into two.

Dorsal area The upper or back surface of an organism.

Dorso-ventrally From the back to the belly of an organism.

Echinodermata The phylum of marine animals that includes starfish, sea urchins, sea cucumbers and brittlestars.

Ecology The relationship of living organisms with their environment and each other.

Ecosystem A living community of organisms sharing an environment. This can be on the scale of a rockpool or of the global ecosystem.

Effluent An outflow of water (or gas) from man-made sources.

Ephyra The first swimming stage of a medusa in the life cycle of a jellyfish.

Epifaunal Fauna that live on the substrate, such as anemones on rocks.

Epiphyte An organism that lives on another.

Eulittoral The mid part of the shore between high and low tide.

Eutrophication A state where water bodies receive excess nutrients from agriculture, which cause excess growth of algae and jellyfish.

Exhalant siphon An organ that is used for the exhalation of water, such as the siphon of a mollusc.

Exoskeleton The external skeleton that protects and supports the body, such as a crab's.

Exposed shore A shore unprotected from aggressive winds, currents and swells.

Foreshore The area between the high and low tides, also known as the intertidal zone.

Frond A leaf-like blade of a seaweed.

Galathidae The family name for squat lobsters.

Gamete A mature haploid cell that fuses with another of the opposite sex during fertilisation, such as the sperm and egg.

Gastropoda The class within the molluscan phylum that includes the sea snails and sea slugs.

Gastrovascular Having both digestive and circulatory functions.

Gastrozooid The feeding zooids of a bryozoan.

Gonotheca A capsule on athecate hydroids which contains the reproductive structures.

Gonozooids A zooid containing a gonad.

Gorgonacea An order of cnidarian that includes sea fans.

Hermaphrodite An organism that has both male and female reproductive organs.

High tide The point where the tidal cycle has reached its uppermost point on the seashore.

Holdfast The structure that acts as the point of attachment for seaweeds.

Holothuroidea The class of echinoderm also referred to as sea cucumbers.

Hydranth A feeding zooid in a hydroid colony.

Hydrozoa A class of cnidarian – colonies of polyps, including the Portuguese Man o'War and the bryozoans.

Inhalant The opening structure of a sponge or mollusc used to draw water and nutrients into the organism.

Intertidal The zone between the high- and low-tide marks on the seashore.

Invasive Term used to describe non-native species that have a negative effect on an economy or environment.

Invertebrate Lacking a backbone or spinal column.

Iridescent The property of a surface to reflect light, appearing to illuminate and change colour.

Isomorphic To be of identical or similar shape or structure.

Laminaria Genus of brown algae commonly called kelp.

Lobule A small, rounded lobe-like structure.

Lophophore The feeding apparatus or tentacles of bryozoans.

Low tide The lowest point of the tide on the seashore within a tidal cycle.

Lusitanian species Warm water southern species at their most northerly limit in the British Isles.

Macroalgae Algae or seaweeds that are visible without the use of a microscope.

Macroscopic Large enough to be seen with the naked eye.

Madreporite An opening valve in the echinoderms that lets in water for their vascular systems.

Maxillae Modified limbs that work as a pair of accessory jaws.

Medusa The swimming stage of cnidarians or another term for jellyfish.

Megalopa The final larval stage of decapod crustaceans, such as crabs, lobsters, shrimps and prawns.

Meiosis A cellular division which produces half the genetic material of the parent cells, resulting in gametes or eggs and sperm.

Mesoglaea The jelly-like substance that fills jellyfish and other cnidarians.

Midrib The central vein of a seaweed blade.

Mid shore The central zone between the high and low tides.

Morphology The form and structure of an organism's specific features.

Nacreous layer The lower layer of a mollusc shell, also known as mother-of-pearl.

Native species A species that is naturally present in a given area, with no human intervention.

Nauplius The free-swimming first stage of crustacean larvae which use appendages on the head for swimming.

Naupliar Of or pertaining to the nauplius stage.

Naturalised species A non-native organism that, over time, can thrive in an ecosystem that differs from its place of origin.

Neap tides Weak tides at the quarter-moon phases of *high* low tides and *low* high tides.

Nematocysts The stinging cells used by cnidarians for defence and predation.

Nemertea The phylum of ribbon worms or proboscis worms.

Nephropidae The family of crustaceans also known as lobsters.

Non-native species A species living outside its native geographical range.

Nudibranchia A sub-order of the marine molluscs, also called sea slugs.

Ocean acidification The increase in the acidity of the ocean as a result of excessive production of carbon dioxide from the burning of fossil fuels.

Ocellus (plural **ocelli**) The relatively complex eye of some chitons, which includes a lens and retina cells.

Ochrophyta The group of seaweeds also known as brown seaweeds.

Operculum A small lid-like structure on gastropods and other species to protect vulnerable body parts and openings.

Ophiuridae The family of echinoderms better known as brittlestars.

Ostia The opening pores of a sponge.

Ormering The tightly controlled process of gathering Ormer in the Channel Islands.

Oscula A large opening of a sponge which excretes water and waste material.

Ovigers or **ovigerous legs** A pair of appendages in the pycnoginids that carry egg masses and are used for cleaning.

Pallial Of or pertaining to the mantle of a mollusc.

Pallial groove The region where the gills are found in (for example) chitons.

Palp A sensory appendage in annelid worms, crustaceans and pycnogonids.

Parapodia The pairs of paddle-like extensions from the sections of polychaete worms.

Pedal disk The large sucker-like attachment of an anemone.

Pedicellariae Pincer-like structures on the uppermost surfaces of echinoderms.

Pelagic Living in open oceans or seas close to neither the bottom or the shore by drifting (planktonic) or swimming (nektonic).

Pereopod A leg or appendage from the thorax.

Periostracum Outer thinner layer of shell of a mollusc produced by the mantle.

Perisarc An outer protective layer of certain hydrozoans.

Pharynx The section of the digestive system that extends from the back of the mouth to the larynx.

Photosynthesis Process of harnessing the sun's energy to split carbon dioxide and combine with water molecules to make glucose and oxygen.

Phylum A taxonomic rank below kingdom and above class.

Phytoplankton Marine algae that photosynthesise producing approximately half of our atmospheric oxygen.

Planula larva An oval larva of the cnidarians.

Platyhelminthes The phylum of flatworms.

Pleopoda Appendages on the abdomen used for swimming and/or copulation.

Polyclaphora The chitons.

Polyp A cup-like form of cnidarian, which includes anemones and corals, or stages within the life cycle of other cnidarians.

Porifera The phylum also known as sea sponges.

Priapulida A phylum of marine worms, also called penis worms.

Pulmonates The molluscan group of sea snails and sea slugs.

Pycnogonida The class of sea spiders.

Pyloric stomach A part of the stomach connected to the small intestine.

Radula A specialised tongue-like structure of a mollusc used to rasp algae off rocks.

Receptacle The expanded reproductive part of a seaweed.

Rhinophores The pair of tentacles on the heads of nudibranchs.

Rostrum An extension of the carapace in shrimps, crabs and lobsters.

Scyphozoa The class of cnidarian jellyfish.

Sessile Permanently attached and immobile.

Sheltered shore A shoreline protected from aggressive winds, currents and swell.

Siphonophore A colony of hydroids, such as the Portuguese Man o'War.

Sinistral Of or facing the left side (the opposite of dextral), e.g. a sinistral mollusc shell has its aperture on the left-hand side.

Spring tide The point in the lunar tide when the moon is full or new and the tide has very *low* low tides and *high* high tides.

Spermatophore A package containing sperm.

Stipe The main stem-like stalk of a seaweed.

Stolon A tube-like structure in a bryozoan.

Strombus A genus of conch shells.

Subtidal Below the tidal regions of the seashore.

Sublittoral The regions of the shore that are only exposed on the low spring tides.

Substrate A surface on which a species grows or to which it is attached.

Test The fused skeletal plates of a sea urchin.

Thecate A type of bryozoan that has a cup-like theca into which the polyp can withdraw.

Transect A path or line that is used to record the occurrence of species or objects.

Tube feet or **podia** The small hydrostatic locomotory and feeding appendages of echinoderms.

Umbilicalis In gastropods this is a hollow tube at the centre of the spiral of the shell which runs to the apex.

Uropods The appendages on the last sections of the abdomens of crustaceans.

Ventral area In most species the side facing downwards. In bivalves it is the side farthest from the hinge.

Vertebrate Having a backbone or spinal column.

Vibraculum In some bryozoans this whip-like zooid keeps the bryozoan clean of settling organisms.

Whorl One complete spiral on a shell. The first whorl is situated at the apex and the last (the body whorl) at the aperture.

Zoea (plural **zoeae**) The larval stage of a crustacean larva characterised by appendages on its thoracic region for swimming.

Zooid A single individual of a bryozoan colony.

Zooplankton Plankton that consists of small animals and the immature stages of larger animals.

Further reading

This book is a starting point on your journey to understanding the marine world. Here are some complementary books that might also enhance and advance your knowledge of all things marine and coastal. I would also urge you to look to some of the historical seashore guides and marine-related books that are often found in secondhand bookshops, for some inspirational and historical perspectives of the seashore and our marine and coastal environment.

Barnes, R. S. K. and Hughes, R. N. 1999. *An Introduction to Marine Ecology* (3rd edn). Blackwell Science, Oxford.

Barnes, R. S. K., Calow, P., Olive, P. J. W, Golding, D. W. and Spicer, J. J. 2001. *The Invertebrates: a Synthesis* (3rd edn). Blackwell Science, Oxford.

Bunker, F. D., Maggs, C. A, Brodie, J. A and Bunker, A. R. 2012. *Seaweeds of Britain and Ireland*. Wild Nature Press, Plymouth.

Clarke, R. B. 2001. *Marine Pollution* (5th edn). Oxford University Press, Oxford.

Eilperin, J. 2012. *Demon Fish: Travels Through the Hidden World of Sharks*. Duckworth, London.

Fish, J. D. and Fish, S. 2011. *A Student's Guide to the Seashore* (3rd edn). Cambridge University Press, Cambridge.

Hayward, P. J. and Ryland, J. S. 1995. *Handbook of the Marine Fauna of North-West Europe*. Oxford University Press, Oxford.

Karleskint, G. 1998. *Introduction to Marine Biology*. Saunders College Publishing, Philadelphia.

Kirby, R. R. 2010. *Ocean Drifters: A Secret World Beneath the Waves*. Studio Cactus Books, London.

Little, C. and Kitching, J. A. 1996. *The Biology of Rocky Shores*. Oxford University Press, Oxford.

Lobban, C. S. and Harrison, P. J. 1994. *Seaweed Ecology and Physiology*. Cambridge University Press, Cambridge.

Naylor, P. 2003. *Great British Marine Animals*. Sound Diving Publications.

Porter, J. S. 2012. *Seasearch Guide to Bryozoans and Hydroids*. Marine Conservation Society, Ross-on-Wye.

Raffaelli, D. and Hawkins, S. 1996. *Intertidal Ecology*. Kluwer Academic Publisher, London.

Roberts, C. 2007. *The Unnatural History of the Sea: The Past and Future of Humanity and Fishing*. Gaia Books Ltd, London.

Roberts, C. 2012. *The Ocean of Life: The Fate of Man and the Sea*. Viking Books, London.

Shirihai, H. and Jarrett, B. 2006. *Whales, Dolphins and Seals: A Field Guide to the Marine Mammals of the World*. A & C Black, London.

Wood, C. 2005. *Seasearch Guide to Sea Anemones and Corals of Britain and Ireland*. Marine Conservation Society, Ross-on-Wye.

Useful websites

These offer an additional source of inspiration for and knowledge of our marine world.

Algaebase .... www.algaebase.org
Database of algae including the marine seaweeds.

British Divers Marine Life Rescue .... www.bdmlr.org.uk
International marine animal rescue organisation.

Basking Sharks .... www.baskingsharks.org
Information on distribution, research, sightings and guidelines around Basking Sharks and other shark species.

Inshore Fisheries and Conservation Authorities ... www.defra.gov.uk/environment/marine/wwo/ifca
Regional fisheries and management of inshore waters.

Irish Whale and Dolphin Group .... www.iwdg.ie
Irish whale and dolphin news, sightings, research and conservation.

Learn To Sea .... www.learntosea.co.uk
Marine education in South Devon.

Marine Biological Association .... www.mba.ac.uk
Scientific research, education and conservation.

Marine Conservation Society .... www.mcsuk.org
Marine conservation, beach cleans, sustainable fish guides and sightings.

Marine Life Information Network .... www.marlin.ac.uk
Information for marine environmental management, protection and education.

Marine Management Organisation .... www.marinemanagement.org.uk
Marine planning, legislation and licences.

National Lobster Hatchery .... www.nationallobsterhatchery.co.uk
Promoting sustainability of fisheries and aquaculture, particularly lobsters.

Scottish Strandings .... www.strandings.org
Scottish marine animal stranding scheme

Sea-changers .... www.sea-changers.org.uk
Marine conservation and protection.

Seasearch .... www.seasearch.co.uk
Reporting scheme for British divers for marine habitats and species.

Seawatch Foundation www.seawatchfoundation.org.uk
National charity for dolphin and whale conservation.

Shark Trust .... www.sharktrust.org
Information on shark conservation, sightings and science.

Sir Alister Hardy Foundation of Science .... www.sahfos.ac.uk
Plankton monitoring science and research.

The Great Eggcase Hunt Project .... **www.eggcase.org**
Information and reporting of mermaid's purses/shark egg cases.

The Royal Society for the Protection of Birds **www.rspb.org.uk/ourwork/policy/marine**
The RSPB works to save threatened birds and wildlife across the UK and overseas.
Information on its marine and coastal policies can be found here.

UK Cetacean Strandings .... **www.ukstrandings.org**
Reports and research on cetacean, Basking Shark and turtle strandings.

Whale and Dolphin Conservation Society **www.wdcs.org**
Worldwide conservation of whales and dolphins, including guidelines, reports and news.

Welsh Strandings .... **www.strandings.com/wales.html**
Information on Welsh strandings of cetaceans and turtles.

WiSE Scheme .... **www.wisecheme.org**
Training, accreditation and guidelines for marine wildlife operators.

World Register of Marine Species .... **www.marinespecies.org**
International database of marine species and their synonyms.

Author acknowledgements

First of all, I would like to thank the many marine scientists and natural philosophers, young and old, who have inspired me during and before the writing of this book. The efforts of these individuals to help generate a better understanding of our marine environments should not be underestimated or undervalued.

I would like to thank my University of Plymouth lecturers and friends who further sparked my enthusiasm in marine sciences. They have continued to be very helpful throughout my working career. I would also like to thank individual marine scientists who have been incredibly helpful, providing information and support. They include Dr Ceri Lewis, Dr Emma Sheehan, Dr Stacey DeAmicis, Dr Alex White, Dr Alex Ford, Dr Jennifer Loxton, Dr Joanne Porter, Dr David Wilcockson and Dominic Boothroyd of the Lobster Hatchery. I would also like to thank the Marine Biological Association for its continued help and support. Its library of books, both new and old, is a constant inspiration, and the existing and previous staff at the Marine Biological Association are exceedingly helpful and kind – Dr Gerald Boalch and Linda Noble, their librarian, being great examples.

I would not have written this book had it not been for the power of Twitter and the sharing of comical rude scientific names with Bloomsbury's commissioning editors Jim Martin and Julie Bailey. Thanks to Jim and Julie for allowing me this opportunity to become better acquainted with the seashore. Thanks also to the RSPB for endorsing the book, to the illustrator Marc Dando and designer Julie Dando, and to all who have provided photographs for the book.

Finally, I would like to thank my friends, the inspiring marine educators I met on Midway atoll PA'A and my family. Thanks go to my mother for her lifelong support, and to my husband and daughter for their endless patience while I was writing this book and for allowing me my marine obsession. This book is for you, Niamh – you are my finest and most perfect inspiration.

Index

A

Acanthochitona crinita 111
Acorn Barnacle 148
Actinia equina 81
    fragacea 81
Actinothoe sphyrodeta 84
Aeolidia papillosa 130
Alaria esculenta 48
Alcyonium digitatum 88
Alpheus macrocheles 159
Alyconidium diaphanum 178
Ammodytes tobianus 217
Anemonia viridis 82
Angulus tenuis 138
Anomia ephippium 136
Aphrodita aculeata 99
Aplysia punctata 129
Aporrhais pespelecani 126
Archidoris pseudoargus 130
Arctic Cowrie 122
Arenicola marina 100
Ascophyllum nodosum 46
Asparagopsis armata 62
Asterias rubens 186
Asterina gibbosa 185
    phylactica 185
Astropecten irregularis 188
Atrina fragilis 141
Aulactinia verrucosa 82
Aurelia aurita 95

B

Baked Bean Sea Squirt 203
Balanophyllia regia 88
Balanus perforatus 149
Ballan Wrasse 218
Banded Wedge Shell 139
Batters 57
Beadlet Anemone 81
Bispira volutacornis 103
Bittium reticulatum 125
Black Brittlestar 191
Black-footed Limpet 118
Bladder Wrack 45
Blennius ocellaris 211
Bloody Henry 187
Blue-rayed Limpet 120
Blunt Gaper Clam 141

Bollan Cross 226
Bootlace 49
Bootlace Worm 104
Boring Sponge 75
Botryllus schlosseri 202
Breadcrumb Sponge 73
Broad-clawed Porcelain Crab 166
Brown Shrimp 158
Buccinum undatum 128
Buoy Barnacle 226
Butterfish 216
Butterfly Blenny 211
By-the-wind Sailor 222

C

Calliostoma zizyphinum 117
Callophyllis laciniata 56
Cancer pagurus 166
Candy Striped Worm 104
Carcinus maenas 164
Carrageen 55
Caryophyllia smithii 87
Celtic Sea Slug 131
Cerastoderma edule 137
cetaceans 228
Chamelea gallina 138
Chameleon Prawn 157
Channelled Wrack 44
Chinese Mitten Crab 169
Chondrus crispus 55
Chorda filum 49
Chrysaora hysoscella 95
Chthamalus montagui 148
Ciliata mustela 208
Ciocalypta penicillus 74
Ciona intestinalis 203
Cladophora rupestris 66
Clavelina lepadiformis 202
Cliona celata 75
Codium tomentosum 66
Colpomenia peregrina 52
Common Brittlestar 191
Common Cockle 137
Common Goby 209
Common Goose Barnacle 225
Common Limpet 118
Common Lobster 172
Common Mussel 135

Common Otter Shell 139
Common Pelican's Foot 126
Common Periwinkle 123
Common Piddock 140
Common Prawn 157
Common Starfish 186
Common Sunstar 187
Common Tortoiseshell Limpet 119
Common Wentletrap 125
Common Whelk 128
Compass Jellyfish 95
Coral Weed 61
Corkwing Wrasse 218
Corralina officinalis 61
Corynactis viridis 83
Coryphella browni 131
Coryphoblennius galerita 210
Corystes cassivelaunus 165
Cotton Spinner 199
Crangon crangon 158
Crassostrea gigas 136
Crenilabrus melops 218
Crepidula fornicata 127
Crossaster papposus 187
Cushion Star 185
cuttlefish bone 223
Cuvie 50
Cystoseira tamariscifolia 47

D

Dabberlocks 48
Dahlia Anemone 83
Dead Man's Fingers 88
Delesseria sanguinea 57
Dendrodoa grossularia 203
Devonshire Cup Coral 87
Didemnum vexillum 204
Dilsea carnosa 58
Diodora graeca 119
Dog Whelk 127
Donax vittatus 139
Dosima fascicularis 226
Drachiella spectabilis 56
Dulse 58
Dynamena pumila 91

E

Echiichthys vipera 217

Echinocardium cordatum 196, 225
Echinus esculentus 195
Edible Crab 166
Edible Sea Urchin 195
Egg Wrack 46
Electra pilosa 178
Ensis ensis 140
Epitonium clathrus 125
Eriocheir sinensis 169
Estuary Ragworm 99
Eulalia clavigera 100
Eunicella verrucosa 227
Euspira catena 124

F

Fan Mussel 141
Fan Weed 56
Fifteen-spined Stickleback 213
Five-bearded Rockling 208
Flat Periwinkle 124
Flat Top Shell 116
Flustra foliacea 179
Fried Egg Anemone 84
Fucus serratus 45
    spiralis 44
    vesiculosus 45
Furbellows 50

G

Gaidropsarus mediterraneus 208
Galathea squamifera 172
Gem Anemone 82
Gibbula cineraria 117
    umbilicalis 116
Gobius paganellus 209
Golfball Sponge 74
Goose-necked Barnacle 149
Grantia compressa 73
Great Pipefish 214
Great Scallop 137
Green Leaf Worm 100
Green Ormer 120
Green Sea Urchin 195
Grey Chiton 111
Grey Sea Slug 130
Grey Top Shell 117
Gutweed 65

H

Hairy Crab 168
Halichondria panicea 73
Halidrys siliquosa 46
Haliotis tuberculata 120

Harpoon Weed 62
Heart Urchin 196
Heart Urchin test 225
Hediste diversicolor 99
Henricia oculata 187
Hermit Crab 164
Heterosiphonia plumosa 60
Himanthalia elongata 47
Hippocampus guttulatus 216
    hippocampus 215
Hippolyte varians 157
Holothuria forskali 199
Homarus gammarus 172
Honeycomb Worm 103
Hornwrack 179

I

Irish Moss 55

J

Janthina janthina 126
Jewel Anemone 83

K

Keel Worm 101
Keyhole Limpet 119
Knotted Wrack 46

L

Labrus bergylta 218
Laminaria digitata 49
    hyberborea 50
Lanice chonchilega 102
Leathery Sea Squirt 204
Lepadogaster purpurea 213
Lepas anatifera 225
Lepidochitona cinerea 111
Leptopsammia pruvoti 87
Lesser Sandeel 217
Lesser Weever Fish 217
Light Bulb Sea Squirt 202
Ligia oceanica 153
Lineus longissimus 104
Liparis montagui 212
Lipophrys pholis 211
Lithophyllum incrustans 62
Littorina littorea 123
    obtusata 124
    saxatilis 123
Long-clawed Porcelain Crab 167
Long-spined Sea Scorpion 212
Lugworm 100

Luidia ciliaris 188
Lutraria lutraria 139

M

Maerl 61
Maja squinado 169
Mantis Shrimp 159
Marsh Samphire 69
Masked Crab 165
Marthasterias glacialis 186
Melarhaphe neritoides 122
mermaid's purse 222
mermaid's tears 224
Metridium senile 84
Montagu's Barnacle 148
Montagu's Blenny 210
Montagu's Crab 167
Montagu's Sea Snail 212
Moon Jellyfish 95
Mya truncata 141
Mytilus edulis 135

N

Nassarius reticulatus 128
Native Oyster 135
Necklace Shell 124
Necora puber 165
Needle Whelk 125
Nerophis lumbriciformis 214
Netted Dog Whelk 128
Nilson's Pipefish 215
Nucella lapillus 127
Nymphon gracile 175

O

Oarweed 49
Obelia longissima 92
Ocenebra erinacea 129
Onchidella celtica 131
Ophiocomina nigra 191
Ophiothrix fragilis 191
Oscarella lobularis 75
Osilinus lineatus 116
Osmundea pinnatifida 55
Ostrea edulis 135
Oyster Drill 129
Oyster Thief 52

P

Pacific Oyster 136
Padina pavonica 52
Pagurus bernhardus 164
Painted Top Shell 117

Paint Weed 62
Palaemon serratus 157
Palmaria palmata 58
Parablennius gattorugine 210
Paracentrotus lividus 196
Patella depressa 118
     pellucidum 120
     vulgata 118
Pawsonia saxicola 199
Peacock's Tail 52
Peacock Worm 102
Pecten maximus 137
Pelvetia canaliculata 44
Pencil Sponge 74
Pentapora fascialis 179
Pepper Dulse 55
Periclimenes sagittifer 158
Pheasant Shell 121
Pholas dactylus 140
Pholis gunnellus 216
Phycodrys rubens 57
Phymatolithon calcareum 61
Physalia physalis 92
Pilumnus hirtellus 168
Pisidia longicornis 167
Pistol Shrimp 159
Pleurobrachia pileus 224
Plumose Anemone 84
Pollicipes pollicipes 149
Polysiphonia lanosa 59
Pomatoceros triqueter 101
Pomatoschistus microps 209
Porcellana platycheles 166
Porphyra umbilicalis 59
Portuguese Man o'War 92
Prosthecaraeus vittatus 104
Psammechinus miliaris 195
Purple Laver 59
Purple Sea Urchin 196
Purse Sponge 73
Pycnogonum littorale 175

R

Rainbow Weed 56
Rainbow Wrack 47
Razor Clam 140
Red Rags 58
Rhodothamniella floridula 60
Rissoides desmaresti 159
Risso's Crab 168
Rock Goby 209
Ross 179

Rough Periwinkle 123

S

Sabella pavonina 102
Sabellaria spinulosa 103
Saccharina latissima 48
Saccorhiza polyschides 50
Saddle Oyster 136
Salicornia europaea 69
Sand Binder 60
Sand Hopper 153
Sand Mason 102
Sand Star 188
Sargassum muticum 51
Scarlet and Gold Star Coral 88
Scarlet Lady 131
sea beans 227
Sea Beech 57
Sea Chervil 178
Sea Fan 227
Sea Fir 92
Sea Gherkin 199
Sea Gooseberries 224
Seagrass 69
Sea Hare 129
Sea Lemon 130
Sea Lettuce 65
Sea Mat 178
Sea Mouse 99
Sea Oak 46, 57
Sea Slater 153
sea wash ball 223
Semibalanus balanoides 148
Serrated Wrack 45
Seven-armed Starfish 188
Shanny 211
Shore Clingfish 213
Shore Crab 164
Shore Rockling 208
Short-snouted Seahorse 215
Slipper Limpet 127
Small Periwinkle 122
Snakelocks Anemone 82
Snakelocks Shrimp 158
Spider Crab 169
Spinachia spinachia 213
Spiny Seahorse 216
Spiny Starfish 186
Spiral Worm 101
Spiral Wrack 44
Spirorbis spirorbis 101
Spotted Cowrie 121
Squat Lobster 172

squid eggs 228
Star Ascidian 202
Strawberry Anemone 81
Striped Venus Clam 138
Styela clava 204
Sugar Kelp 48
Sunset Cup Coral 87
Syngnathus acus 214
Syngnathus rostellatus 215

T

Talitrus saltator 153
Taurulus bubalis 212
Tectura testudinalis 119
Tethya aurantium 74
Thick Top Shell 116
Thin Tellin 138
Thongweed 47
Tompot Blenny 210
Tricolia pullus 121
Trivia arctica 122
     monacha 121
Tubularia indivisa 91
Twin Fan Worm 103

U

Ulva intestinalis 65
     lactuca 65
Undaria pinnatifida 51
Urticina felina 83

V

Velella velella 222
Velvet Horn 66
Velvet Swimming Crab 165
Violet Snail 126
Volcano Barnacle 149

W

Wakame 51
Wireweed 51
Worm Pipefish 214

X

Xantho hydrophilus 167
Xantho pilipes 168

Z

Zostera marina 69

Photographic credits

Bloomsbury Publishing would like to thank the following for providing photographs and for permission to reproduce copyright material. While every effort has been made to trace and acknowledge all copyright holders, we would like to apologise for any errors or omissions, and invite readers to inform us so that corrections can be made in any future editions of the book.

1 Bob Gibbons/FLPA; 3 Maya Plass; 4 Erica Olsen/FLPA; 5 Andy Sands/NPL; 6 Scott Tibbles; 10 John Shaw/NHPA; 11 Adam Burton/NPL; 12 top Maya Plass; 12–13 Terry Yarrow/SS; 14 D P Wilson/FLPA; 13 Graham Prentice/SS; 17 Sion Roberts; 18 Paul Kay; 20 Nicholas and Sherry Lu Aldridge/FLPA; 21 Maya Plass; 22 Roger Tidman/FLPA; 23, 24 and 26 Maya Plass; 27T Mike Lane/NHPA; 27B Meelis Endla/SS; 28T Laurie Campbell/NPL; 28M S Charlie Brown/FLPA; 28B Michael Pitts/NPL; 29T FotoNatura/FN/Minden/FLPA; 29M British Divers Marine Life Rescue; 29B Maya Plass; 31 Gary K Smith/FLPA; 31 Adam Burton/NPL; 34 Ross Hoddinott/NPL; 35 D P Wilson/FLPA; 36 Maya Plass; 37 Juriah Mosin/SS; 38 Paul Kay/NHPA; 41 Maya Plass; 42 Maya Plass; 44T D P Wilson/FLPA; 44B Angela Hampton/FLPA; 45 both Steve Trewellha/FLPA; 46T Maya Plass; 46B Sion Roberts; 47T Andrew Bailey/FLPA; 47T inset Bill Coster/FLPA; 47B Steve Trewellha/FLPA; 48T Steve Trewellha/FLPA; 48B David Fenwick; 49T Chris Gomersall/2020Vision/NPL; 49B Nick Upton/NPL; 50T Nick Upton/NPL; 50B Steve Trewellha/FLPA; 51T Nature Production/NPL; 51B Adrian Davies/NPL; 51B inset Sion Roberts; 52T D P Wilson/FLPA; 52B Jose B. Ruiz/NPL; 53 Sally Sharrock; 54 Nick Upton/NPL; 55T Nick Upton/NPL; 55B Laurie Campbell/NHPA; 56T David Fenwick; 56B Paul Kay; MWPA1808; 57T David Fenwick; 57B Lin Baldock; 58T D P Wilson/FLPA; 58B Sion Roberts; 59T Steve Trewellha/FLPA; 59B Sion Roberts; 60T Sion Roberts; 60B Lin Baldock; 61T Sion Roberts; 61B Maya Plass; 62T Sion Roberts; 62B Sue Daly/NPL; 63 Adrian Davies/NPL; 65T D P Wilson/FLPA; 65B Sion Roberts; 66T Paul Kay; 66B Nick Upton/NPL; 67 Paul Naylor; 68 Steve Trewellha/FLPA; 69T Imagebroker/FLPA; 69B Sue Daly/NPL; 70 Sue Daly/NPL; 73T D P Wilson/FLPA; 73B David Fenwick; 74T Andre Pascal/Biosphoto/FLPA; 74B Steve Trewellha/FLPA; 75T Steve Trewellha/FLPA; 75B Nick Upton/NPL; 75B inset Sion Roberts; 76 Sue Daly/NPL; 78 Sue Daly/NPL; 80 Paul Kay/NHPA; 81T D P Wilson/FLPA; 81T inset David Fenwick; 81B Maya Plass; 81B inset Bill Coster/FLPA; 82T Paul Naylor; 82B Maya Plass; 83T Hans Leijnse/FN/Minden/FLPA; 83B Robert Thompson/NPL; 84T Robert Thompson/NPL; 84B Dan Burton/NPL; 85 Linda Pitkin/2020Vision/NPL; 87 all Sue Daly/NPL; 88T Christophe Courteau/NPL; 88B Sue Daly/NPL; 89 Wild Wonders of Europe/Lundgren/NPL; 91T D P Wilson/FLPA; 91B Linda Pitkin/2020Vision/NPL; 92T Nick Upton/NPL; 92B Charles Hood/NHPA; 93 Wim Van Egmond/Visuals Unlimited Inc/SPL; 95T Paul Naylor; 95B S Charlie Brown/FLPA; 96 David Shale/NPL; 98 D P Wilson/FLPA; 99T both D P Wilson/FLPA; 99B David Fenwick; 100T both Sion Roberts; 100B Pierre Petit/NHPA; 101T Nick Upton/NPL; 101B Christophe Courteau/NPL; 102 both Sue Daly/NPL; 103T Sue Daly/NPL; 103B Sion Roberts; 104T Sion Roberts; 104B Steve Trewellha/FLPA; 105 D P Wilson/FLPA; 106 Erica Olsen/FLPA; 108 Alex Mustard/2020Vision/NPL; 109 both Daniel Speiser; 111 both David Fenwick; 112 Paul Naylor; 114 Jason Smalley/NPL; 116T Sion Roberts; 116B D P Wilson/FLPA; 117T David Fenwick; 117B Robert Thompson/NPL; 118T Gary K. Smith/NPL; 118B David Fenwick; 119T David Fenwick; 119B David Fenwick; 120T Sion Roberts; 120B Sue Daly/NPL; 121T David Fenwick; 121B Nick Upton/NPL; 122T Sion Roberts; 122B Nick Upton/NPL; 123T Steve Trewellha/FLPA; 123B Gary K. Smith/NPL; 124T Paul Naylor; 124B Philippe Clement/NPL; 124B inset Sion Roberts; 125T Philippe Clement/NPL; 125B David Fenwick; 126T Steve Trewellha/FLPA;

126B David Fenwick; 127T Simon Colmer/NPL; 127B Steve Trewellha/FLPA; 128T Elaine Whiteford/NPL; 128B Nick Upton/NPL; 128B inset Sue Daly/NPL; 129T David Fenwick; 129B Paul Naylor; 129B inset Jason Gregory; 130T Sue Daly/NPL; 130B Nick Upton/NPL; 131T Jason Gregory; 131B Steve Trewellha/FLPA; 132 Graham Eaton/NPL; 134 Richard Marsh; 135T Philippe Clement/NPL; 135B David Fenwick; 136T David Fenwick; 136B David Fenwick; 137T Maya Plass; 137B Sion Roberts; 138T Philippe Clement/NPL; 138B David Fenwick; 139 both David Fenwick; 140T ImageBroker/FLPA; 140B David Fenwick; 141T Steve Trewellha/FLPA; 141B Steve Trewellha/FLPA; 142 Maya Plass; 144 Wayne Hutchinson/FLPA; 145T all Maya Plass; 145B Dominic Boothroyd; 146 Rob Spray/Seasearch; 148T Bill Coster/FLPA; 148B David Fenwick; 149T Nick Upton/NPL; 149B Jason Stone/NHPA; 150 Jany Sauvanet/NHPA; 152 University of Aberdeen; 153T Andy Sands/NPL; 153B Christophe Courteau/NPL; 154 David Fenwick; 156 Steve Trewellha/FLPA; 157T David Fenwick; 157B Jason Gregory; 158T David Fenwick; 158B Reinhard Dirscherl/FLPA; 159T Rohan Holt; 159B David Fenwick; 160 Maya Plass; 163 both Maya Plass; 164T David Fenwick; 164B David Fenwick; 165T David Fenwick; 165B Maya Plass; 166–168 all David Fenwick; 169T David Fenwick; 169B Mike Lane/NHPA; 170 Sue Daly/NPL; 172T Sue Daly/NPL; 172B Sue Daly/NPL; 173 Christophe Courteau/NPL; 175T Christophe Courteau/NPL; 175B Andrew J. Martinez/Science Source/FLPA; 176 Sue Daly/NPL; 178 both Nick Upton/NPL; 179T Steve Trewellha/FLPA; 179B Sue Daly/NPL; 180 Maya Plass; 182 Laurie Campbell/NPL; 183 Sue Daly/NPL; 185T Robert Thompson/NPL; 185B David Fenwick; 186T Sion Roberts; 186B David Fenwick; 187T Nick Upton/NPL; 187B Photo Researchers/FLPA; 188T David Fenwick; 188B Maya Plass; 189 Wild Wonders of Europe/Lundgren/NPL; 191T David Fenwick; 191B Robert Thompson/NPL; 192 Philippe Clement/NPL; 194 Sue Daly/NPL; 195T Sue Daly/NPL; 195B Georgette Douwma/NPL; 196T Robert Thompson/NPL; 196B David Fenwick; 197 Paul Naylor; 199T Paul Naylor; 199B David Fenwick; 200 D P Wilson/FLPA; 201 Christophe Courteau/NPL; 202T Nick Upton/NPL; 202B Jason Gregory; 203T D P Wilson/FLPA; 203B David Fenwick; 204T David Fenwick; 204B Rohan Holt; 205 Steve Trewhella/FLPA; 207 Linda Pitkin/2020Vision/NPL; 208 both David Fenwick; 209T David Fenwick; 209B Paul Kay; 210 both Paul Naylor; 211T D P Wilson/FLPA; 211B Paul Naylor; 212T David Fenwick; 212B Sue Daly/NPL; 213T David Fenwick; 213B D P Wilson/FLPA; 214 both David Fenwick; 215T Paul Kay; 215B Wild Wonders of Europe/Zanki/NPL; 216T Steve Trewhella/FLPA; 216B Jason Gregory; 217T Paul Naylor; 217B David Fenwick; 218 both Paul Naylor; 219 Maya Plass; 221 Maya Plass; 222T Sion Roberts; 222B Steve Trewhella/FLPA; 223T Sion Roberts; 223B Christian Hütter/Imagebroker/FLPA; 224T Sion Roberts; 224B Maya Plass; 225T Sion Roberts; 225B Maya Plass; 226T Sion Roberts; 226B Steve Trewhella/FLPA; 227T Maya Plass; 227B Steve Trewhella/FLPA; 228T Claire Minett; 228B Peter Reynolds/FLPA.

Front cover (main): Maya Plass; bottom (left to right): Sue Daly/NPL; David Fenwick; Nick Upton/NPL. **Back cover** (top to bottom): Jason Gregory; Nick Upton/NPL; Sion Roberts; Jason Gregory; Sue Daly/NPL.

Abbreviated sources in full: David Fenwick aphotomarine.com; FLPA flpa.co.uk; Jason Gregory britishmarinelifepictures.co.uk; Paul Kay marinewildlife.co.uk; Paul Naylor marinephoto.co.uk; NHPA photoshot.com; NPL naturepl.com; Sion Roberts flickr.com/photos/gwylan; SPL sciencephoto.com; SS shutterstock.com.

Newport Community
Learning & Libraries